Creative Entrepreneurship

Creative Entrepreneurship is an essential guide for artists, makers, and designers, offering practical tools and strategies to transform creative talents into successful business ventures.

This book provides a comprehensive, step-by-step roadmap for entrepreneurial success, tailored specifically for the creative industries. It covers essential topics such as opportunity recognition, market research, branding, financial management, and operational strategy. Each chapter is designed for hands-on application, featuring learning outcomes, actionable activities, and real-world case studies. By introducing classic business tools in an accessible and pragmatic way, this book bridges the gap between creativity and business, empowering readers to confidently navigate the entrepreneurial landscape. Additionally, it emphasizes the unique challenges and opportunities within the creative economy, ensuring relevance to artists, designers, and makers. Whether you are developing a new venture or refining an existing one, *Creative Entrepreneurship* equips you with the knowledge and skills to succeed.

Perfect for students and practitioners alike, this book is ideal for courses in arts entrepreneurship, creative industries, and professional practice.

Instructor resources, including slide decks, sample syllabi, and activities, provide a seamless teaching and learning experience.

Jennifer A. Reis is a creative entrepreneur, artist, author, trainer, and teaching textile artist with 30 years of experience in cultural entrepreneurship and non-profit management. Her earned degrees include a BFA from Columbus College of Art and Design, and graduate work in arts management, instructional design, studio art, and arts education from Syracuse University, UNC-Greensboro, and Morehead State University. As an arts entrepreneurship curricular consultant, her clients have included Nest NYC, MassArts, Ringling College of Art and Design, Kauffman Foundation, Triangle Artworks, Tremaine Foundation, West Virginia Creative Economy Network, AIR Collaborative, and the Tamarack Foundation. Formerly arts entrepreneurship faculty at UNC-Greensboro, she utilizes years of experience teaching artists and artisans creative venture development and has authored and co-authored numerous academic journal articles on creative entrepreneurship research, education, and practice. Through her consulting company Make Do Creative, she works with community and economic development, trade, governmental, and cultural organizations to design, manage, and deliver creative entrepreneurship curriculum for makers of all kinds to develop sustainable ventures. She has served on the Board of Directors for the Society for Arts Entrepreneurship Education and numerous community, arts, and economic development boards and committees on the international to local level.

Marie Segares is a career intrapreneur in the non-profit sector with expertise in program development, launch, and expansion. She is a Robert P. Stiller Endowed Chair and an Associate Professor of Business and Management in the Stiller School of Business at Champlain College. She earned her AB in Sociology from Barnard College, her MPH in Sociomedical Sciences from Columbia University, her MBA in Leadership and Change Management and in Entrepreneurship and Innovation from New York University, and her EdD in Organizational Leadership Studies from Northeastern University. Her areas of research interest include artisan entrepreneurship, creative business, microenterprises, and leadership. She conducts qualitative research using a variety of approaches and has written teaching cases for multiple publishers. She is also an artisan entrepreneur, creating digital content to self-publish and for major crafts manufacturers and publishers. Her craft industry work includes coordinating content creator activity on behalf of brands, providing professional development workshops at trade shows, and writing for industry publications.

Sara Hartmann is the Program Director for Creative Entrepreneurship at Massachusetts College of Art and Design (MassArt), where she also holds a faculty position. She holds a BFA from MassArt and an MBA from Simmons University. In her current role, she oversees the Creative Economy Business Incubator, a scale-agnostic program she founded to support the unique needs of art, design, and cultural ventures. She also directs the Business of Creative Industries minor and the student-run brand program. Additionally, she co-produces professional development programs for working artists and designers in partnership with organizations like the Boston Mayor's Office of Arts and Culture and the Harvard Ed Portal. Prior to academia, she worked as a costume designer for theater and opera and as a digital marketer for apparel and consumer product startups. Her experience moving between the cultural and innovation economies has inspired her work addressing the resource gaps faced by would-be founders in creative industries.

Creative Entrepreneurship

Building Your Creative Venture

Jennifer A. Reis, Marie Segares, and Sara Hartmann

Routledge
Taylor & Francis Group
LONDON AND NEW YORK

Designed cover image: Courtesy of Aaliyah Taylor/Exalting in Beauty / Courtesy of Geoff and Kristen Zephyrus/Cognitive Surplus / Photo by Melissa Ostrow. Courtesy of Massachusetts College of Art and Design

First edition published 2026
by Routledge
4 Park Square, Milton Park, Abingdon, Oxon, OX14 4RN

and by Routledge
605 Third Avenue, New York, NY 10158

Routledge is an imprint of the Taylor & Francis Group, an informa business

British Library Cataloguing-in-Publication Data
A catalogue record for this book is available from the British Library

ISBN: 9781032962511 (hbk)
ISBN: 9781032962504 (pbk)
ISBN: 9781003588771 (ebk)

DOI: 10.4324/9781003588771

Typeset in Times New Roman
by codeMantra

Access the Support Material: www.routledge.com/9781032962504

Contents

About This Book

by Jennifer A. Reis

Hello! We are excited you are engaging with this book, whether as a traditional student or instructor, as a maker who wants to scale their creative practice into an entrepreneurial venture, or a facilitator working with cohorts of learners interested in doing so.

This book was inspired by decades of experience by the authors of working with both traditional college populations in arts and business, high school students in STEAM and entrepreneurship, and adult learners looking for resources to start (or scale) their arts- and crafts-based businesses. In my professional experience, I was tasked to develop arts entrepreneurship curriculum for higher education many years ago, and when designing the course noted there was a significant lack of "plug and play" resources that could be embedded within a sequence of learning. The ends of the creative entrepreneurship education continuum were heavy: one end was leaden with scholarly journal publications focusing on research and data that – while worthwhile to academics in the field – was unwieldy to translate into the learning environment. The other end was weighted down with more aspirational work that was sometimes light on details and logistics and often promised a successful entrepreneurial dream untethered from business realities. I spent so many hours creating a curriculum that would thread the needle between these two extremes. When thinking through this potential book project, I immediately thought of asking the co-authors, Dr. Marie Segares and Sara Hartmann to join the writing team as they are experts in the field. Thankfully they accepted and have contributed an abundance of expertise and professional writing experience.

As mentioned prior, this book seeks to be accessible and user-friendly while providing useful, pragmatic, and grounded information to ideate, design, plan, and execute a creative entrepreneurial venture based on both business best practices and the particulars of being a working creative maker. We as the authors collectively have four decades of experience of providing creative entrepreneurship education to college and adult learners in a variety of contexts; we have witnessed the rubber hitting the road so to speak. We have all separately designed and implemented (and pivoted!) our own creative entrepreneurship curriculum as well as engaged with multiple other entrepreneurial education programs. This wealth of experience has informed this book and the sequence of chapters with associated activities, resources, and composite maker studies drawn from people we have had the privilege of teaching and learning from. You can read more about us individually in our biographies.

This book was intentionally designed and sequenced to fit within a three-month, semester-long timeframe as a standard college learning structure. Starting from an introduction to entrepreneurial concepts, venture ideation, and issues pertaining to creative microenterprise, we move onto business modeling, market research, branding, and marketing to financials and business logistics. Finally, interviews with a range of creative makers in both discipline and entrepreneurial life stage, including emerging, mid-career, and 20+ years into their ventures, have been crafted into case studies. This chapter sequence was developed out of the authors' experience of leading learners through their entrepreneurial journey as creative makers. All that being said, we encourage readers and instructors to access the information as they need, engaging with the chapters as is relevant to them.

Each chapter was designed to provide multiple means of engaging with the content, with introductions to concepts, maker narratives to illustrate specific topics, and learner activities to use either within an instructional context or on your own. **Bolded** words in the chapters can be found with definitions in the glossary. We also included additional resources at the end of each chapter. While each chapter was individually authored, we worked together to ensure multiple perspectives and robust information were included throughout this book.

Chapter 1 introduces creative entrepreneurship for makers and explains why having an entrepreneurial mindset helps you adapt to new technologies and spot opportunities in a changing world.

Chapter 2 is about coming up with and refining business ideas using different thinking approaches. You'll learn what makes a good business model, how to define what makes your offering unique, and explore some proven business models that creative ventures have used successfully. It also covers how to research your market and competitors.

Chapter 3 teaches you to analyze what's happening in your business environment and find opportunities. You'll learn about competitive advantage and different strategies to achieve it, plus useful tools like the five forces analysis to understand competitive pressures and matrices to plan product growth. It also touches on digital entrepreneurship.

Chapter 4 focuses on understanding your customers and their problems. It emphasizes creating prototypes to test your ideas with real users and introduces design thinking as a process for solving customer problems.

Chapter 5 walks you through building your brand and marketing strategy. You'll learn how to position yourself in the market, craft a compelling value proposition, understand what drives your customers' decisions, and create marketing plans that actually work.

Chapter 6 teaches you the financial basics to figure out if your business idea can actually make money. You'll learn to analyze unit economics, do breakeven calculations, and think strategically about pricing based on what customers value.

Chapter 7 covers day-to-day financial management, including how to read financial statements and explore different funding options like investors, loans, crowdfunding, and grants.

Chapter 8 helps you organize your business operations using value chain analysis. It addresses the balance between efficiency and creativity, plus practical stuff like business structures, outsourcing decisions, and protecting your assets. Sustainability is also covered.

Chapter 9 is about strategic planning using frameworks like PESTLE, SWOT, and SOAR to understand your situation and set meaningful goals. You'll learn to create SMART objectives and track the right metrics to measure success.

Chapter 10 features ten real case studies of creative entrepreneurs sharing their actual journeys, challenges, and wins, with reflection questions to help you think about and apply what you've learned.

Appendix A includes a detailed glossary of over 500 business terms you can use as a reference. Appendix B includes helpful organizations for makers and entrepreneurs, and tips for finding more support locally. Appendix C includes information about business taxes.

Closing

For learners of all ages, whether in a traditional education context, a community cohort, or on your own, we are excited to share this book with you. It's my hope personally that this book makes creative entrepreneurship (and creative entrepreneurship education) accessible, practical, and is a primer on making your maker's business as successful as possible!

Acknowledgments

Jennifer would like to thank all the folks and organizations who generously shared creative entrepreneurship professional expertise, opportunities, and perspectives over the years. The Society for Arts Entrepreneurship Education has been invaluable for relationship building and support especially in the early days of developing creative entrepreneurship curriculum. The fellowship of other makers, learning from their struggles and successes as well as having sounding boards for developing entrepreneurial concepts and curriculum, has been a true gift. She would like to thank her husband Pete for the support and encouragement through this journey from a seed of an idea to publication. Finally, a special note of gratitude to Sara Hartmann and Dr. Marie Segares in accepting the offer to collaborate on this book – their expertise, professional advice, and general patience and perseverance are so very much appreciated!

Marie wishes to thank her partner, Matthew, and her cat, Cappuccino, for their patience and care while she was working on this book. She also wants to thank the hundreds of makers and creative entrepreneurs who have inspired her, shared business advice, and commiserated with her over the years, and the dozens who gave their time, photos, and stories to make this book possible. And, of course, she would like to thank Jennifer Reis for inviting her to work on this book and Sara Hartmann for being such a collaborative co-author. It has been a joy to work with both of them on this project.

Sara would like to thank the inspiring community of creative entrepreneurs she has been fortunate to work with; watching the amazing things they create and the way they show up for each other is a constant source of inspiration. She extends her deepest gratitude to her family, especially her husband, Alex, and children Thea and Jordan for their encouragement and support throughout the process. To her co-authors, Jennifer and Marie, thank you for making the collaboration on this text a genuine pleasure. Thank you to Sondra, Dan, Anne Marie, Carol, and Maryellen at MassArt, for their early support and steadfast advocacy for arts entrepreneurship education in the days when business classes at art school were still unorthodox. Finally, sincere thanks to Sarah, Kenlyn, and Jen for their invaluable day-to-day work in building and sustaining the program that inspired Sara's work on this book.

1 The Entrepreneurial Maker

An Introduction to Motivations and Concepts

Jennifer A. Reis

Introduction

Welcome to your journey as an entrepreneurial maker! This book is designed to give you the **mindsets** and tools to navigate a creative path through the landscape of entrepreneurship, focused on makers who are developing and implementing micro-enterprises. Being an entrepreneurial maker has both rewards of developing your own career path through creative venture creation and maintaining ownership of your capacity and **capital** as well as risks related to going it alone in the **marketplace**.

Entrepreneurial mindsets and motivations vary among creative makers. Some makers may have a strong leaning toward engaging with the marketplace. Others might be comfortable with making for making's sake, selling occasionally when the situation arises or in a stark example, refusing to engage with the exchange of capital for their work in any context. Participating in a creative practice on its own is valuable. However, this book focuses on creating an entrepreneurial venture on the foundation of your creative capacities.

Learning Outcomes

- **Define** the concept of an entrepreneurial maker
- **Identify** entrepreneurial motivations and business types
- **Compare and contrast** micro-enterprise with other business models
- **Develop** a basic business model using key concepts.

What Is Creative Entrepreneurship? What Is a Maker?

What is **creative entrepreneurship**? It is a term that refers to creative ventures that seek to earn financial **capital** in a marketplace. **Ventures** that participate in creative entrepreneurship are businesses that hold creative value at its core, often through the artist and artisan-based expertise and vision of the founder/owner/operator.

This can look like:

- a landscape painter who has gallery representation in a retail art space,
- a quilter who does commission work for a fashion designer,
- a ceramicist who develops a production line of planters for an upscale shop,
- a maker of bath and body products for sale at regional farmers' markets,
- a content creator for podcasts and streaming,
- any product/service intended for the **market** whose core value is grounded in creative ideation and generation (Figure 1.1).

DOI: 10.4324/9781003588771-1

Figure 1.1 Makers at work resin casting, woodworking, and crafting pottery.
Source: Thirdman, Ono Kosuki, and Quang Nguyen Vinh via Pexels

In the context of this book, the term **maker** includes artists, artisans, designers, and others whose primary form of expression is through the making of goods and/or services. Additionally, the text focuses on **micro-enterprises**, typically concerning small-scale ventures that are driven by one person, potentially with the involvement of assistants or delegating out business-related tasks to other professionals, or a modest creative collective of a limited group of people.

Entrepreneurship in the creative sector can look quite different than traditional entrepreneurship. For example, creative entrepreneurship can be on a much smaller scale than a large corporation. It often has priorities outside the profit-only motive; it can be seen as akin to social enterprise where there are two motivations: providing value to your market through your expertise as well as generating capital through your creative capacities. Creative entrepreneurs might not have the ultimate **exit strategy** of selling out to a larger corporation or have the goal of "**scaling** up" from small-batch production to mass produced and distributed products.

Entrepreneurial Mindsets and Motivations

For some makers, being entrepreneurial in their creative practice comes as second nature – they are driven to create products and services through **opportunity recognition** to develop new clients within their market. Others might feel uncomfortable about calling themselves entrepreneurs or seeming too financially focused in fear of appearing to "sell out" their work for the sole benefit of making money. Wherever creatives fall on this continuum, it is valuable to consider societal issues related to monetizing our creative practice as well as defining **entrepreneurial mindsets** and **entrepreneurial motivations**.

There are structural issues to consider related to our creative practice whether or not we put our work out there as a business venture. Within a capitalistic society, money is a validation of success and worth, creating pressure to monetize our work. Additionally, there is friction between the terms and identities of hobbyist versus business owner, and amateur versus professional. A watercolorist might say, "it started as a hobby and now it's a business," a statement that implies that the motivation and perhaps validity of the artistic practice has pivoted. Furthermore, you might find that traditional business resources and convenings prioritize the CEO/Founder model where the entrepreneurial effort is a 100%, "all in" effort necessitating a full-time commitment and significant startup capital in hand (or through investors). Sometimes the **side hustle** model is the accessible business option for creative **solopreneurs** who may need to continue to work a day job at least for the time being, or who do not have access to large amounts of capital.

In his book, *The Entrepreneurial Mindset: Preparing Our Next Generation for the Future of Work*, Kyle Garman provides an important list of traits and behaviors found in entrepreneurs noted below:

- **Future Orientation**
- **Creativity & Innovation**

- **Comfort with Risk**
- **Communication & Collaboration**
- **Flexibility & Adaptation**
- **Critical Thinking & Problem-Solving**
- **Initiative & Self-Reliance**
- **Opportunity Recognition**

Let's look at each of entrepreneurial characteristics and how they could appear in the sector of creative entrepreneurship and questions you may want to ask yourself associated with your possible venture.

Future Orientation

We can't predict the future, but if we are active in our creative discipline as well as aware of the world around us, we can make assumptions about trends and issues that might show up in the near future. This could include a creative maker reflecting on the evolving opportunities to utilize AI to automate administrative tasks or participate in diversifying revenue streams using Print-on-Demand to generate passive income. How could your venture be forward looking to take advantage of evolving opportunities?

Creativity and Innovation

Even though it seems counter-intuitive, some makers need a mindset pivot and new skills to apply creative thinking to their own business design, development, strategy, and implementation. A ceramist may be wedded to creating only pieces for use in the domestic kitchen for instance and miss opportunities to be expansive and creative in their practice to develop new product lines. Reflect on your own tendencies regarding creativity and innovation in your venture concept and related logistics. Do you feel open to trying out different ideas and modes of operation or are you locked into a specific concept without room to pivot and evolve?

Comfort with Risk

This is a necessary emotional skill to navigate what can be a **saturated market**, an economic space where there may be many others also determined to sell their products and services. A jeweler may utilize creative thinking as mentioned prior to develop a new product line only to take it to an arts market where there is limited interest. Further in this book, we will discuss the value of **market testing** with a limited product or service by designing and implementing a **minimum viable products**. Ask yourself about your comfort with potential failure as well as choices you could make that could mitigate risk.

Communication & Collaboration

Creatives run the gamut as **introverts** to **extroverts**; however, the ability to communicate and collaborate are important abilities. All micro-enterprises must communicate the value they provide to the market and partner with other people and entities to translate their vision to a viable business venture. It is tempting to buy into the concept of the entrepreneur as the "lone wolf," but no maker exists alone. Consider the teaching artist who must meet with program directors, be responsive and collaborative with developing instructional opportunities, answer emails and sign contracts in a timely manner, communicate effectively in an instructional environment, and receive and reflect on constructive feedback from workshop participants and administrators. Ask yourself (and answer honestly) how well you communicate and collaborate when working with others.

Flexibility & Adaptation

Both are necessary in an evolving market landscape and can be challenging when the core value of the venture can be strongly integrated into the maker's sense of self and creative practice. Also, it can be difficult to think objectively about one's personally engaged venture and setting **key performance indicators** related to a successful business: it is easy to be emotionally misdirected. A weaver might be focused on making large works for functional domestic use only to become aware that smaller wall-mounted artworks are more in demand and the clientele has a capacity to purchase due to a lower price. How flexible and adaptable are you in facing facts that challenge your initial assumptions?

Critical Thinking & Problem-Solving

These are skills that help creative makers take a step back and reflect from an outsider's perspective on what is and is not working for the creative venture, why that is the case, and how to problem solve and potentially "pivot" a product or service. A ceramicist could be focused on making soup bowls only to realize with a quick cut on the side of the vessel, they now have a "yarn bowl" to hold balls of knitting yarn and can be sold for double the price. How comfortable are you with being a detective, anthropologist, and problem-solver with your potential creative practice?

Initiative & Self-Reliance

Even though makers do collaborate and communicate with partners and **stakeholders**, managing a micro-enterprise can be a solo endeavor some of much of the timea. A graphic novelist invests **sweat equity** into a book: they often perform unpaid labor in the process of character and plot development, writing initial drafts and creating primary sketches, and finishing the book. This author would need to be a salesperson as well, pitching the book, building relationships with retail partners, and developing **distribution channels**. Ask yourself: how self-motivated are you, do you have (or have the will/means to develop) project and time management skills/tools, and have the internal drive to push through challenges and barriers for your creative venture?

Opportunity Recognition

Other forms can the venture's core value take to provide benefits to the **end user**? If a natural dyer has a full production line and is often asked about the dyeing process, this may be a perfect "opportunity recognition moment" to consider the viability of offering natural dyeing classes locally and on a small scale for market testing for **proof of concept**. How open are you to build a **portfolio** of revenue-generating opportunities that are aligned with your venture's creative vision but may be outside of your initial business concept?

Additional Entrepreneurial Mindsets

In addition to this list, a capacity for **entrepreneurial pivoting** is a useful characteristic of a successful entrepreneur. An entrepreneurial pivot is when a venture has learned, based on market reaction, that its products and/or services are not as desirable or in demand as assumed or had been in the past. In that case, the venture may strategically shift its offerings for increased market relevance (Figure 1.2).

Figure 1.2 Kathy Cano-Murillo, founder of Crafty Chica (profiled in Case 10.1), at work in her studio.
Source: Courtesy of Kathy Cano-Murillo/Crafty Chica.

Another helpful mindset to consider is **effectuation** developed by Saras Sarasvathy, which posits that entrepreneurs should lean into uncertainty and collaborative **ideation** through action, partnerships, and **pivoting**. It suggests that successful entrepreneurs begin with their existing means – who they are, what they know, and whom they know – and then explore opportunities that arise from those means. This approach emphasizes flexibility, experimentation, and the ability to adapt to changing circumstances. This is in contrast to our initial inclination to set a rigid intention and grasp onto it regardless of capacity or market interest, or through **causal logic** of setting a goal and then planning toward it. Using effectuation, entrepreneurs can practice five core principles:

- **Bird-in-Hand Principle:** Who are you, what are your current tangible and intangible assets (like your expertise and talent), and who do you know? If we inventory and leverage these existing elements, we can move forward to opportunities rather than getting stuck on looking for the perfect opportunity.
- **Affordable Loss Principle:** Given that all entrepreneurial efforts have risk baked in, this principle directs you to determine what you can afford to lose rather than focusing on what you expect to gain in returns.
- **Crazy Quilt Principle:** As we will discuss in further chapters, collaborating with stakeholders and perceived competitors can be an effective means to leverage resources which might be scarce, especially in the creative sector.
- **Lemonade Principle** (Leverage contingencies): This principle encourages us to embrace the unexpected or unassumed and to transform them into opportunities rather than denying and/or resisting them.
- **Pilot-in-the-Plane Principle:** Entrepreneurship is a creative endeavor: we can operate with an agency mindset and actively develop and leverage actions and assets within our control to shape our progress.

Ironically, we can neglect to bring the creativity from our artistic practice in the design of a **unique value proposition** for our entrepreneurial venture. This approach to entrepreneurship, focusing on process and practice rather than a predetermined outcome, reflects the creative process. It encourages a mindset of experimentation and discovery, mirroring the way many artists work in their studios.

Money Mindsets and Hidden Scripts

We all have mental models and internal narratives about money and financial concerns, be them positive or negative. For a considerable portion of the population, money serves as a salient source of stress. This phenomenon transcends professional and socioeconomic boundaries, affecting individuals across diverse occupations and life circumstances. The genesis of financial stress can be multifaceted, stemming from personal lived experiences, deeply ingrained cultural narratives, and patterns learned within familial contexts. However, for aspiring entrepreneurs to achieve sustainable success, a critical examination and understanding of their personal relationship with financial anxiety is paramount. Stress can impede rational decision-making processes by diminishing the activity of the prefrontal cortex, the region of the brain responsible for logical thought. When you cultivate an awareness of your relationship with money and identify personal financial stress triggers, you can be informed and judicious about the financial management of your venture.

A helpful framework for initiating this self-reflection is the Klontz **Money Script Inventory**, a theoretical construct proposed by psychologist Brad Klontz. His research posits that individuals harbor internalized narratives and beliefs about money, termed **money scripts**, which profoundly influence their thoughts, feelings, and behaviors concerning financial matters. Engaging in an inventory of your money beliefs can serve as a potent tool for mitigating financial anxiety.

Klontz identifies four primary categories of money scripts:

- **Money Worship:** The conviction that increased financial wealth will inevitably lead to greater happiness.
- **Money Status:** The belief that an individual's self-worth is directly proportional to their net worth.
- **Money Vigilance:** The belief in the paramount importance of meticulous financial management and diligent saving for future contingencies.
- **Money Avoidance:** The association of negative emotions and connotations with the concept of money.

Klontz suggests that these money scripts are shaped by both the explicit and implicit financial lessons learned from our family members and close associates, as well as from significant personal financial experiences. Episodes of financial hardship, for instance, can indelibly shape financial behaviors for years to come and may even be transmitted across generations. Artists and creative professionals are particularly susceptible to experiencing financial stress due to the inherent income variability and the prevalence of gig-based work within the creative sector. Over time, this can engender a chronic stress response, making proactive financial planning and analysis feel increasingly daunting.

Furthermore, the cultural landscape surrounding art and money is often fraught with contradictory narratives that many creatives internalize to varying degrees. The sentiment that "money corrupts the creative process" stands in stark contrast to the equally pervasive notion that "if you're not getting paid for your work, then it's just a hobby." These opposing viewpoints create a precarious "lose-lose" situation for creatives. As creatives, there are competing narratives of pursuing financial gain can be perceived as "selling out" and diminishing one's status as a "genuine" artist, while a lack of financial compensation can lead to the invalidation of their artistic endeavors as mere pastimes. Both of these stories cultivate anxiety around money and establish the expectation that financial success plays a defining role in validating an artist's identity. This additional layer of financial stress can further impede meaningful engagement with financial planning and analysis.

The significant stress associated with money can lead you to avoid the close monitoring of your financial data or the careful analysis of potential financial outcomes during the planning process. If financial success is perceived as a critical determinant of artistic validation, the prospect of confronting potentially unfavorable financial realities can feel overwhelmingly frightening. However, this avoidance can incur substantial **costs**. A lack of robust understanding of one's financial standing can result in missed opportunities for strategic growth and leave the creative venture vulnerable to unforeseen risks. Over the long term, this pattern of avoidance can increase the likelihood of financial instability and ultimately limit the ability to fully realize your creative aspirations. It is crucial to recognize that money, in its essence, is a morally neutral and theoretical tool intended to empower and facilitate the pursuit of creative goals.

Entrepreneurial Motivations

As mentioned prior, some creative practitioners are highly entrepreneurial and others are not. Entrepreneurial motivations and types, like mindsets, can be innate or developed through education, experience, or external circumstances. Here is a list of a few entrepreneurial types and motivations:

- **Nascent entrepreneurship:** early ideation stage, emerging entrepreneurship
- **Necessity entrepreneurship:** a need to fill a personal financial gap in earnings
- **Social entrepreneurship:** developing a low-profit, high social impact venture
- **Serial entrepreneurship:** a path of developing multiple ventures over time.

Many makers are in the category of nascent entrepreneurship. They have honed their craft/practice, are eager to enter the marketplace with a business they have designed, and now seek to operate it. However, with many small business development resources focused on non-creative ventures, it can be difficult to translate what is relevant to you when developing a creative venture. A sculptor might be interested in pivoting their work to a production line of water-feature sculptures that are intended for private lawns. As a nascent entrepreneur, they would want to do their **market research**, understanding competitors, end users, and **market demand**. Running the **costs of goods sold** and **overhead costs** would also be valuable because it will test the venture's viability. If you fall into this category, what would be some important first steps to investigate issues that will impact your potential venture?

Necessity entrepreneurship can be an unfortunate situation you may find yourself, a situation in which people, whether through income loss, debt hardship, cost of living pressures, or a host of other financial stressors that individuals need to develop and implement an entrepreneurial endeavor to make ends meet. Aaliyah Taylor, profiled in Case 10.4, started as a necessity entrepreneur. When she needed cash urgently, she would walk through neighborhood barber shops and hair salons with her jewelry on a display board. Her prices were very low, set to encourage purchasing, so that she was guaranteed to sell most or all of her inventory in a short amount of time. What entrepreneurial endeavors could you undertake if necessity entrepreneurship was.... necessary? How could you determine whether this was worth the time and capacity you need to invest in order to create a side hustle offering to increase personal revenue? Remember to

Figure 1.3 A pair of earrings designed by Aaliyah Taylor, founder of Exalting in Beauty (profiled in Case 10.4).
Source: Courtesy of Aaliyah Taylor/Exalting in Beauty.

consider the **cost-benefit analysis** aspect of your necessity entrepreneurship efforts to ensure you are being properly compensated (Figure 1.3)!

You might be a maker who is interested in a socially engaged venture which is commonly referred to as social entrepreneurship. Social entrepreneurs are those business creators who identify a social or community problem to identify a profit- as well as purpose-based solution. This can take the form of a **multi-sided business model** where the venture is funded both through **earned income** in the form of buyers seeking a service or products which is partially subsidized through **contributed income** by way of grants, foundation, private individual, or corporate support. Chris, a street art muralist, could design a collaborative, community-engaged public art project implemented through grassroots feedback and participation to transform an abandoned alleyway into a shared space for public gatherings as a means of **creative spacemaking**. A substantial portion of the artist's stipend and mural supplies would be underwritten through grants and corporate sponsorship. The public art reveal event could include a pop-up sales opportunity for the artist and other project participants, and the mural artist's profits from the sale of smaller works would be considered earned income. Could your venture have elements of a multi-sided business model where financial capital comes from both earned and contributed income?

If you are a maker who is highly entrepreneurially driven and have ideas for, or even already developed multiple ventures, you may fit the term of a serial entrepreneur.

Serial entrepreneurs are individuals who create multiple businesses over time, sometimes with elements of the previous entrepreneurial effort bleeding or building into the next. It is more expansive than a soap maker adding a new production line of candles for example. A serial entrepreneur, Jane, might initially have a small plant and herb store with an artisanal brand. The venture does well in early to mid stage; however, the trend of people wanting multiple plants in their domestic environment begins to lag. Jane has always carried other sustainability-designed home accessories in her shop and when she looks critically at the sales data and profit margins, she determines that focusing on those products would be more lucrative and in market demand. Therefore, Jane makes the decision to close up the plant business and establish an environmentally oriented home accessories venture. In the past or potentially in the future, do you see yourself with the inclination to be a serial entrepreneur, moving through cycles of different businesses over time?

Differentiating Micro-Enterprise from Other Entrepreneurial Business Models

As mentioned prior, the text focuses on creative makers who desire to create a micro-enterprise. Micro-enterprise is defined as a venture with a limited number of people engaged in the business, often ten or less. In this context, the maker is often especially in early stages operating as a business of one with potential outsourcing of professional expertise and production assistance. The term **solopreneur** is also used in this context, and these ventures can start as a **side hustle**. Other entrepreneurial business models like a tech startup are larger in scale employing many people and the CEO/Founder is focused full time on the business. The goal might be to reach a financial goal with the company and then have an **exit strategy** to sell to a larger entity. Micro-enterprises (and/or side hustles) may not have that goal, be associated with one person only, and in some cases might be considered negatively by other entrepreneurial endeavors as a "vanity project."

> Jay is a fashion designer focusing on one-of-a-kind upcycled clothing and accessories and is the primary venture visionary, designer, and maker. They develop and control the clothing style and brand aesthetics and identify the target members and related distribution channels. They might hire production assistants to increase inventory volume as well as contract professional photographers for visual assets in branding and marketing; these folks are part of the team in a part time, contractual manner. Branding and marketing strategy may be hired out as well. Despite the various professional partners Jay contracts with, it is sole endeavor that unless they are intentional about selling the business or having a successor to take over, will naturally end with Jay's involvement in the venture.

Managing a micro-enterprise has its strengths and weaknesses. Micro-enterprises can be highly nimble, need limited capital to launch, and can be able to operate as a side hustle in the startup phase. Technology has enabled micro-enterprises to have a low threshold to launch through the abundance of digital marketing and e-commerce opportunities. On the other hand, as in the book *The E-Myth Revisited* by Michael E. Gerber, with micro-enterprise, the venture is the Technician (the maker), the Manager (the business operator), and the Entrepreneur (the visionary and salesperson). Not surprisingly, if the designer of the venture is not careful about strategy and implementation, burnout can happen very quickly especially in tandem outward-facing success leading to the venture's capacity collapse.

Closing

Becoming an entrepreneurial maker is an exciting prospect with both rewards and risks. The intention of this chapter as well as the book as a whole is to foster venture ideation, research, planning, and execution to prepare creative entrepreneurs to have a foundation for future success.

Mini Case: Serial Entrepreneurship at Magners Farm

Kylie Woodham is an Australian-educated entrepreneur who now resides in Ireland. Kylie worked as a stud hand, a work rider, and a yard foreperson in Australia and Japan while in college before transitioning into public relations jobs. After moving to Ireland, Kylie worked as a media director and in advertising, met her husband, Billy, and went on to have four children together.

Kylie decided to break into the entrepreneurial world, intending to remain at home and raise her children. Kylie established an advertising and marketing agency in 2010. The business provides services such as website creation, social media services, consultancy, brand creation, and brand management. Kylie has worked on projects throughout Europe and Australia. Seven years later, Kylie and Billy founded Magners Farm in County Tipperary, Ireland. This family-owned farm sells pasture-raised eggs, bone broth from chickens, chickens, beef, pork, and lamb. Magners Farm is an organic farm that has received awards for its high-quality products and emphasizes regenerative farming, sustainable agricultural systems, and nutrient-dense food produced locally. Kylie was a participant in the Irish program Accelerating the Creation of Rural Nascent Start-ups, which assists budding female entrepreneurs in rural Ireland. Farming is an important aspect of Kylie's life and has also had an impact on her home life. Both her job and her way of life are inextricably linked, and in many ways her lifestyle is inseparable from her profession. Ultimately, Kylie has no desire to alter the world drastically. Instead, she wishes to uphold her principles and serve healthy products to her customers.

Remixed with permission from Kelley, J.N. (2021). Kylie Woodham. In Gupta, V.K. (Ed.), *WE: The inspiring stories of entrepreneurial women from around the world* (pp. 49-51). University of Alabama

Activities

Activity 1: Meet Your Maker Presentation or Visual Board

Pick a creative entrepreneur that you admire who is currently managing a venture (and the venture doesn't have to align with what you might do, just make sure it is of interest to you!). Create a presentation or visual board that includes the following:

- Who are they and what specifically do they do?
- How did they start their creative entrepreneurial journey? How long have they been running their business?
- Who are the primary type(s) of clients that they engage with regularly (knowing there are always outliers)?
- How do they communicate with their clients? What's the vibe of the overall branding and marketing? What specifically do they use to reach their clients in digital and print assets?
- How do they generate revenue for their venture? Is there more than one revenue stream? Do you know what they charge for their work and/or potentially how much money they make (don't be surprised if, especially for a service-based business, this is difficult to ascertain!)?
- Why do you admire this creative entrepreneur and what can you learn from them?

Activity 2: Your Creative Entrepreneur Story: Written Reflection + Peer Share

- Why do you want to be a creative entrepreneur?
- Which of the entrepreneurial motivations resonates strongest with you, and why?
- Your three strongest entrepreneurial mindset qualities and how will you leverage them? Your three weakest and how will you improve or mitigate them?
- What are the benefits and risks to you as a creative entrepreneur? How will the benefits improve your life and creative practice? How will you plan to tackle risks involved?

Activity 3: Venture Iteration Chart – Introduction to Developing Unique Value Propositions

Use the table below to brainstorm three venture concepts. These concepts are mini side hustles and something you could do as a monetized hobby.

- *The heart* = what you love to do. List three things you do in your free time – or you would happily do for free! For example, baking from scratch.
- *The person* = for each heart, note one type of person who might be interested. For example, people who love homemade baked goods but lack the time/capacity to do it themselves.
- *The lightbulb (idea)* = for each of the heart/person you listed, come up with a short, unique value proposition. For example, hosting a pop-up muffin table at the local farmers market (Figure 1.4).

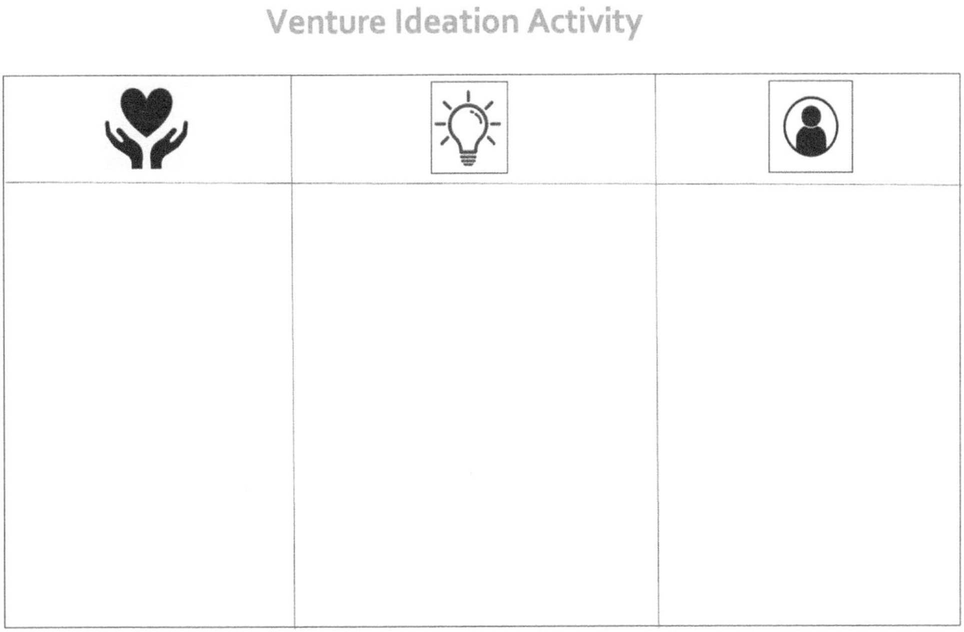

Figure 1.4 Venture ideation map.

Source: Jennifer A. Reis.

Activity 4: Klontz Money Script Writing Reflection

Do reflective writing using the following prompts. If you are comfortable, share with a peer, friend, or partner. Don't be surprised if answering these questions causes emotions to surface!

- What were you taught about money as a child?
- What behaviors around money did you observe from adults?
- What "financial flashpoints" (trauma/challenges) have you experienced?
- What "financial flashpoints" (trauma/challenges) are in your family history?
- When has spending brought you joy?
- Reflecting on your Money Scripts results, reflect on where those scripts might come from. How can you work within those mindsets productively/intentionally?

Resources and References

de Leon, P. (2022). *Finance for the people: Getting a grip on your finances*. Penguin Books.

Garman, K. (2020). *The entrepreneurial mindset: Preparing our next generation for the future of work*. New Degree Press.

Gerber, M. E. (2017). *The E-myth revisited: Why most small businesses don't work and what to do about it*. Harper Business.

Guillebeau, C. (2019). *SIDE HUSTLE: Build a side business and make extra money - without quitting your day job*. Macmillan.

Klontz, B., Britt, S. L., Mentzer, J., & Klontz, T. (2011). Money beliefs and financial behaviors: Development of the Klontz money script inventory. *Journal of Financial Therapy*, *2*(1), 1.

Klontz Money Scripts Test. (n.d.). Brad Klontz. https://www.bradklontz.com/moneyscriptstest

NPR. (2022). How I built thisNPR cookie consent and choices. *NPRpr.org*. https://www.npr.org/series/490248027/how-i-built-this

Sarasvathy, S. D. (2001). Causation and effectuation: Toward a theoretical shift from economic inevitability to entrepreneurial contingency. *Academy of Management Review*, *26*(2), 243–263.

2 Venture Ideation and Market Research

Jennifer A. Reis

Introduction

Where do creative **venture** ideas come from? They might be rooted strongly in an artistic practice: as an oil painter, there is a wish to create and sell paintings at a high-end retail art gallery. Or as a fashion designer, a desire to create a sustainable clothing line to be sold on an independently managed e-commerce site. Some creatives might have a clear vision of how entrepreneurial activity is intrinsic to their practice, others may have concerns about negative perception as a "commercial artist." Regardless of the level of enthusiasm for developing business venture concepts related to the creative practice, it is valuable to investigate other modes of ideation to develop a more creative and innovative venture concept and business model.

Your venture ideation should include potentially disruptive practices like **opportunity recognition** and **divergent thinking** as well as **convergent thinking**. Using these practices will help you with coming up with innovative venture concepts which evolve from the initial idea but could prove more sustainable and marketable. Eventually, your creative venture needs to develop the important **unique value proposition (UVP):** the core, **competitive advantage** that sets the particular entrepreneurial endeavor apart from others in the market. Once the UVP has been established, the exercise of business modeling through different **modeling canvas** examples as well as the review of defined **business models** that have commonly been utilized by creative ventures is extremely helpful in mapping out a new business concept.

Finally, if you employ the basics of **primary market research** including investigating exemplars and competitors and explore the potential value of **secondary market research** tools for market and industry sector data and trends like Mintel and Ibis, the information you discover will inform whether (or not) the creative venture has the **market demand** and capacity to support the venture.

Learning Outcomes

- **Describe** the process of venture ideation and opportunity recognition
- **Develop** a structured process for creative problem-solving using both divergent and convergent thinking
- **Construct** a business model canvas for a new venture.
- **Analyze** a business's UVP.
- **Utilize** market research tools to find relevant data.

DOI: 10.4324/9781003588771-2

Venture Ideation

Creative makers exist on a continuum of entrepreneurial drive. You might be a "born entrepreneur," driven to be in the marketplace with your creative practice. Or, you may be the opposite: shying away from entrepreneurial activity, considering it as "selling out." Regardless of enthusiasm for or reluctance to entrepreneurship, makers need to *ideate* their venture concept thoughtfully and consider opportunities to evolve initial ideas into the creation of a financially sustainable business that meets market demand.

Some makers come to ideation with a specific idea in mind that might be rooted in traditional and perhaps limited business models. For instance, Janey, a weaver who graduated with a college degree in a textile arts program might have been trained to pursue relationships with high-end contemporary craft galleries or art and craft fairs as the sole means of generating a career and related financial support. This route might be sustainable if access to those markets is available, and the intermediaries (the galleries and art/craft fair organizations) are viable and sustainable. However, with the rise of e-commerce and other digital offerings coupled with the high costs of gallery overhead and limited organizational capacity, Janey at the very least should consider diversifying her portfolio of **revenue streams** to offset potential liabilities.

When your seed of a venture concept is at its origin stage, it is important to both hold that idea as well as pursue other modes of investigation and evolution. Researching other creative entrepreneurs and offerings, opportunity recognition through observation, and use of divergent thinking are all means of pivoting the initial concept into a business model that captures more market demand.

- **Researching offerings:** Other creative products and services generated by similar makers are an excellent education. What do they make, how is it distributed, what is the pricing and marketing strategy, and how do they communicate their brand?
- **Opportunity recognition:** Market opportunities are constantly evolving with trends and technology: being an entrepreneurial anthropologist is a very important first step in exploring different creative business models.
- **Using divergent thinking:** Divergent thinking is also of value and is the opposite of where many early-stage entrepreneurs begin. Its opposite "twin" is convergent thinking, when as a maker there is an assumption that the origin idea is the concept of significance and, thereby, they jump into planning and logistics. Divergent thinking is a cognitive activity of generating iterations of the origin idea in order to explore multiple products and/or service opportunities. It forces creative makers to, ironically, be creative with their entrepreneurial venture. Consider market offerings that are adjacent or even contrary to the origin idea. It is not unlike working within a series of artworks that sprout from an initial concept but then evolve into other forms. Convergent thinking is important toward the mid-point and summation of business planning; however, creatives should fully explore divergent thinking activities as a means of generating alternative market offerings.

> How do we think like an anthropologist? This perception is led by curiosity, exploration, and critically reflecting on the makers we are researching. It is easy to fall into "compare and despair" when we look into the creative entrepreneurship practice of others who may appear to be years away from us in the level of success they have achieved. It is important to use a learning mindset when exploring exemplars and competitors and consider as objectively as possible their UVP, offerings, marketing and communication, pricing, and other information relevant to our own potential venture

Using divergent thinking is also helpful at building a venture with a **portfolio business model**. Using a portfolio point of view with business planning and execution results in having a diverse range of market offerings that assist with venture sustainability. When there is a package of products/services at different price points, **distribution channels**, and **target markets**, micro-entrepreneurs can continue to be nimble, financially sustainable, and resist dependency on a single mode of operation. Trends, technology, and markets move rapidly and operating within a portfolio mindset can ensure ventures stay consumer relevant and financially healthy.

What's the Venture's Unique Value Proposition?

A UVP is a strategic communication tool necessary to any venture. It is a clear and concise statement of the following: your venture's product(s) and/or service(s), its target market, and its competitive advantage in the market. A UVP serves as a compass statement both for the venture in planning and execution as well as an underlying narrative for marketing assets.

Developing a UVP for your venture can be daunting and often evolves through multiple iterations. In the creation of a UVP, focus first on brainstorming with short statements of information rather than diving into "wordsmithing." Generate information related to the value the venture brings to the market focusing on the benefit to the end user, who is assumed to be the target market and their potential motivation to engage with the product(s)/service(s), and how the venture's offerings are distinct from and superior to current market options. The "anthropologist" work mentioned earlier in the chapter might assist with generating information useful to the UVP.

Another Way to Think about Unique Value Propositions – The Belonging Framework: A Creative Value Proposition by Sara Hartmann

As a creative entrepreneur, being told to "figure out what problem you're solving for customers" can sometimes feel like the most frustrating advice. How can we explain the profound value of art or creative work using a framework that seems better suited to an infomercial product? Yet, at the same time, it is crucial to understand how we create value for our audience and to center this value in everything we do if we want our businesses to grow. The **Belonging Framework** offers a unique lens through which to explore and better understand the deep value others may be finding in our work, enabling us to maximize its impact.

Consider the artwork or artists that have been most impactful for you in your own life. Can you truly explain your love for a favorite song or a movie you've watched over a hundred times by clinically stating what "problem" it solves for you? Of course not. The complex emotional bond between a fan and an artist cannot be fully explained by a short, objective formula. While this framework won't provide a formulaic explanation either, it can help you come closer to understanding the **psychographics** – the attitudes, values, and lifestyles – of your most enthusiastic audience members.

We'll continue this information in Chapter 4 when we discuss venture **benefits** versus **features** aligned with your **target markets**.

Business Models and Modeling

Understanding and using business modeling is essential for venture success. As noted prior with the importance of utilizing divergent thinking for creative ideation prior to jumping into convergent thinking focused on logistics, business modeling can create space for mapping out and trouble-shooting exactly how the venture will operate with intention. Consider a business model to be the expanded version of a UVP. In short, business modeling consists of the following for a creative venture: what are the product(s)/service(s) on offer and associated benefits; who is the target market; how are the product(s)/service(s) distributed; how it is operated; how is revenue generated; and what are the venture's incurred costs of doing business? There are different business model canvases available to use, but all follow a similar format of being a visual tool to use in planning. After reviewing each, think about which one is most appropriate for you to use at this point in your business planning. There are four business model "canvases" we will look at in this section: the **value proposition canvas**, the **business model canvas**, the **lean canvas**, and the **creative micro-enterprise canvas**.

Using the Value Proposition Canvas

The first business modeling canvas comes from the book *Value Proposition Design* by Alex Osterwalder, Yves Pigneur, Greg Bernarda, and Alan Smith. Outlined in more detail farther into this chapter, modeling canvases are helpful tools to help you outline critical aspects of your creative venture in a concise and more informal manner than a lengthy traditional **business plan**. In short, the value design process takes us through the steps of ideating potential UVPs, designing a method to test the market, and reflecting on the results of said testing to continue on or pivot to another UVP iteration or start anew with another idea. By being thoughtful about our UVP at the very beginning, we can attempt to gauge whether or not our concept is strong enough (with market demand!) to move forward with investing our valuable time and financial resources.

This canvas is the most simple in design of the ones we will address. To see a visual of the canvas, refer to the link provided at the chapter's end under resources. It comprises two primary components: **customer profile** in which you establish an understanding of your ideal client and **value map** where you articulate the UVP. According to the book mentioned above, when these two aspects are in alignment, you achieve **fit**, basically an assumption that there is market demand associated with your UVP and the clientele you seek to engage.

The value map continues three core elements: a list of the **products** and **services** your venture will provide, the ways in which those products and services will address client **pain points**, and how the products and services will provide **gains** for your assumed clients. It is a concise box that you can use to capture the primary details of the UVP. The customer profile also focuses on three key aspects with the assumed client avatar in the middle of the circle. First, what is the client attempting to solve for in their professional and personal life? Second, what are the pains associated with that journey? And lastly, what is the ideal outcome to that responsibility?

Sara, a woodworker, could create a production line of cutting boards that are attractive enough to be used in charcuterie. The solution for a pain point could be making hosting a get-together easier and more stylish. She plans on gaining traction and promoting these products by partnering with a wine bar that serves snacks as well as sells cheeses, meats, and other premade hors d'oeuvres. Her assumed client is a very busy working professional who has personal obligations to host occasional happy hours at their house. Their pain consists of yet another responsibility on top of a very busy agenda. Extra money to buy nicer objects to make life easier is not an issue, time and capacity is. The gain would match (the fit!) the pain point noted above – a solution to pulling together a nice spread that appears to have taken effort and care to their guests.

The book *Business Model Generation: A Handbook for Visionaries, Game Changers, and Challengers*, authored by Alexander Osterwalder and Yves Pigneur (yes, two of the authors from the aforementioned value proposition canvas), pioneered the use of a canvas template as a means of mapping out business models. In lieu of a dense, text-based business plan, the business model planning tool popularized by the book introduced a visual method of getting a "30,000 foot" view of a venture's business model. Subsequently, other iterations of the original business model canvas were created to meet additional entrepreneurial needs, two of which are noted below. A link to the business model canvas is provided at the end of the chapter under resources (Figure 2.1).

The business model canvas is more detailed than the value proposition canvas mentioned earlier in the chapter. It comprises nine blocks, and in the middle of the canvas sits a long vertical block titled value proposition (your UVP). In the design of the canvas, this is the spine of the whole venture which should make sense given the attention we have thus far given to creating a compelling UVP. On the right side are a cluster of three outward-facing content blocks: **channels** – how you

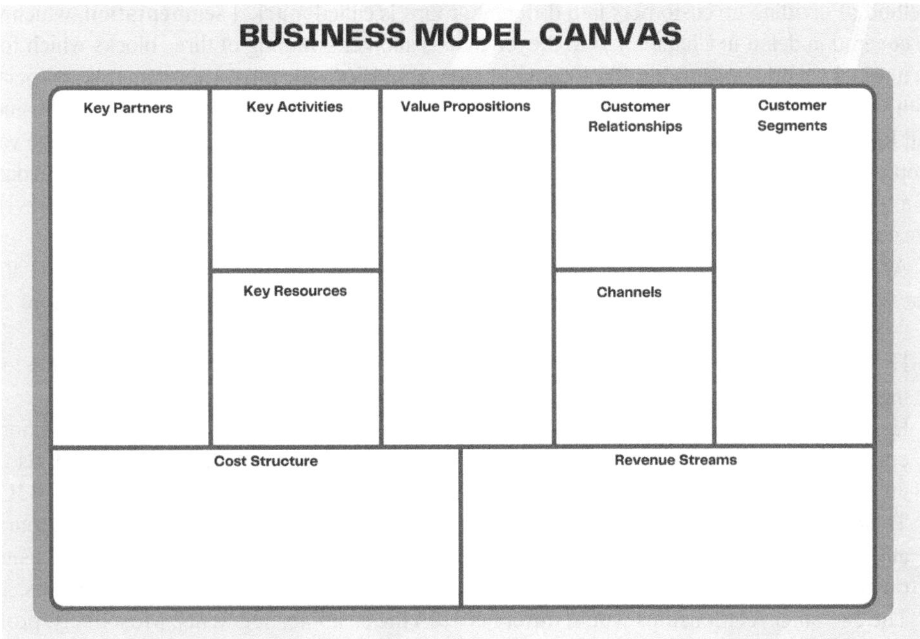

Figure 2.1 The business model canvas.

Source: Adapted from the business model canvas by Strategyzer.com.

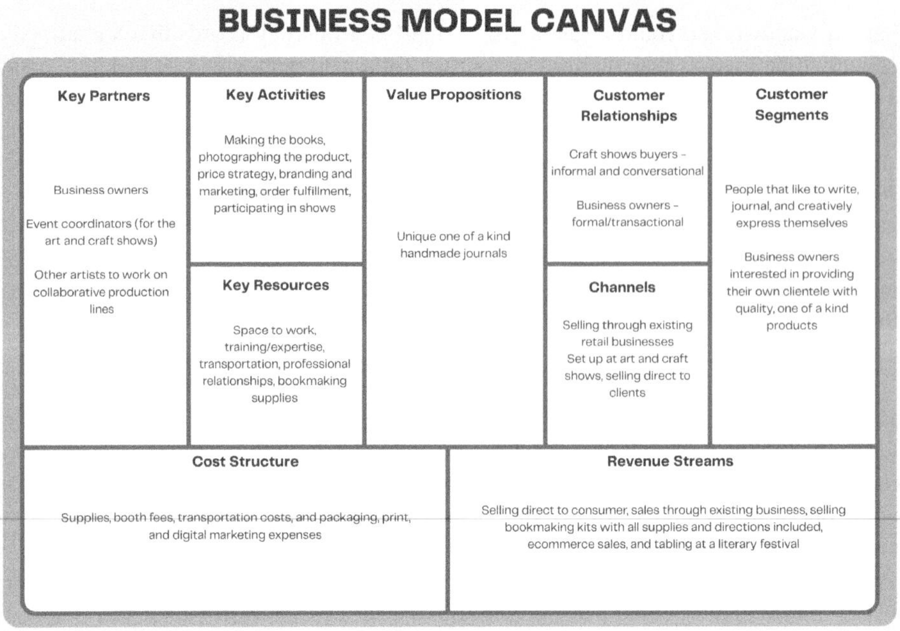

Figure 2.2 Business model canvas: handmade book artisan example.

Source: Adapted from the business model canvas by Strategyzer.com.

will distribute and deliver that value to your clients, **customer relationships** – how you will engage with those folks, and customer segments – what type or types of clients do you seek to serve? (This method of dividing up customers into different groups is called **market segmentation**, which will be covered in detail in Chapter 4.) On the left side is another grouping of three blocks which focus on internal venture **operations**. They consist of **key activities** – the most important tasks associated with your venture, **key resources** – those tangible and intangible **assets** necessary to do business, and **key partners** – who you need to work with in order to operate the venture. Finally, the value proposition block as well as the outward- and inward-facing components sit upon the foundation of a viable venture: **cost structure** – the costs associated with running the business, and revenue streams – the ways in which you will generate funds through your entrepreneurial efforts.

As an illustration, let's consider Sam who crafts and sells handmade books. We'll look at the canvas with concise information followed by a narrative that provides more detail (Figure 2.2).

- His value proposition (the UVP) could be well made, one of a kind, journals for people looking for a product to foster creativity and personal reflection.
- His channels might include selling through existing retail businesses like a contemporary craft shop or a bookstore which would be **business-to-business (B2B)**. He could also set up at art and craft shows, selling direct to clients, known as **business-to-consumer (B2C)**.
- The customer segments, based on the above, would include people who like to write, journal, and creatively express themselves. Additionally, a segment would also include other business owners interested in providing their own clientele with quality, one-of-a-kind products.
- The customer relationships would differ between the customer segments. Most likely, professional communication and customer service would be consistent; however, the interaction at the craft show with buyers would probably be more informal and conversational whereas interactions with the business owner would be more formal and transactional.

- The key activities would include making the books, photographing the product, price strategy, branding and marketing the books, fulfillment of orders, participating in art and craft shows, developing and maintaining relationships with B2B buyers, and the tasks involved with operating a business in good standing with financial and governmental requirements.
- His key resources could include a space to work, his training/expertise, a mode of transportation, his network/relationships, and of course bookmaking supplies.
- In Sam's venture, he might partner with other business owners, event coordinators (for the art and craft shows), and other artists to work on collaborative production lines.
- The cost structure to this entrepreneurial endeavor could include the costs associated with the supplies, booth fees, transportation costs, and packaging, print, and digital marketing expenses.
- Sam could make money off his handmade journals by selling direct to consumer, wholesale, or commission-based sales through existing business, selling bookmaking kits with all supplies and directions included, e-commerce sales, and tabling at a literary festival where he is a demonstrating vendor.

The Lean Canvas

The next modeling canvas we will address is the lean canvas by Ash Maurya, author of *Running Lean.* The lean canvas is an iteration of the business model canvas. The most compelling difference between the canvases is that the lean canvas is problem and solution focused rather than only about value propositions and business operations. It also includes areas to reflect on differentiating your venture from competitors and **key performance indicators** (Figure 2.3).

Similar to the original business model canvas, there is a core vertical block titled UVP in the middle which sits on the foundation of two blocks for cost structure and revenue streams. Customer segments and channels are also situated in the same location. However, in the upper right cluster of outward-facing boxes is a block called **unfair advantage** which is another way of addressing competitive advantage. On the left side of the canvas is where we see the significant

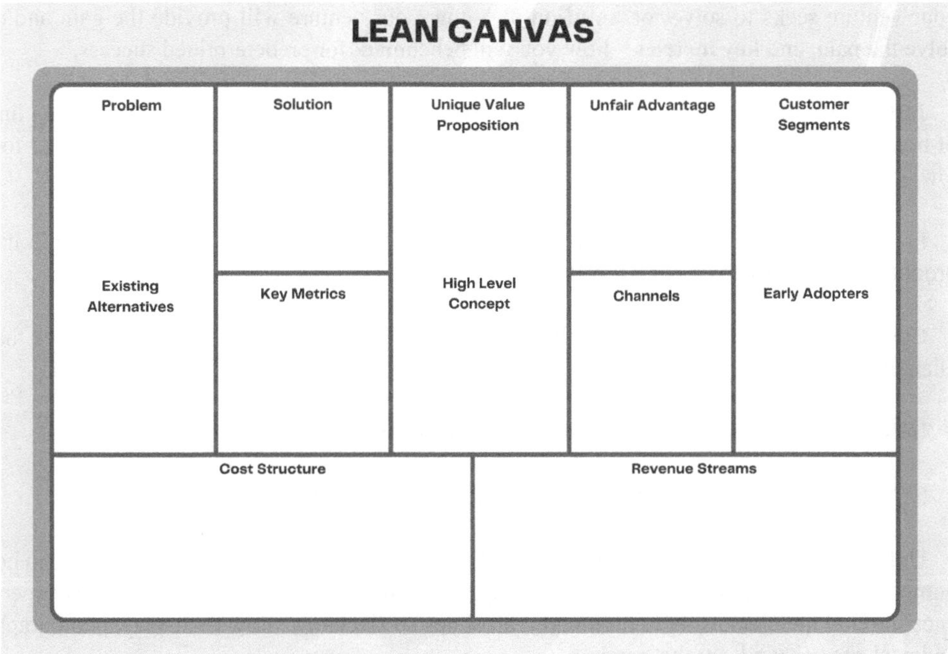

Figure 2.3 The lean canvas.

Source: Adapted from the business model canvas by Strategyzer.com and the lean model canvas by Ash Maurya.

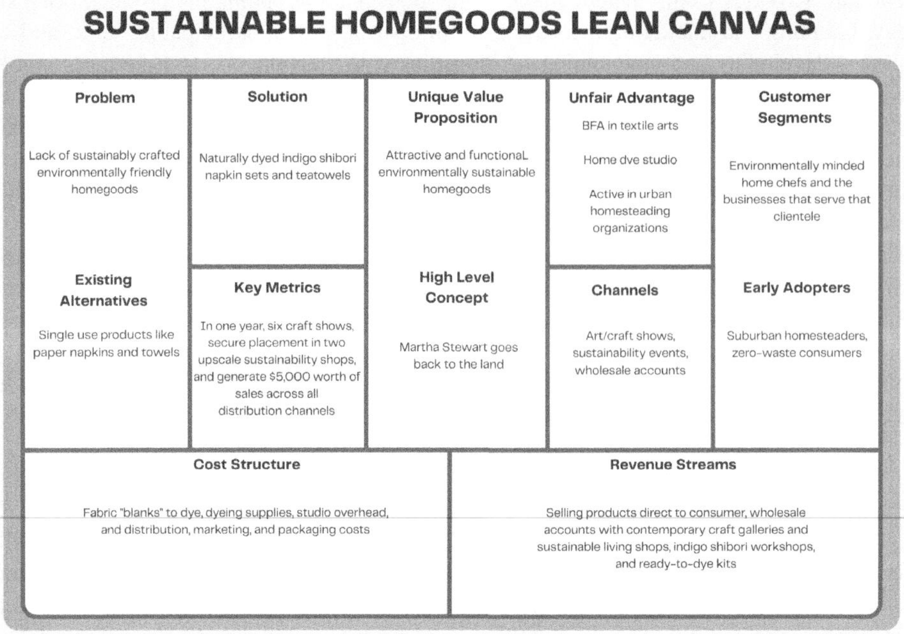

Figure 2.4 The lean canvas: environmental sustainable textiles example.

Source: Adapted from the business model canvas by Strategyzer.com and the lean model canvas by Ash Maurya.

difference with this canvas. The three blocks in this area are: **problem**(s) – identifying what your venture seeks to solve for, **solution**(s) – how your venture will provide the gain and/or solve the pain, and **key metrics** – how you will benchmark for predetermined success.

Just like we did with Sam the bookmaker, let's look at Latala's natural dyed production line of homegoods, particular cloth napkins and tea towels. Here is the illustrated canvas, and following is a list ordered in Ash Maurya's suggested sequence (Figure 2.4).

Problem: A lack of sustainably crafted environmentally friendly alternatives to single use products like paper napkins and towels.

Customer segments: Environmentally minded home chefs and the businesses that serve that clientele.

UVP: Attractive and functional sustainable homegoods.

Solution: Naturally dyed indigo shibori napkin sets and tea towels.

Unfair advantage: Latala has a Bachelor of Fine Arts (BFA) in textile arts, a dye studio in her home, and is active in urban homesteading organizations where she lives. She also has experience in retail merchandising in high-end craft shops so she knows how to display, photograph, and package her work for that market.

Revenue streams: Selling products B2C, wholesale accounts with contemporary craft galleries and sustainable living shops (business to business, aka B2B), and she might even want to teach indigo shibori workshops – and sell even more product to workshop participants or ready-to-dye kits to take home.

Cost structure: Fabric "blanks" to dye, dyeing supplies, studio overhead, and distribution, marketing, and packaging costs.

Key metrics: Latala has mapped out one year's worth of success. She wants to participate in six craft shows, secure placement in two upscale sustainability shops, and generate $5,000 worth of sales across all distribution channels.

Channels: Art/craft shows, sustainability events, wholesale accounts.

Creative Micro-Enterprise Canvas

Our last canvas was designed by the author of this chapter. While the canvases noted above are helpful entrepreneurial tools, they were informed by and designed within the context of the tech sector as well as traditional entrepreneurial development. Even though the other canvases are helpful for us to learn and use, some adaptation and translation were always needed to make them truly useful in the space of creative micro-enterprise. Much like the inspiration for this book, I needed to develop a tool that was bespoke for this specific cohort, relatable, and practical. Like Ash Maurya, my canvas illustrated below obviously is inspired by the business model canvas but has been tweaked to reflect the practicalities of being a creative entrepreneur (Figure 2.5).

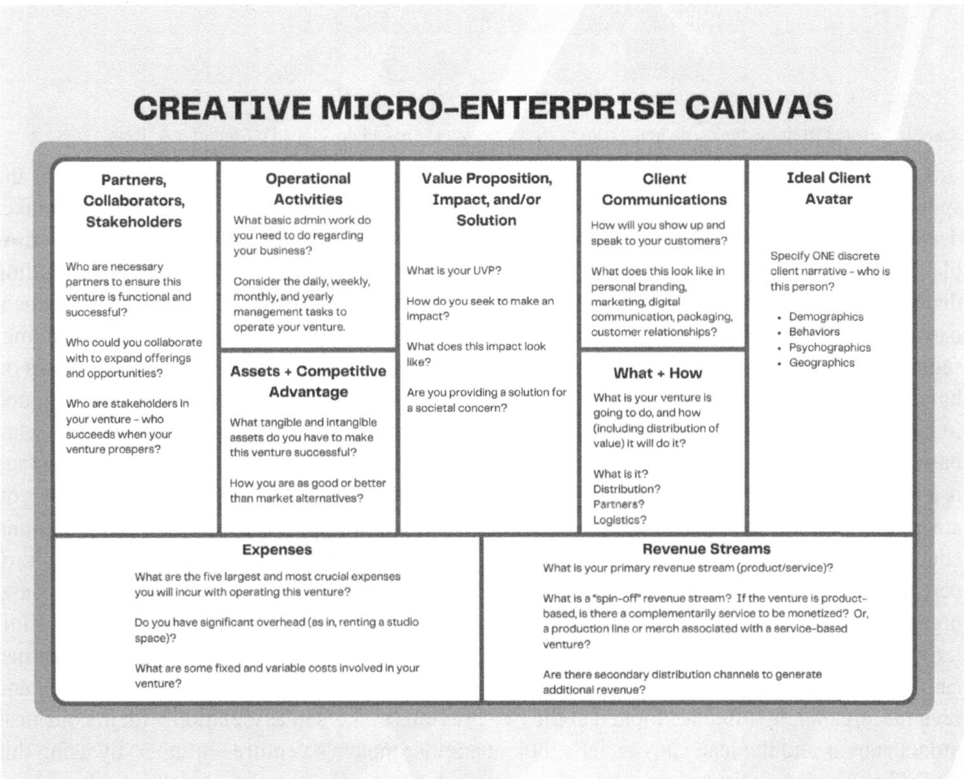

Figure 2.5 Creative micro-enterprise canvas.

Source: Adapted from the business model canvas by Strategyzer.com and developed by Jennifer A. Reis.

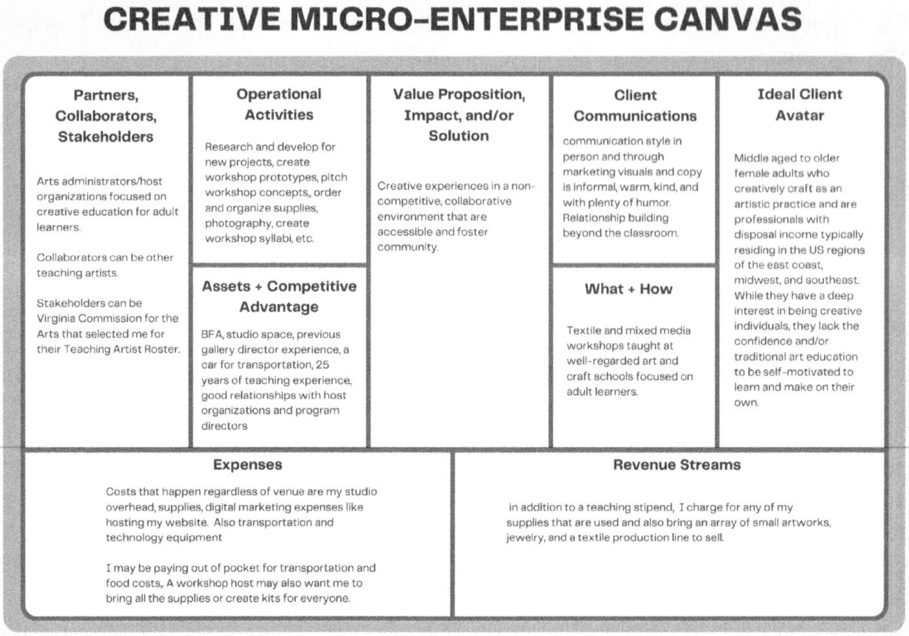

Figure 2.6 Creative micro-enterprise canvas: teaching artist example.

Source: Adapted from the business model canvas by Strategyzer.com and developed by Jennifer A. Reis.

Like the business model canvas and the lean canvas, the value proposition block sits as the spine in the middle. It also includes **impact** and solution if that's pertinent information the maker decides to include, so it is open to **social entrepreneurship** efforts as well. The **what + how** block is an opportunity to detail exactly what your venture is going to do, and how (including distribution of value) it will do it. **Ideal client** avatar is an area to specify ONE discrete client narrative – who is this person? – in lieu of attempting to come up with several different customer segments. Coming up with one can be challenging enough! **Client communications** focuses on how we will show up and speak with our customers depending on who that person is assumed to be. As far as business tasks, that is dealt with using the **operational activities** block – what basic admin work do you need to do regarding your business? Assets + competitive advantage is a space to detail what you bring as value being the **solopreneur** to this venture and how you are as good or better than market alternatives. While traditional entrepreneurship activity and education focused solely on competitors, this canvas expands that concept into the collaborator perceptive in the partners/stakeholders/collaborators block. Instead of seeing other makers and organizations through the zero sum lens of competition only, often folks and entities doing similar work can be excellent partners and allies. Finally, as in the other two previously described canvases, the venture design rests on top of a foundation of financial viability: expenses and revenue streams. Just like we looked at the two previous makers in association with the business model canvas and the lean canvas, let's look at another maker's venture – mine! – by using this tool. The descriptive list below is based on my work as a teaching artist, something I have been professionally active in for decades (Figure 2.6).

Value proposition/impact/solution: Creative experiences in a non-competitive, collaborative environment that are accessible and foster community.

What + how: Textile and mixed media workshops taught at well-regarded art and craft schools focused on adult learners.

Ideal client avatar: Middle aged to older female adults who creatively craft as an artistic practice and are professionals with disposal income typically residing in the U.S. regions of the east coast, midwest, and southeast. While they have a deep interest in being creative individuals, they lack the confidence and/or traditional art education to be self-motivated to learn and make on their own.

Client communications: My communication style in person and through marketing visuals and copy is informal, warm, kind, and with plenty of humor. It is definitely more conversational and casual than my communication style in the college classroom! The workshop participants see me as a mentor and a friend, more of a facilitator of a creative experience rather than a professor assessing a final project or presentation. Adult learners can carry educational trauma baggage especially with the pressure of making art "correctly" and I come into the workshop environment understanding there might be anxiety about me and the overall situation. Finally, my client communications is about relationship building – I often have repeat students in my classes and in a large part it is because they enjoy learning from me.

Operational activities: I need to do research and development for new projects, learn new skills, create workshop prototypes, identify and pitch workshop concepts, develop pricing strategy, order and organize supplies, do photography (including process shots), create workshop syllabi, communicate with the participants prior as an introduction and to identify any individual issues/questions, transport myself and supplies, organize the workshop space, deliver the instructional content being mindful of participant's cognitive capacity and physical limitations, take photos during the workshop, sell supplies and product, and engage with prior workshop participants via digital marketing like social media and email campaigns.

Assets + competitive advantage: Like Latala, I too have a BFA, but mine is from a traditional art and design college in painting and printmaking so I bring an understanding of color, composition, aesthetics, and art history plus contemporary art and craft. Since I was a gallery director (for far too long…) who specialized in contemporary craft, I have a knowledge base associated with exhibiting art and how to prepare works for display, especially those requiring alternative preparation. I have been hand-stitching from a young age, and the conceptual content as well as aesthetic which focuses on vintage ephemera and feminine imagery appeals to my ideal client.

Partners/stakeholders/collaborators: Given what I stated for my what + how, I clearly need to partner with arts administrators focused on creative education for adult learners. This means that my valuable partners and stakeholders are often program directors at art and craft schools. They need their instructors to be good communicators, professional (as in signing and returning contracts in a timely manner), and represent the school well considering the school's reputation. Collaborators can be other teaching artists – which I could easily pigeonhole as competitors. However, I try to be expansive to see them as potential collaborators – could we team-teach together perhaps? Or at least, if they are generous enough to share, would they have tips on other places they have taught that might be a good fit for me?

Expenses: When I first started teaching at numerous and diverse organizations, I realized some of my expenses would vary although some would stay the same. Costs that happen regardless of venue are my studio overhead, supplies, and digital marketing expenses like hosting my website. However, if I am doing a one day or weekend class, I may be paying out of pocket for transportation and food costs, which really adds up. A workshop host may also want me to bring all the supplies or create kits for everyone. I have developed a pricing strategy to offset differing costs based on the context.

Revenue streams: As a young teaching artist, I left a lot of money on the table! Having learned the hard way, I had to think creatively about revenue generation. So, in addition to a teaching stipend, I now charge for any of my supplies that are used and also bring an array of small artworks, jewelry, and a textile production line to sell. Given my ideal client has disposable income, often they want to leave with a souvenir of our time together – and of course now they have a story to share about their new artist friend.

Identifying the Venture's Market, Target Market, Competitors, and Sectors

After doing the work of venture ideation and business modeling in which the focus is on the internal value and operations, a creative entrepreneur needs to invest in the context whereby it exists – aka, a **market**. This is accomplished by identifying the venture's market, **target market(s)**, **exemplars**, **competitors**, and the **sector** in which it operates. This information will be further discussed in Chapter 3; however, this is an introduction of basic concepts to get you thinking about early venture design and implementation.

> For Scott, an illustrator who creates acrylic paintings for role-playing card games (RPGs), this could look like the following. The market consists of people interested in RPGs who have the capacity and are allowed by law to purchase and engage with those games. The target market (ideal clients) are players interested in tabletop games that are narrative, collaborative, and often played "IRL" (in real life). The sector the illustrator engages with is the RPG **industry** which can include in-person as well as virtual iterations of gaming.

If a creative entrepreneur can identify their market, target market, and sector, they can research all three to further inform the venture and the value it offers. Particularly with target markets, understanding and empathic engagement with the end user is the foundation of primary market research further discussed below. When investigating a venture's target market, it is valuable to create an avatar of the expected end user. Prompts to consider when crafting a venture's target market avatar include reflecting on the **demographic, behavioral**, and psychographic profile of someone who could be an ideal client. Additionally, creative entrepreneurs should focus on the consumer motivations related to the target market – why are they purchasing and engaging with this product/service (Figure 2.7)?

Lastly, a creative entrepreneur should investigate other operators in the sector in which they wish to participate. Researching exemplars, those entrepreneurs who are doing what you want to do but at an established level of success, can serve as an inspiration and assist with future goal setting and expand opportunity recognition. Competitors are those individuals/ventures at an earlier stage of business that might be a direct alternative to the venture being created. While it is extremely valuable to understand who is already engaged with the market to create competitive advantage with existing ventures, the venture's competitors could at some point be collaborators on future endeavors. There are DIRECT competitors and INDIRECT competitors as well. Direct competitors are those ventures doing exactly or nearly what you are doing. Indirect competitors are businesses that are providing value which is analogous. For example, if you are a painter hosting an art reception at a gallery, another artist doing similar two-dimensional work down the street would be a direct competitor especially if the pieces are of similar aesthetic and market demand. However, consider there's a painting class being taught as well a few blocks away that same night – that would be an indirect competitor. It's not an art exhibition opening where people are passively looking at paintings but it is a painting experience nonetheless which is active engagement in art. Both are competitors for attention and revenue but within different means of engaging with painting.

Figure 2.7 Janeise Harmon, founder of Hello unto You, with weaving demo.

Source: Jennifer A. Reis

Primary and Secondary Market Research

Once you identify and investigate the market and, more importantly, the target market, you can utilize primary research and, in some cases, when appropriate, secondary research. We all need to be aware, however, of the dangers of bias leading to bad intel from research. For instance, confirmation bias leads us often to gravitate toward information that aligns with our current beliefs and gives it more weight than information that contradicts our beliefs. Furthermore with acquiescence bias, research subjects in surveys, interviews, and focus groups subconsciously lean toward the answers they think the researcher is looking for. Be aware of biases that might become barriers for you as the receiver and analyzer of information as well as those coming from people from which you might solicit information.

Primary market research consists of engaging with and listening to end users. In the case of a venture operating as a B2B, this would include interacting with other businesses that would be potential buyers. For example, if a ceramist was creating a production line of one of a kind lamp bases for a home décor business, the maker might want to identify and reach out to potential retailers for informational interviews or with a survey to collect information pertaining to market interest, price points, and aesthetics. If a creative venture is within a business model of B2C, the entrepreneurial maker might engage with ideal clients through social media posts, IRL interactions through conversations focused on end user needs and wants, and general observations of their behavior. Primary research is ongoing, and creative entrepreneurs should always be investigating their target markets and, most importantly, listen and reflect on the information gleaned to persevere or pivot their venture's product(s) and/or service(s).

Finally, you as a creative entrepreneur might avail yourselves of resources through **secondary market research**. Secondary market research is information collected and sometimes analyzed through established entities, often in the form of large databases. These can include governmental entities focused on demographic data for a particular geographic area, private for-profit companies researching market trends affecting specific industry sectors, and technology companies tracking and reporting on Internet search queries and traffic patterns. This can be helpful for creative entrepreneurs operating in large, well-known sectors like publishing, fashion, and technology. For other creative entrepreneurs, especially those in artisanal or fine art and craft work, the information provided especially by for-profit research companies like Ibis and Mintel can have limited usefulness as the database information is often focused on large industry sectors. Additionally, access can be restricted due to the high cost of purchasing subscriptions or reports from such entities; this is often limited to business development centers and university libraries due to the expense.

Closing

From initial venture ideation to market research, creative entrepreneurs should both understand their UVP as well as be receptive to external information. They need to develop and pivot their business models by being adaptive to the context in which the venture exists. Early stages of market research by considering one's market, target market, and sector data inform the evolution of the venture's UVP. In closing, this stage of venture ideation is flexible to market context and demand in order to develop a sustainable creative entrepreneurship venture idea.

Mini Case: Key Partners, Stakeholders, and Collaborators at Look at What I Made by Marie Segares

Dedri Uys, founder of Look At What I Made, is originally from South Africa and currently lives in England. Dedri is a crochet pattern designer, author, and teacher best known for Sophie's Universe Crochet Along, a free crochet pattern for a continuous square blanket that was released in parts over 20 weeks in 2015. Sophie's Universe is the fifth most favorited crochet pattern of all time on Ravelry, a social network and pattern marketplace for the fiber arts with more than 9 million members. On Ravelry, Sophie's Universe has over 8,400 user-submitted projects and has been favorited by over 40,700 members (Figure 2.8).

Look At What I Made specializes in creating stunning patterns using advanced crochet skills and techniques that are accessible to adventurous beginners, combining clearly written instructions, alternative options (such as availability in multiple languages and varied sizes), and step-by-step photos with video tutorials. Look At What I Made's partners/stakeholders/collaborators include Scheepjes, Facebook and Ravelry group moderators, and several European YouTubers. Scheepjes is a popular Dutch yarn brand that Dedri has collaborated with for more than a decade. Scheepjes sponsored the original Sophie's Universe Crochet Along, and Dedri designed the patterns for their annual crochet alongs in 2018 and 2025. She is highlighted on their website in the "Friends" menu as an independent designer that the company frequently works with. Over the years, several fan-led and unofficial Facebook and Ravelry groups have formed for her patterns, including ones that Dedri has partnered with directly. One Facebook group for sharing pictures of blankets made with her series of Sophie's patterns has over 18,000 members. These groups provide community and belonging along with pattern support, answering questions from beginners during her crochet alongs, and reducing Dedri's need to provide technical assistance. Although Dedri has a YouTube channel and has created video tutorials for some of her patterns, she has also partnered with different

European crochet YouTubers – including It's all in a Nutshell Crochet and Mike's Creatieve Wereld – to create video tutorial series in English and Dutch to support her crochet alongs.

Sources: Christina Crochet Coach. (2025, May 8). *Ep 31: The science behind crochet stitches with Dedri Uys | Part One* [Video]. YouTube. https://youtu.be/UvYPj1ypdk0; Look At What I Made lookatwhatimade.net; Ravelry www.ravelry.com; Scheepjes www.scheepjes.com

Figure 2.8 Dedri Uys, founder of Look at What I Made, with several crochet blankets.
Source: Courtesy of Dedri Uys/Look At What I Made

Activities

Activity 1: Be an Entrepreneurial Anthropologist Presentation or Digital Board

Identify one exemplar (high success level) and one competitor related to your venture concept. Whether through a presentation to your peers, or a digital board/presentation you create for yourself, explore the following for both the exemplar and the competitor. FYI – your exemplar should be DIFFERENT than the creative entrepreneur you researched for the Meet Your Maker activity in Chapter 1.

Venture Exemplar (a creative business similar to yours, two to three years out and successful)

- Who are they?
- What do they sell: their product(s)/service(s)?
- Who do they sell it to?
- How do they price it?
- How do they distribute the product/service? E-commerce model/platform?
- What's their marketing strategy including DIGITAL MARKETING?

Venture Competitor (a creative business similar to yours when you launch)

- Who are they?
- What do they sell: their product(s)/service(s)?
- Who do they sell it to?
- How do they price it?
- How do they distribute the product/service? E-commerce model/platform?
- What's their marketing strategy including DIGITAL MARKETING?

Activity 2: Unique Value Proposition (UVP) Creation – Write and Share

It's time to write your venture's UVP! This is a clear and concise statement that, akin to an elevator pitch, you can say to someone in one breath. This is iterative writing and you are encouraged to continue to wordsmith and tweak this UVP over multiple versions. This type of writing can be daunting – remember that you are at a starting point with this first iteration of a UVP. Given that we can let perfect be the enemy of the good, you can start by using this "mad libs" diagram for your first try!

Mab Libs UVP:

Venture/Personal Name is a what the venture does that serves target market(s) through product(s)/service(s) by what makes this venture UVP competitive to what is the venture's impact.

As an example, here's a UVP using the Mad Libs exercise for a makers shop offering supplies and classes:

The Magpie is a makers' shop that serves creative crafters through high-quality art and craft supplies and workshops by creating an inclusive and kind environment to support personal expression and community.

Activity 3: UVP Disruption

In this chapter, we addressed the importance of divergent thinking. It is difficult to expand on your original venture concept idea solo. This two-part activity will help you think outside the box with the help of a peer, partner, or friend.

1 Swap UVPs with a peer or hand yours over to a partner/friend. Have them review the idea outlined in the UVP. They will then provide three related ideas as follows:

   - One product/service related to the UVP that is an obvious idea. As in, a clothing designer includes a fashion accessory line.
   - One product/service related to the UVP that is a stretch idea. As in, a clothing designer includes a line of pet clothing.

- One product/service related to the UVP that is a silly idea. As in, a clothing designer's production line of dolls wearing miniature outfits related to human designs.

2 Look over the ideas created for you and ideate on how to incorporate information from either the stretch or silly idea. You don't have to embed it verbatim into your venture concept, instead use it as inspiration to develop a new product/service line or to pivot your initial idea. This is an exercise only so you don't have to wed yourself to this new concept. However, it helps us think more expansively!

Activity 4: Create Your Creative Micro-Enterprise Canvas

Our convergent thinking activity for this chapter is to begin to model your creative venture with the Creative Micro-Enterprise Canvas. Add information to the blocks associated with the following. No need to do full paragraph or an excessive amount of information – this is a sketch of your business model (Figure 2.9).

- Value proposition/impact/solution
- What + how
- Ideal client avatar

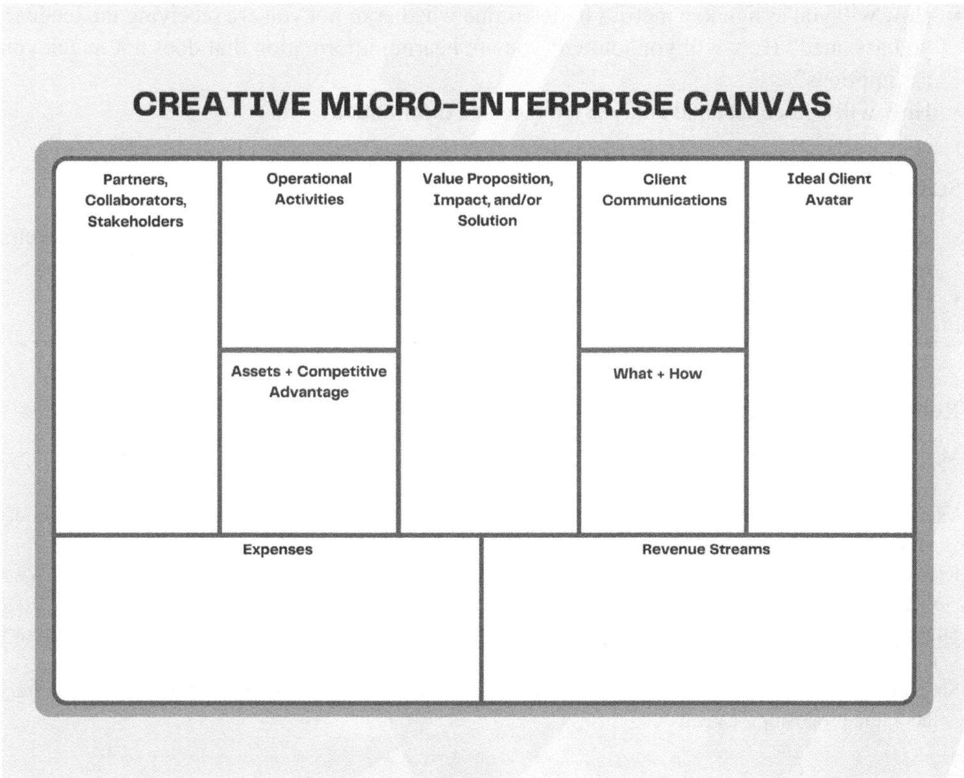

Figure 2.9 Creative micro-enterprise canvas: blank.

Source: Adapted from the business model canvas by Strategyzer.com and developed by Jennifer A. Reis.

- Client communications
- Operational activities
- Assets + competitive advantage
- Partners/stakeholders/collaborators
- Expenses
- Revenue streams

Activity 5: Primary and Secondary Research Collection

The last activity for this chapter is to do your research! Primary research is investigating assumptions about your venture out in the market and with your ideal client(s)/target market(s). Secondary research, if appropriate to your venture and available to you, is using data already collected and analyzing it.

Primary Research

- What is an assumption about your market and your ideal client(s)/target market(s)? Write that down as your research question.
- How will you test that assumption? One-on-one interviews? Focus groups? Surveys? Social media engagement?
- How will you assign key metrics to determine whether or not you are receiving the feedback you assumed? How will you know if you are hearing information that does not match your assumptions?
- How will you collect and analyze the received information?

Secondary Research

- What do you wish to know about your sector, market, and ideal client(s)/target market(s) from the research already collected?
- How will you analyze that data in comparison with your initial venture idea?
- How will you use it to adapt your venture?

Resources and References

Maurya, A. (n.d.). Build your business model in 20 minutes + Learn the method. *LeanFoundry*. https://www.leanfoundry.com/tools/lean-canvas

Maurya, A. (n.d.) What is the right fill order for a lean canvas? *LeanFoundry*. https://www.leanfoundry.com/articles/what-is-the-right-fill-order-for-a-lean-canvas

Reis. (2025, August 1). Micro-enterprise for creatives canvas. *Make Do Creative LLC*. https://www.makedocreative.com/micro-enterprise-for-creatives-canvas

Strategyzer. (2025, February 11). Business model canvas. *Strategyzer*. https://www.strategyzer.com/library/the-business-model-canvas

Strategyzer. (2025, February 11). Value proposition canvas. *Strategyzer*. https://www.strategyzer.com/library/the-value-proposition-canvas

3 Strategy

Tools to Thrive in a Competitive Market

Sara Hartmann

Introduction

In creative fields, the path to excellence is often seen as a personal and individual journey. The mythology of a lone genius laboring away in the studio looms large in our popular imagination. However, succeeding in business requires us to study, understand, and adapt to the external business environment. Business success does not happen in a vacuum; it is not the inevitable outcome of creative achievement. It is the combined result of the entrepreneur's own effort *and* favorable market conditions. While your creative work may be entirely your own vision, how it is received in the marketplace is ultimately subject to economic influences that are often outside of your direct control.

The world of big business understands that market forces and competitive dynamics shape outcomes more profoundly than individual performance alone. To navigate these complexities, many tools and frameworks have been developed to help leaders of large businesses craft and execute competitive strategies. This chapter will introduce some of these key frameworks, discussing and interpreting them specifically through the lens of the creative small business.

Learning Outcomes

- **Define** competitive advantage.
- **Explain** the factors that support generic strategy.
- **Analyze** a competitive situation using a Five Forces analysis.
- **Evaluate** creative focus points within a competitive strategy (BCG and Blue Ocean).
- **Formulate** growth strategies using an Ansoff matrix.

What Is Competitive Advantage?

A company's **strategy** can be defined as its action plan for achieving a **competitive advantage** over its rivals. But what exactly do we mean by competitive advantage? At its most basic level, there are only two fundamental types of advantages that one company or its product can possess over another: either the company's products or services are **better** than similar offerings or they are **cheaper**.

Businesses compete with rivals by organizing their business around either offering **products** or **services** that provide superior value to customers, or by delivering their products and services to customers at a lower cost. If a business is able to develop an advantage that persists over time, despite competitor efforts to match or surpass that advantage, then the company has achieved a **sustainable competitive advantage**. This is the ultimate goal of **strategic planning**.

DOI: 10.4324/9781003588771-3

At its core, strategy asks a fundamental question: What will you do better than anyone else? It delves into identifying that distinctive feature, unique skill, or compelling point of view that will cause customers to actively seek out your offerings and consistently choose them over the available alternatives in the marketplace.

The Five Basic Competitive Strategies

In crafting a strategy, businesses can employ one of five basic **generic competitive strategies**. These strategies are built upon fundamental trade-offs: whether to compete by offering differentiated products or services that better serve customer needs or by offering products and services at a lower price; and whether to compete for a broad market audience or focus on a narrow, niche audience. These trade-offs between "better" versus "cheaper" and "large audience" versus "small audience" define the five basic generic strategies:

- **Low-Cost Provider Strategy:** The business strives to achieve lower overall costs than its rivals for comparable products or services and competes to attract a broad spectrum of customers. The goal is to be the cost leader in the industry.
- **Broad Differentiation Strategy:** The business aims to differentiate its products or services from competitors by offering superior product attributes or unique features that will appeal to a broad spectrum of buyers. The focus is on creating perceived value that justifies a premium price.
- **Focused Low-Cost Strategy:** The business concentrates on serving a narrow market niche and competes within that niche by offering products or services at a lower price than rivals. This strategy leverages cost advantages within a specific segment.
- **Focused Differentiation Strategy:** The business focuses on a narrow market niche and competes within that niche by offering a highly differentiated product or service with attributes that specifically cater to the unique needs and preferences of this segment.
- **Best-Cost Provider Strategy:** This is a hybrid strategy that combines elements of both low-cost and differentiation. The business aims to provide the customer with more value for their money by meeting key preferences on product attributes while simultaneously beating price expectations relative to competitors offering similar quality (Figure 3.1).

Strategic Competencies

To successfully deploy a chosen strategy, a business must develop core competencies that align with that strategy and possess the necessary resources to implement it effectively. These competencies are the unique capabilities and strengths that allow a company to execute its chosen strategic path better than its competitors (Table 3.1).

What Does This Mean for You as a Creative Entrepreneur?

For most small businesses in creative industries, the choice often leans toward pursuing a **differentiation strategy** rather than a low-cost strategy. This is in part because creativity itself is a natural advantage in the pursuit of differentiation. Furthermore, the resources necessary to successfully pursue a sustainable advantage in low-cost competition often necessitate **economies of scale**, which are typically beyond the reach of most small creative ventures.

Competing on the basis of being "better" is generally a more sustainable strategy for many entrepreneurs in the long run. If you are competing solely on the basis of being a low-cost provider, it's always possible for a larger business with more resources to copy your product and sell it at an even lower price than you can afford. However, while "cheaper" is an objective

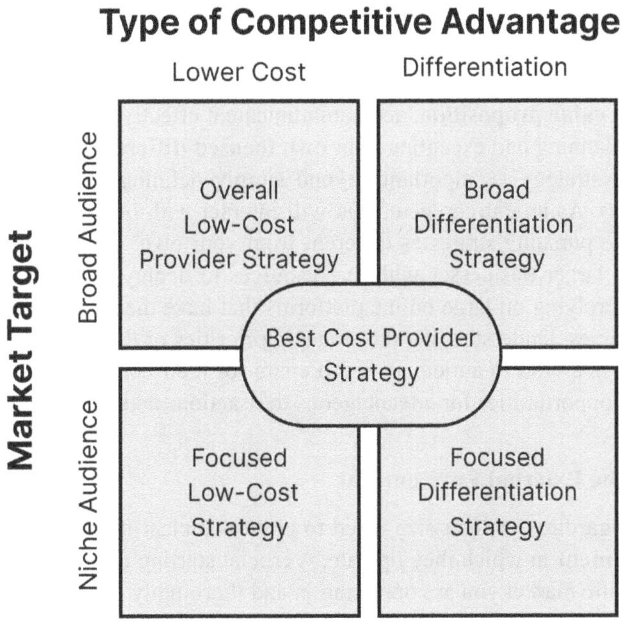

Figure 3.1 The five generic competitive strategies.

Source: Sara Hartmann

Table 3.1 Resources and Competencies for Deploying Strategy

Strategy	*Resources Needed*	*Key Competencies*
Differentiation	• Strong research and development capabilities or creative talent • Appealing brand • Premium quality materials or components • Defensible Intellectual property	• Innovation and product development • Brand building and marketing prowess • Superior customer service and experience design • Quality control and assurance • Ability to understand and anticipate customer needs
Low Cost	• Access to low-cost raw materials • Highly efficient production systems • Strong bargaining power with suppliers • Lean operational infrastructure • Large distribution network	• Exceptional cost management and control • Process optimization • Supply chain management • High-volume production capabilities • Ability to standardize products/services
Best Cost	• Hybrid production capabilities (e.g., some automation, some customization) • Efficient supply chain with some flexibility	• Balancing cost efficiency with quality enhancement • Agility in adapting to market demands • Effective communication of "value for money" to customers

measure that we can understand just by comparing two prices, "better" is inherently in the eye of the beholder. What is considered "better" to one group of consumers may not be "better" to another. The foundational work you will do in chapters four and five to define your audience, craft your **unique value proposition**, and communicate it effectively through your brand are all integral parts of planning and executing your own **focused differentiation strategy**.

Understanding strategy is important beyond simply defining the strategic positioning of your own business. As an entrepreneur, you will interact with other organizations, both large and small, that are pursuing strategies different from your own. You may find yourself facing competition from larger businesses with the resources to deploy different strategies, and you may find yourself relying on large online platforms that have their own strategic priorities and competitive strategies. Understanding the strategic priorities of these other businesses that you interact with will help you to anticipate and prepare for their competitive moves and can also help you identify opportunities for advantageous transactions and collaborations.

Understanding the External Environment

All businesses, regardless of their size, need to possess a clear understanding of the **external business environment** in which they operate. A crucial starting point for this understanding is to define the specific market you are operating in and thoroughly examine its characteristics.

Defining Your Market

What do we mean when we refer to a **market**? A market is a place, whether real or theoretical, where buyers and sellers come together to exchange goods or services. This can range from a highly formal structure, like the New York Stock Exchange, to an informal gathering, such as a neighborhood yard sale. In the context of business strategy, the term "market" most commonly refers to all of the transactions within a particular category of goods or services, occurring within a specific geographic area, over a defined period of time. For example, if we talk about "the craft beer market in the US," we are referring to the total value of all craft beer sold across the United States within a given year.

Key Market Characteristics to Examine

When studying a market, there are several fundamental characteristics that you should examine to gain a comprehensive understanding:

Market Size: This characteristic asks: "How big is this market?" In other words, what is the total value of sales (usually expressed in currency) within the most relevant geographic market for your business during a recent year? For example, if you are opening a tattoo shop, you might focus on a local geographic market and research the total sales volume of all tattoos in your city, state, or province in a recent year. Alternatively, if you are starting a jewelry business that will sell custom wedding bands online, you might research the total nationwide sales for wedding bands or fine jewelry in your country over the last year. Quantifying your market size provides a baseline for estimating potential revenue.

Market Growth: Once you are able to quantify the size of your market, the next crucial question is its growth trajectory. Market growth measures how much a market is increasing or decreasing in total sales volume year over year, typically expressed as a percentage. Market growth is closely tied to a market's stage of development, as each distinct stage carries its own unique competitive dynamics.

Market Stages: These distinct phases describe the typical life cycle of a market, from its inception to its eventual decline.

- **Introductory Stage:** When a product or service is completely new, or new to a specific geographic area, it is in its introductory stage. At this stage, market growth is often uncertain and unpredictable. There may be fewer competitors in the market as the newness and inherent uncertainty deter others from joining immediately.
- **Growth Stage:** If a market successfully takes off from its introductory stage, market growth accelerates and becomes more certain. The market has entered its growth stage. At this point, new players and competitors are likely to enter to compete for a share of the expanding pie. Growth rates for companies within the market may be in double or even triple digits for an extended period.
- **Mature Stage:** When a market enters its mature stage, the rate of growth slows down but typically becomes more predictable. Competition between existing market players may intensify significantly, as they will now need to capture market share from each other in order to grow, rather than simply benefiting from overall market expansion.
- **Decline Stage:** In the declining stage, the market begins to experience negative growth and starts to contract in overall size. Competition becomes even more intense as the total number of customers has reduced. Many competitors may emerge, merge, or exit the market entirely as profitability becomes increasingly challenging (Figure 3.2).

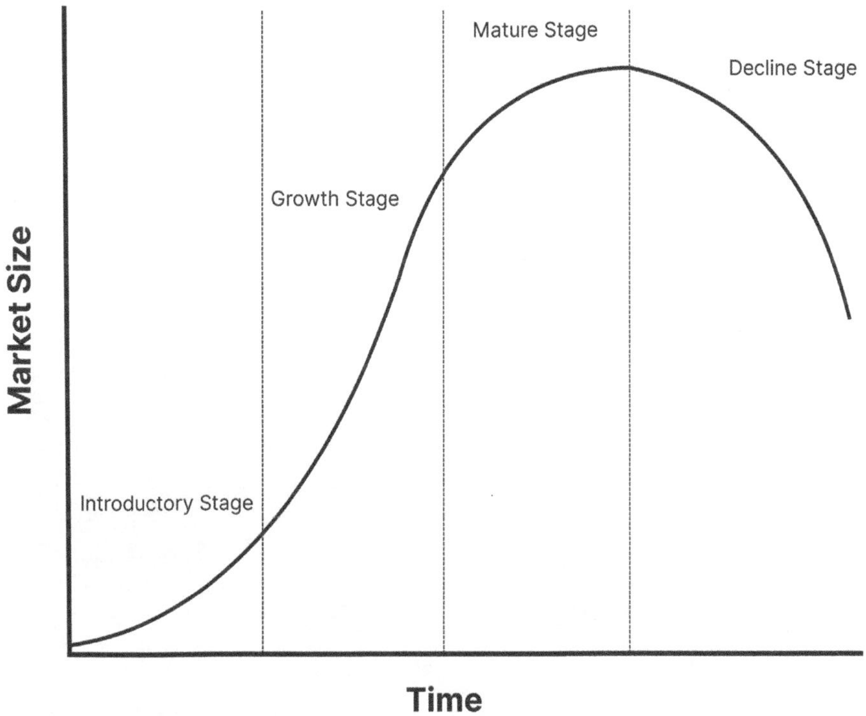

Figure 3.2 The stages of market growth.

Source: Sara Hartmann

Market Concentration: Market concentration asks: "How many competitors exist within this market, and how is market share distributed among them?" A **highly concentrated market** may have just a small handful of businesses with dominant shares of the market, meaning customers have fewer choices. Conversely, if the market is **fragmented** rather than concentrated, there are many smaller competitors, and less concentration of market share among a few large players. (**Market share** is defined as the percentage of a market that a single business controls.)

Market Trends and Cycles

Once you've identified the market you are operating in and noted its key characteristics like size, growth stage, and degree of concentration, it's a good idea to continuously monitor your market for major trends reported in business news and trade publications. When you notice a trend occurring in your market, a key question to ask yourself about this trend is: **Is it structural or is it cyclical?**

- **Structural trends** reflect major, permanent shifts in market dynamics, indicating a fundamental change in consumer behavior, technology, or industry structure.
- **Cyclical trends**, on the other hand, are temporary fluctuations that can be expected to pass as the broader business cycle changes or as specific, short-term conditions abate.

For example, in 2020, when COVID-19 lockdowns spread around the globe, there were some immediate and dramatic shifts in consumer behavior and resulting market impacts. For instance, the market for streaming services increased significantly, while the market for movie theaters plummeted. Many who studied these markets debated whether these changes were **structural** (meaning that many customers would permanently continue to prefer streaming over going to the theater even after lockdowns had passed) or whether they were **cyclical** (meaning that once the business cycle dominated by COVID-19 lockdowns had passed, consumers would largely return to their pre-COVID consumption habits, and there would be no permanent changes to either of these markets). Understanding this distinction is vital for making long-term strategic decisions (Figure 3.3).

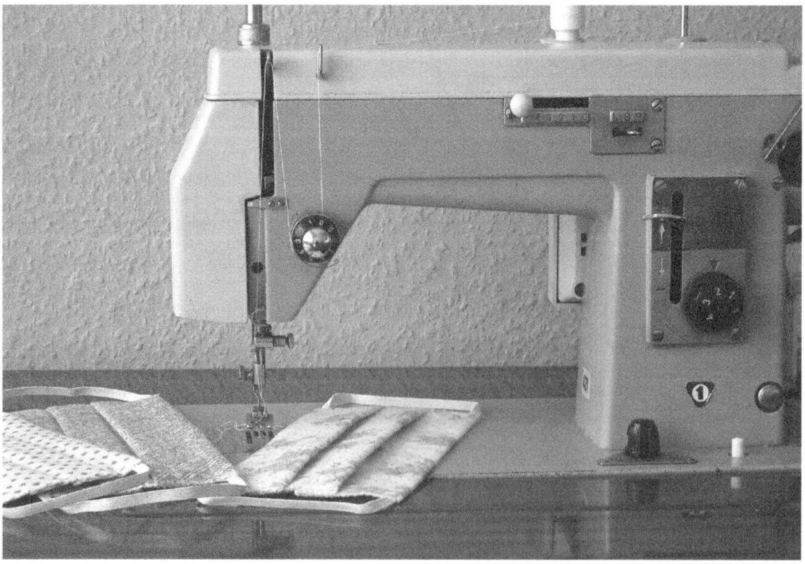

Figure 3.3 Many entrepreneurs made and sold facemasks in 2020.

Source: MrGajowy3 via Pixabay

During the same period, many crafters and small business owners took advantage of the sudden and immense demand for face masks. Some entrepreneurs correctly recognized that this demand was a cyclical trend, meaning it was a short-term opportunity based on temporary market conditions that would not persist. These businesses may have temporarily pivoted their operations to produce masks in order to increase short-term cash flow during a turbulent period.

However, other creative entrepreneurs launched new businesses that were wholly focused on mask production, mistakenly assuming that the demand for face masks would be a long-term structural trend that would persist beyond the COVID-19 emergency. When this assumption proved inaccurate, most of these new businesses had to either **pivot** their product offerings significantly or shut down entirely. This case study underscores the importance of accurately distinguishing between cyclical and structural trends when making strategic business decisions.

Porter's Five Forces Analysis

Another important tool for understanding the external environment and its potential impact on a given business is a **five forces analysis**. Business theorist Michael Porter recognized that businesses experience competitive pressure on their ability to make a profit from a range of sources that extend beyond just direct competitors. His five forces framework is a powerful tool for understanding the degree of competitive threats posed from five key sources of pressure within an industry. For each of the five forces, you will consider the degree of competitive pressure it exerts on a business and determine if that pressure is high, moderate, or low for the business at that particular time (Figure 3.4).

Bargaining Power of Buyers: This force assesses the leverage customers have over a business. This doesn't necessarily refer to literal bargaining or haggling, but rather to a buyer's ability to choose alternative options. The more choices a buyer has – whether to purchase something similar from a different provider, to switch to a **substitute**, or to opt not to purchase at all – the more power they possess in their relationship with the company. High buyer power can force

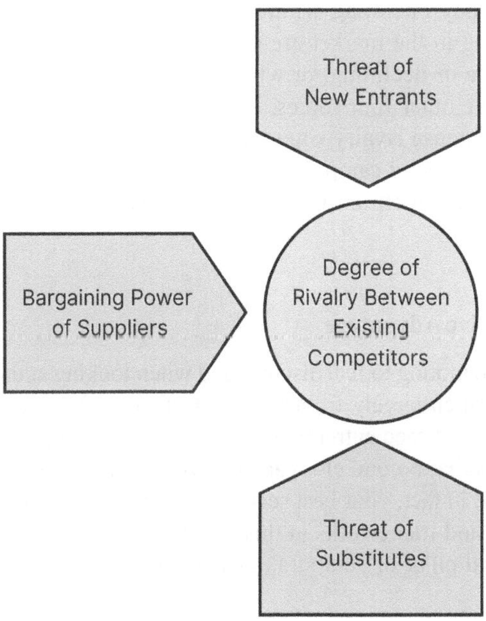

Figure 3.4 Porter's five forces framework.

Source: Sara Hartmann

prices down, demand more features, or push for better service, thereby eroding a company's profitability.

Bargaining Power of Suppliers: Supplier power refers to the leverage that providers of inputs (like raw materials, labor, or services) have over the businesses they supply. Similar to buyer power, the more options a company has to choose between competing suppliers, the more power they have in that relationship. Conversely, if a company relies on a key supplier for a critical resource that is unique, scarce, or difficult to switch from, then that supplier has a high degree of power over the company, potentially dictating terms, raising prices, or limiting supply, which can impact the company's costs and profitability.

Threat of New Entrants: This force examines how easily new competitors can enter an industry and exert competitive pressure. The key question here is: What are the **barriers to entry**? Barriers to entry are obstacles or difficulties that make it harder or more costly for new businesses to enter an existing market. Examples of high barriers to entry include high capital requirements, strong brand loyalties, intellectual property, and government regulations. Many small businesses operating in creative industries, particularly those requiring less upfront capital or specialized equipment, often face a high degree of pressure from the threat of new entrants.

Threat of Substitutes: This force considers the likelihood of customers switching to alternative products or services from *outside* the industry that fulfill the same basic need. It refers to the competitive pressure that arises when customers will skip purchasing from your product or service category altogether in favor of choosing a different product or service that meets similar underlying needs. For example, the traditional camera market has faced significant competitive threats from substitutes, as many consumers have opted to use the high-quality cameras built into their smartphones rather than purchasing a separate, dedicated camera. Similarly, a live concert might face a substitute threat from a high-quality streaming performance or a video game, as all fulfill the need for entertainment. A high threat of substitutes can limit an industry's pricing power and profitability.

Degree of Rivalry between Existing Competitors: This force assesses the intensity of competition among companies already operating within the same market. It refers to how aggressively businesses participating in the market are competing with each other for market share. In a market that is mature or declining, or where there is substantial competitive pressure and unprofitability from the other four forces, the degree of rivalry between existing firms tends to be higher. This intense rivalry often manifests in various forms, such as aggressive price wars, extensive advertising campaigns, rapid product innovation, increased customer service offerings, or fierce competition for distribution channels, all of which can erode industry profitability.

Creativity as a Source of Competitive Advantage

As a creative entrepreneur, it can be tempting to feel discouraged when looking at theories about strategy and competition that are written largely from the point of view of large corporations with vast resources. However, as an arts-based entrepreneur, you possess a unique and powerful ability: to envision and create things that no one else can. The very creative practice and skill set that you bring to your business is, in fact, your best secret weapon in the pursuit of strategic differentiation. The remaining tools and frameworks in this chapter are specifically focused on leveraging your creativity as a central pillar of your strategy and a driving force for your business's growth.

Blue Ocean Strategy

In 2005, W. Chan Kim and Renée Mauborgne introduced the theory of **Blue Ocean Strategy**, which offered a compelling alternative to Michael Porter's traditional view of competitive trade-offs between cost and differentiation. They suggested that established markets, where businesses were primarily competing with incremental approaches to either low-cost or differentiated offerings, were akin to **red oceans** – overcrowded market spaces with intense competition, limited potential for growth, and diminishing returns for all players.

Kim and Mauborgne proposed that entrepreneurial businesses could instead use a systematic approach to creative thinking to discover or create what they termed **blue oceans**. These are new market spaces, or uncontested market segments, where products or services are so innovative and distinct from current offerings that they effectively create new demand and render existing competition irrelevant. The goal is not to beat the competition but to make the competition irrelevant by creating entirely new value.

Kim and Mauborgne outlined a framework to help businesses and entrepreneurs break away from existing market spaces and create something truly new and different. They identified ways that innovators can study existing markets and then strategically reconstruct market boundaries to create uncontested new spaces.

Key Principles of Blue Ocean Strategy

1 Serve **Noncustomers:** Instead of fighting over existing customers in a red ocean, a core principle of blue ocean strategy is to identify and serve noncustomers. These are individuals or groups who currently don't purchase in the existing category, or whose needs are not adequately catered to by current offerings. By understanding why they are noncustomers, innovators can design new solutions that unlock new demand.

2 The **Four-Action Framework**: Blue Ocean companies utilize a "Four-Action Framework" to systematically challenge existing industry logic and create new value. This framework guides innovators in rethinking what to do with existing factors of competition and what new factors to introduce:

- Raise: What existing factors or points of competition within the industry need to be significantly improved upon, well above the industry standard?
- Reduce: What existing factors, standard practices, or points of competition within the industry can be reduced well below the industry standard?
- Eliminate: What existing factors or points of competition can be eliminated altogether, as they no longer add value or are taken for granted by the industry?
- Create: What new factors that don't presently exist in the industry can be introduced to create entirely new value for buyers and unlock new demand?

Mini Case: Cirque du Soleil

The remarkable rise of Cirque du Soleil from a local circus troupe in Montreal to a global entertainment phenomenon was one of the foundational case studies used to help introduce the Blue Ocean Strategy theory. At the time, the traditional circus market was in decline: three-ring circus productions were costly to produce, and audiences were shrinking due to competition from other forms of entertainment and changing public tastes (e.g., concerns about animal cruelty) (Figure 3.5).

Figure 3.5 A Cirque du Soliel performance.
Source: Michelle_Pitzel via Pixabay

Cirque du Soleil created a Blue Ocean by strategically applying the Four-Action Framework:

- Eliminated: They eliminated costly features like three-ring tents (reducing infrastructure costs) and animal performers (addressing ethical concerns and reducing training/care costs).
- Reduced: They reduced the prevalence of star performers and traditional clowns, which were standard but increasingly less appealing to a broader audience.
- Raised: They significantly raised the theatricality of performances, emphasizing storytelling, artistic expression, and human acrobatics.
- Created: They created entirely new elements, including elaborate sets and costumes, original musical scores, and sophisticated lighting design, transforming the circus into a theatrical experience.

The net result was that Cirque du Soleil created a new and unique type of performance that appealed to a new segment of noncustomers (adults and corporate clients seeking sophisticated entertainment, rather than just children and families). This innovative approach brought in large audiences, commanded premium prices, and became the basis for a global brand that operates in a largely uncontested market space.

The Growth-Share Matrix for Creative Work

The **Growth-Share Matrix**, often referred to as the BCG Matrix, is a strategic framework first introduced by the Boston Consulting Group. It was designed to help large businesses analyze their diverse portfolios of products and business units to decide where to invest, maintain, or divest resources. Let's examine how this tool is used by large businesses first, and then we'll explore a modified version for creative entrepreneurs.

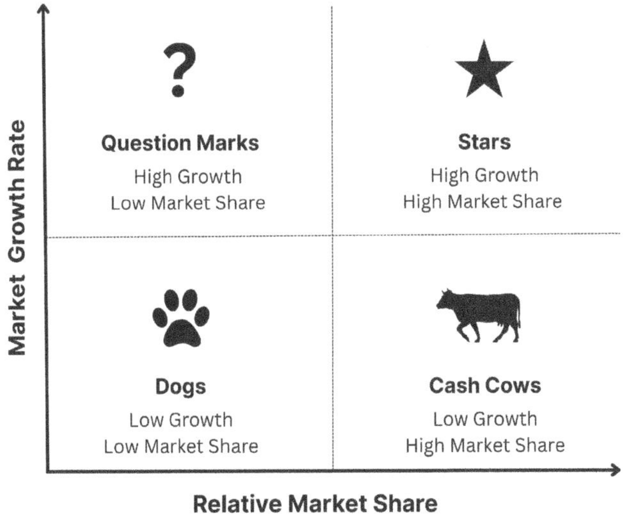

Figure 3.6 The growth-share matrix.

Source: Sara Hartmann

The growth-share matrix plots products or business units into one of four quadrants based on two key dimensions: their relative market share (compared to the largest competitor) and their market growth rate (the annual growth of the market in which they operate) (Figure 3.6).

- **Question Marks:** These are products or business units with a relatively low market share but operating in a high-growth market. They are speculative ventures that require significant investment to grow. Businesses must decide whether to invest heavily to turn them into Stars or to divest them if their potential is uncertain.
- **Stars:** These are products or business units with a relatively high market share in a high-growth market. They are leaders in their rapidly expanding industries. Businesses should prioritize investing in Stars due to their high future potential, aiming to maintain their leadership as the market matures.
- **Cash Cows:** These are business units with a high relative market share but in a low-growth, mature market. They are typically well-established and generate more cash than they consume, requiring minimal investment to maintain their position. Businesses should "milk" these Cash Cows for profit to invest in other business units, such as Stars or promising Question Marks.
- **Dogs:** These business units have relatively low market share and operate in low-growth or declining markets. They typically generate low profits or even losses and consume more cash than they produce. Businesses should consider liquidating these business units or, as the saying goes, "kill off their old dogs," to free up resources for more promising ventures.

The Adapted Matrix for Creative Entrepreneurs

While most creative entrepreneurs are not large conglomerates with multiple business units in the traditional sense, the underlying principle of the growth-share matrix – prioritizing the allocation of assets across multiple activities – is highly relevant. For creative entrepreneurs, an adapted matrix can be particularly useful, using creatively rewarding activities and financially

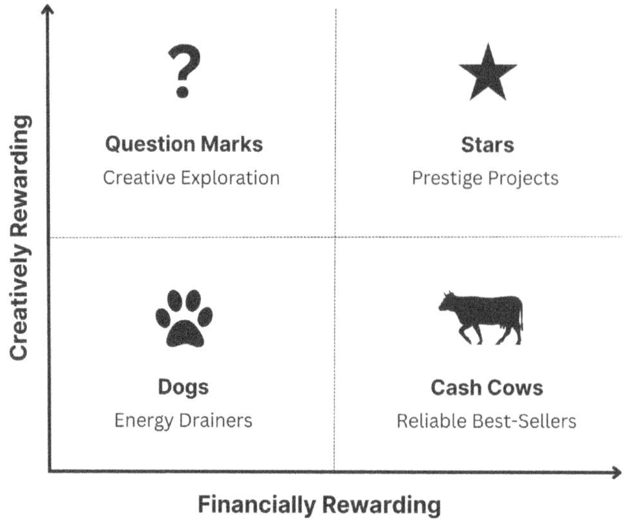

Figure 3.7 The growth-share matrix adapted for creative entrepreneurs.
Source: Sara Hartmann

rewarding activities as its two axes. It's important to think of the resources being invested not just as financial capital, but also as your precious time, energy, and creative focus (Figure 3.7).

Here's how the quadrants translate for a creative entrepreneur:

- **Question Marks:** These become products or activities that are highly creatively rewarding but offer low financial rewards. This is your perfect space for creative exploration and engagement in new pursuits without an immediate plan for monetization. It's where you experiment, develop new skills, and pursue passion projects that may or may not become financially viable in the future.
- **Stars:** These are activities that are highly creatively rewarding and also highly financially rewarding. Your stars are the products or creative outputs that serve as your creative calling card and what you are best known for. While your stars may bring in substantial revenue, it's normal for the profit margins on them to be narrower, as more time, money, and resources often go into executing your unique creative vision and maintaining their excellence.
- **Cash Cows:** These are products, business units, or activities that are highly financially rewarding but may be less creatively rewarding. The primary purpose of your cash cows is to generate a steady profit stream that can support the more creative and exploratory sides of your business. It's important to note that many cash cows may have started out as creatively rewarding question marks or stars. They are referred to as being "less creatively rewarding" because most creative entrepreneurs express that regularly doing the same thing or reproducing past works, while profitable, is less creatively exciting than developing new works.
- **Dogs:** These are products or activities that are neither creatively nor financially rewarding. These are the projects or tasks that drain your energy and resources without providing significant artistic satisfaction or financial return. The strategic advice here is clear: get rid of them. Invest your precious time, energy, and financial resources into parts of the business that are rewarding in different ways, whether creatively, financially, or both (Figure 3.8).

Growth-Share Matrix Example: Julia the Ceramics Artist

Let's imagine Julia is a ceramics artist who produces both fine art and consumer-focused craft ceramics. Here's how she might classify her work using the adapted Growth-Share Matrix: (Table 3.2)

Figure 3.8 Studio exploration can be categorized as a question mark.
Source: marcelkessler via Pixabay

Table 3.2 Julia's Growth-Share Matrix

Question Mark: Julia's studio practice and fine art pieces are her "question marks." She finds this part of her work highly creatively rewarding and inspiring, and it's where she explores new ideas. She shows her work regularly at galleries, but it is not yet a major financial contributor to her business.	**Stars:** Julia's "stars" are a line of unique, sculptural vases that have gained significant attention on social media and at craft shows. While the sales volume is lower because they sell at a high price point, these pieces are her creative calling card. They generate excitement and often lead customers to purchase her more accessibly priced items.
Dogs: Based on the popularity of her mugs, Julia also tried to produce a line of plates, thinking they could be another top seller. However, the plates are not selling well, and Julia doesn't enjoy producing them. Since they are neither creatively nor financially rewarding, she should consider eliminating them from her business to free up her time and energy.	**Cash Cows:** Julia's ceramic mugs are her "cash cows." They are consistently popular with consumers and sell at a high volume, accounting for a substantial portion of her cash flow. While they may not be the most creatively exciting things for her to produce anymore, their reliable profitability supports the more experimental sides of her business.

Growth Strategies: The Ansoff Matrix

Opportunities for growth are something that occupies the minds of almost every business owner, regardless of size. Creative entrepreneurs, in particular, are often uniquely excited by the possibilities of new projects, new lines of business, or expanding their artistic reach. After all, entrepreneurs are inherently creative people, and new ideas tend to come naturally to many of us. However, pursuing new ideas always involves some degree of risk. This isn't just the financial risk associated with money spent on a new product; it can also involve the risk of dedicating your precious time and energy, and even reputational risk to your existing business. The **Ansoff Matrix** is a widely used strategic tool for categorizing the types of growth a company may pursue and for considering the associated levels of risk (Figure 3.9).

The Ansoff Matrix posits that a company essentially has four distinct strategies available when it is looking to grow:

- **Market Penetration Strategies:** Market penetration strategies involve selling *more of your existing products or services to the existing markets* that you are already operating in. This is an ideal option for businesses that believe they have not yet reached their full potential with their current offerings and audience. This is generally seen as the **lowest risk** type of growth because the business does not need to risk **capital** on developing new and potentially unproven products, nor on entering new markets or attracting entirely new types of audiences. Instead, it can leverage existing skills, expertise in its product, and established customer relationships.
- **Market Development Strategies:** Market development strategies occur when a business grows by choosing to sell its *existing products or services into new markets*. This is seen

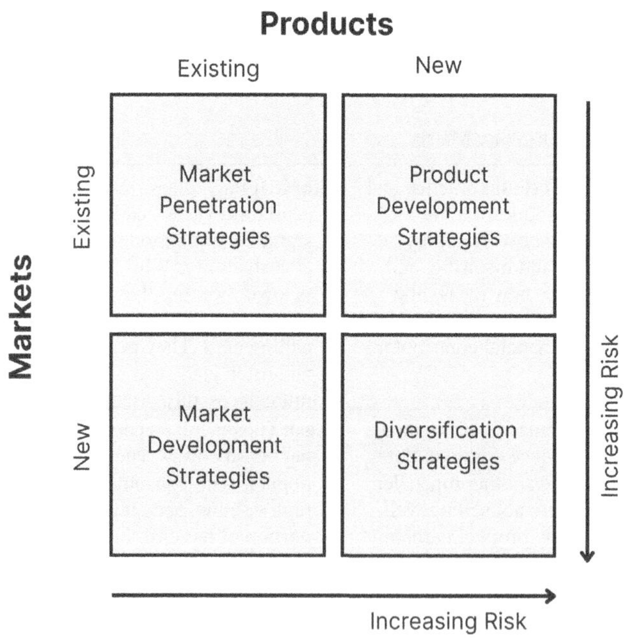

Figure 3.9 The Ansoff Matrix.

Source: Sara Hartmann

as a **moderate-risk** strategy. While the business is utilizing proven products and services and does not have to risk capital on developing new ones, it does need to invest significant resources in the marketing and operational costs of establishing itself in a new market. This new market may present unfamiliar competitive dynamics, different customer needs, and new regulatory environments.

- **Product Development Strategies:** Product development strategies are employed when a business grows through developing *new products and services to sell in existing markets*. This strategy also carries **moderate risk**. The business has to risk resources and capital on the research, development, and launch of new and potentially unproven products. However, the business can leverage its established presence and expertise in customer relationships within its existing markets, and it does not have to risk resources on developing a new market presence or understanding new customer behaviors from scratch.
- **Diversification Strategies:** Diversification strategies are generally considered the **highest risk** approach to growth because a business must simultaneously risk capital on developing *both new and unproven products and services and on developing customer relationships and operational processes within entirely new markets*. In this quadrant, the business cannot leverage existing relationships or expertise on either the product side or the market side, as everything is new. Diversification strategies are typically pursued only when the potential opportunity is attractive enough to genuinely justify the increased risks, or when there is a substantial threat to the company's primary existing business model, making radical action necessary for survival.

To understand the Ansoff Matrix, consider the case of Cognitive Surplus, a business you will learn about in Chapter 10. Using a focused differentiation strategy, they began by selling wrapping paper and stationery specifically for people in STEM fields. Cognitive Surplus has grown its business by successfully applying three of the four growth strategies from the Ansoff Matrix:

- **Product Development:** They expanded their product offerings from stationery and gift wrap to include items like t-shirts and drinkware. They also applied this strategy by broadening their designs to serve a wider list of STEM fields beyond their initial niche.
- **Market Development:** They grew through market development by expanding the distribution of their existing products from the United States to new markets in Canada and the European Union.
- **Market Penetration:** They continue to grow through market penetration by actively participating in trade shows and using advertising to sell more of their existing products within the markets where they already have a presence (Figure 3.10).

Conclusion

The ability to thrive in a competitive market isn't about size, but about strategy. While large corporations rely on these frameworks to manage their vast resources, creative entrepreneurs can apply them to turn their creativity itself into a powerful tool for competitive advantage. The true key to success lies in using your creative focus, time, and energy not just for artistic expression, but as assets to be strategically allocated. By understanding the market and your position within it, you can ensure your unique creative voice stands out and succeeds.

Figure 3.10 Cognitive Surplus has grown through a mix of market penetration, product development, and market development.

Source: Courtesy of Geoff and Kristen Zephyrus/Cognitive Surplus

Mini Case: Cash Cows at Bebemoss by Marie Segares

Bebemoss is a Turkish social enterprise that sells handmade toys made from certified organic yarn and stuffed with filling made from recycled bottles. These materials are ideal "for sensitive newborn skin" while also being environmentally friendly. Bebemoss founder Izabela Ersahin is originally from France and describes herself as "an accidental social entrepreneur." She started crocheting toys while on bedrest during her second pregnancy and began selling them on Etsy and her own site. When demand surpassed her ability to produce toys by hand, Izabela placed an ad which received hundreds of responses from other women in Turkey. She found that "many mothers are excluded from the traditional job market and need a more flexible work model." In a studio outside of Istanbul, she began working with these other mothers to crochet toys. As refugees from Syria, Iran, and Afghanistan moved to Istanbul, Bebemoss expanded its team to include refugee mothers.

In addition to its financial goals, Bebemoss focuses on environmental and social impact. Its most recent impact report indicates that Bebemoss employed 79 women and positively impacted the lives of their 250 children. Bebemoss now ships toys around the world and has several third-party certifications, including World Fair Trade Organization guaranteed member, Nest Ethical Handcraft seal, and People and Planet First verification. Bebemoss is also part of MADE51, a worldwide program of the United Nations High Commissioner for Refugees that connects products made by refugees with international markets.

Since its founding in 2010, Bebemoss has expanded its signature crocheted toy product line from 10 designs to over 50 designs. Additionally, Bebemoss has added two product lines that could be considered cash cows: prints and kits. The prints are reproductions of watercolor paintings of their popular toy designs and inspirational sayings using recycled paper. The "make your own" kits include a crochet pattern booklet with step-by-step photos and instructions with the yarn and stuffing required to make a specific toy, along with a gift bag. Both of these product lines require minimal labor compared to their handmade toys and can produce a steady stream of revenue.

Sources: Bebemoss bebemoss.com; MADE51 Team. (2023, January 24). Founder series: Q&A with Izabela Ersahin of Bebemoss. MADE51. https://shop.made51.org/blogs/news/founder-series-q-a-with-izabela-ersahin

Activities

Activity 1: Applying the Five Strategies

Imagine your creative work is the core of five different businesses. For this exercise, pretend you have access to unlimited resources and support. Think big and don't limit your vision by the practical constraints of a small business. For each of the five generic strategies, you will outline a distinct business concept, how your creative work would be positioned, and what would be required to make it successful.

- *Low-Cost Provider Strategy:* What would a business look like if you focused on being the absolute most affordable option in your market? How would you streamline your creative process or product to achieve this? What specific resources and competencies would you need to make this model profitable at scale?
- Broad Differentiation Strategy: How would you position a business to make your creative work unique and appealing to the widest possible audience? What resources would you need to build a powerful brand, and what competencies would be critical for maintaining your unique edge?
- Focused Low-Cost Strategy: What would a business look like if you concentrated on serving a narrow market niche with the lowest priced creative product or service? What specific resources and competencies would be essential for success within this specific segment?
- Focused Differentiation Strategy: What would a business look like if you aimed to be the most highly differentiated provider for a very specific, niche audience? What unique resources would be needed to serve this particular group, and what competencies would be critical for your business to stand out?
- Best-Cost Provider Strategy: How would you design a business that balances a highly differentiated product with a price point that offers exceptional value? What resources would be necessary to pull this off, and what competencies would be required to balance cost efficiency with a premium offering?

Activity 2: Creating a Blue Ocean

Using the blue ocean strategy framework, create an idea for a new venture that operates in an uncontested market space.

1 Choose an existing market that is either creatively interesting to you or related to your own work. For example, if you are a fiber artist, you could study the market for home textiles.

2 Based on your chosen market, identify a group of noncustomers. Who are the people who currently don't buy or use the products in this market, and what are their reasons for not engaging?
3 Use the four-action framework to analyze this "red ocean," with the goal of creating a solution that appeals to the noncustomer group you identified. For each of the four actions, identify specific factors related to your chosen market:

- Eliminate: What factors that the industry takes for granted should be eliminated?
- Reduce: What factors should be reduced well below the industry standard?
- Raise: What factors should be raised well above the industry standard?
- Create: What new factors should be created that the industry has never offered?

4 Describe the new venture idea you have created. Explain how this new business idea serves your identified noncustomer group and creates a "blue ocean" by making the competition irrelevant.

Activity 3: Growth Brainstorm

1 Brainstorm (ten minutes): Set a timer for ten minutes and list as many growth ideas as possible for your creative business. Don't censor yourself – no idea is too far-fetched for this initial round. Think about:

- New products or services you could create.
- New customer groups you could sell to.
- New places or platforms to sell your work.
- New marketing campaigns to reach different audiences.

2 Sort and Evaluate: After the timer is up, sort each of your brainstormed ideas into the appropriate quadrant of the Ansoff Matrix. As you place each idea, consider the following:

- Market Penetration: This is the lowest risk quadrant. What ideas did you come up with here, and why do they have the highest likelihood of success?
- Market Development: This is a moderate-risk quadrant. Why do these ideas carry more risk than market penetration, and what would be required to succeed?
- Product Development: This is also a moderate-risk quadrant. What makes these ideas riskier than market penetration, and what makes them less risky than diversification?
- Diversification: This is the highest risk quadrant. What ideas did you come up with here, and would it be worth the higher degree of associated risk to try them?

Resources and References

Ansoff, H. I. (1957). Strategies for diversification. *Harvard Business Review*, *35*(5), 113–124.
Boston Consulting Group. (1970). *The product portfolio. Perspectives*, No. 66. Boston Consulting Group.
Kim, W. C., & Mauborgne, R. (2005). *Blue ocean strategy: How to create uncontested market space and make the competition irrelevant*. Harvard Business School Press.
Porter, M. E. (1980). *Competitive strategy: Techniques for analyzing industries and competitors*. Free Press.
Porter, M. E. (1985).*Competitive advantage: Creating and sustaining superior performance*. Free Press.
Porter, M. E. (2008). The five competitive forces that shape strategy. *Harvard Business Review*, *86*(1), 78–93.

4 Understanding Your End User

Ideal Clients, MVP/Prototyping/Market Testing, and Solving for Pain/Gain

Jennifer A. Reis

Introduction

Creative entrepreneurs exist within an entrepreneurial ecosystem of the **market**, other **makers**, and clientele. While often we are internally motivated to produce services and products aligned with our passions, talents, and particular "point of view" (POV), it is necessary to consider the external entrepreneurial landscape in which you as a creative maker are operating to insure market viability and relevance. In Chapter 2, the concept of **target markets** and **ideal clients** was introduced; in this chapter, more emphasis is placed on that concept along with **end-user empathy**, communicating *features* versus **benefits**, and aligning the potential buyer motivation with creative ventures. When a maker is exclusively internally focused on their passion project, they can develop assumptions about **product-market fit** and end-user interest – assumptions that can run up against market realities. **Market testing** is key to avoiding this mismatch: developing a **minimum viable product** (**MVP**, aka, a prototype) as a market testing tool along with systems for developing questions, gathering information, and integrating gained knowledge is invaluable for venture planning and sustainability. MVPs are also a key component of **design thinking**, an iterative system for venture design that works on a cycle of ideation, market testing, reflection, and evolution embedded within the ideal client cohort. Market testing can be scary as you are putting your work (and by extension, yourself) out in the public; however, it is a valuable cyclic process that assists creative ventures in maintaining market relevance and value.

Learning Outcomes

- **Identify** a target market for a new venture
- **Categorize** a venture or product's benefits and features
- **Develop and utilize** an MVP for market testing
- **Apply** design thinking principles to a venture ideation

Target Markets, Market Segmentation, End-User Empathy

The concept of a target market was introduced in Chapter 2; however, deeper investigations on this topic are warranted due to its utility in venture design. Not only is it valuable to understand the definition of a target market – those end users who are interested in what the maker has on offer – but it is also helpful to do a deeper dive into this cohort. First, as mentioned prior, if you can integrate understanding of target markets, it can be tremendously helpful in **product development**, **pricing**, and **marketing**. It is tempting to think that what we make as makers is for everyone, and simply stated, it is not. Not everyone is interested in what an individual maker creates, or said

DOI: 10.4324/9781003588771-4

another way, if everyone is your target audience, you have NO target audience. That does not mean it is exclusive and intentionally designed to limit access to the product and/or service; some people will be fans of work and, for others, it's not of interest. Thinking about what the target market cohort might look like, their motivations, and the different market segmentations within the cohort can be incredibly enlightening when designing and evolving a creative venture.

Market segmentation is the act of dividing up the larger cohort into different batches of interested clients dependent on their interests as well as their **demographic**, **behavioral**, **geographic**, and **psychographic** characteristics.

For example, a contemporary craft maker such as a textile artist will have different market segments based on the portfolio of work produced and services offered. They may have a production line of hand-dyed batik fabrics that would be sold **wholesale** to a **retail** buyer who owns a quilt shop via a **business-to-business** distribution method: market segment 1 would be a business owner looking for authentic and attractive yardage to be sold to quilters. This textile artist may also do music festivals, selling **business-to-consumer**, with "art to wear" finished products like dresses, hats, and bandanas: market segment 2 would be a festival goer interested in expressive clothing and accessories to wear as part of the experience. Finally, they might host fabric batik workshops: market segment 3 might be a creatively minded individual who lacks the creative capacity, confidence, or time to self-teach and also wants a social experience.

Market Segment	*Type*	*Offering*
Market segment 1	business owner	hand-dyed fabric yardage
Market segment 2	product consumer	art-to-wear production line
Market segment 3	service consumer	fabric dyeing workshops

After reflecting on market segmentation per the creative venture, we can use end-user empathy exercises like a client **avatar** activity to create a snapshot of the demographic, behavioral, and psychographic aspects of that particular client. With a client avatar exercise, we can begin to reflect upon this person and what drives them to engage with products/services. Consideration of the end user does not mean a maker is "selling out." Understanding our **unique value proposition** (UVP) keeps the creative vision authentic – however, knowing our clientele and adapting to an evolving culture and market keeps the venture relevant and in-demand.

After careful observation and reflection on target markets and market segmentation, we can think about the value on offer to the cohort and what may motivate different segments to engage with the UVP. In traditional entrepreneurial thinking, this is framed as providing a **gain** or solving a **pain** through the **benefit** the venture provides. Spending time with your end user in real life and using design thinking methodology with testing, observation, and evolution can illuminate motivating factors and behaviors that were not obviously apparent. For instance, an end user of a micro fashion brand may be motivated not only by the style and quality of the garments, but additionally by the "gain" of early adopter status.

We as creative makers might have assumptions about what is actually motivating our buyers that is not true or does not address an underlying desire. For example, Julie is a participant in various art workshops. She tends toward mixed media, collage, and textile workshops as there's a lack of creative confidence and traditional forms of art like drawing and painting are intimidating. While interested in having a creative practice, it is difficult for her to self-motivate and she also lives alone in a studio apartment. Knowing this, we can make some assumptions about Julie's motivations to attend (and pay for!) art workshops. First, she is looking for a supportive art making environment where the instructor is a guide (not a critic). She also might be looking for social opportunities as she lives alone, as well as a **third place** as a community of making. Actually learning the technical skills of the art making process might be secondary to those other issues mentioned prior. These are important issues for teaching artists to be cognizant of prior to developing instructional content – and showing up in the workspace unaware of underlying participant motivations.

Return to the Belonging Framework

Mentioned prior in Chapter 2, the **Belonging Framework** can give makers another lens to think about consumer motivations related to creative ventures. The framework hypothesizes that all people experience some form of alienation, and all actively seek a path to belonging that relieves this sense of exclusion. Creative works that speak directly to our specific experiences with alienation and, in turn, bring us closer to a feeling of belonging, provoke a strong sense of affinity between us and that artwork (Figure 4.1).

Figure 4.1 Kathy Cano-Murillo, founder of Crafty Chica (profiled in Case 10.1) with some of her creations inspired by the Mexican artist Frida Kahlo. Kathy is the author of the non-fiction book, Forever Frida: A Celebration of the Life, Art, Loves, Words, and Style of Frida Kahlo.

Source: Courtesy of Kathy Cano-Murillo/Crafty Chica

The feeling of alienation and exclusion is primal and has deep evolutionary roots. For early humans, being excluded from the group wasn't just an emotionally unpleasant experience; it was a direct threat to survival and safety. From an evolutionary POV, we fear alienation and instinctively seek belonging because the existential threat of alienation was so serious for our ancestors. Humans are inherently social creatures, and when we feel a sense of belonging, our stress responses are calmed, and we feel more physically and emotionally secure.

While the feelings of being threatened by alienation and the desire for belonging are universal human experiences, the specific shapes these feelings take are incredibly varied and unique. Each person's experiences with alienation may stem from childhood or formative experiences, economic or cultural challenges, or any number of lived experiences. Similarly, each person will have their own ideal fantasy or dream of what true belonging would look like. When a creative work in some way helps to process feelings of alienation, or represents a path to the belonging that is sought, it offers something profoundly valuable to its audience. While each individual is unique in their specific experiences of alienation and belonging, if you can identify common themes among the alienation and belonging experienced by the people who gravitate to your work, you can find the unifying message and identity central to the value that you create.

Applying the Belonging Framework to Your Audience

To engage in this exploration, ask yourself the following questions about your audience:

- What do they fear?
- What do they want?
- What do they believe?

One helpful way to understand this framework before applying it to your audience is to apply it to yourself first. Think back to some creative works (music, books, films, art) that were central to your identity during a formative period, such as adolescence or young adulthood. How did these creative works speak to your own wants, fears, and beliefs during that time? How did you experience alienation during that period of your life? What would true belonging have looked like for you, and how did that creative work resonate with that longing?

Identifying and Articulating Benefits and Features

Once you consider the overall target market, market segmentation, and have empathy in considering the needs of your **end user**, articulating **benefits** and **features** of the products and services is crucial. Simply put, benefits are the story of the UVP and the impact and value for the end user as we have discussed prior in this chapter. It describes how the product/service value enhances and/or improves a particular situation for the end user. This might look like providing the gain of status objects, affective benefit in supporting creatives, and/or being part of a community, the development of new skills. On the pain side, as mentioned prior, it could be providing an opportunity to meet new people as a remedy for loneliness or solving the problem of finding a unique gift for some notoriously difficult to please. Features are the "nuts and bolts" of the product or service. For products, things to consider are materials, sizes, care instructions, process, colors, and any product liabilities/constraints. For services, features can include length of time, deliverables, and details about the overall experience. With both products and services, articulating features can level set expectations especially with digital marketing and distribution.

Design Thinking

Popularized by books such as *Change by Design: How Design Thinking Transforms Organizations and Inspires Innovation* by Tim Brown and developed in part by the work of IDEO (www.ideo.com), a Californian and tech-based design firm, design thinking is an iterative design process focused on end-user empathy and human-centered ideation and testing. While design thinking places prototyping toward the back of the ideation cycle, its emphasis on observation, reflection, and understanding of key products/service users is helpful with creative venture design. Design thinking can be helpful for creatives who are working in a sector that is rapidly evolving and those makers who are intensively embedding within their target market (Figure 4.2).

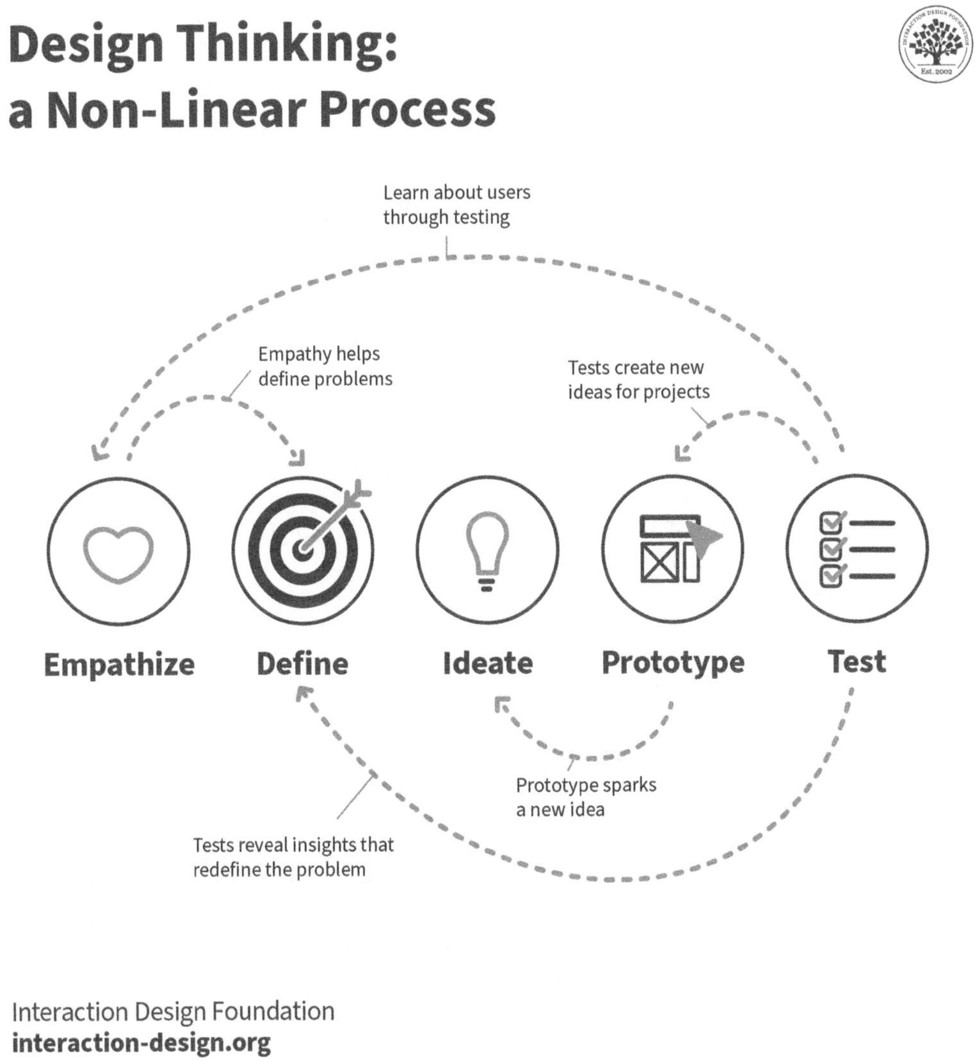

Figure 4.2 Design thinking diagram.

As a non-linear process, design thinking phases include the following for you to reflect on with your venture design and implementation:

- How will you employ means of engagement with potential end users and their needs/wants through empathic thinking?
- How can you articulate the pains/gains identified through end-user research?
- How will you ideate an abundance of solutions, without editing for practicalities?
- How will you develop prototype(s) representing a selection of solutions?
- How can you design an intentional system to market test, collect data, reflect, and iterate for your venture?

John, a video game concept artist, may be interested in branching out to reach gamers directly (in addition to working with a game developer). He is also a gamer who spends an intensive amount of time online engaging with other players including on forums and streaming communication, they may leverage those relationships to learn about the needs and wants of the community currently not being met. They may identify that there is a particular pain/gain unfulfilled (**opportunity recognition**) such as bespoke designed player tokens available for direct purchase that seamlessly embed within existing game contexts. The concept artist could develop a series of solutions, curate a selection of tokens to share with the gamer community, and collect information on the user experience and general feedback on the digital product.

Minimum Viable Product and Market Testing

Earlier in this chapter, it was noted that market testing is a valuable, if not intimidating, action for creative venture designers to undertake. As mentioned previously in the text, primary market testing can be accomplished through surveys, focus groups, and interviews. However, if you as the creative maker seek **proof of concept** in the early stages of venture value design, developing and employing an MVP can be an efficient and honest method of testing the market.

In 2011, Erik Ries authored the book *The Lean Startup: How Entrepreneurs Use Continuous Innovation to Create Radically Successful Business*. While situated in the technology sector, the book's core concept of developing an *asset* associated with the venture's UVP can be extremely impactful to creative venture design. This asset is called an MVP: it is a product/service associated with the venture concept that can be used for market testing and, very importantly, it is developed and distributed with limited investment of time and labor by the entrepreneur. It is limited in scope, easy to deploy, and its activity in the market can give the venture designer information on whether to pivot or persevere. For example, a home business baker might be interested in **scaling** up their venture into a brick-and-mortar open-to-the-public space. Before the major capital investment in infrastructure and equipment, not to mention other **fixed** and **variable costs** like property insurance and utilities, they would be well served to develop an MVP to test market demand. This could look like vending for a temporary amount of time at a local farmers' market or marketing a monthly subscription service for baked goods. Not only does this seek to determine proof of concept, but it is also an opportunity for promotion and developing a foundation of future support.

Here are some important questions/considerations in developing an MVP:

1 What is your venture's UVP?
2 What MVP could be developed that is small scale, needs little financial investment, and can be readily deployed to a target market?

3 What assumptions are being tested? Design, function, aesthetics, price?
4 In what context will it be tested and how will the data be collected?
5 How will the data be integrated into further iterations of the venture design?

James, an illustrator who traditionally does one-of-a-kind watercolor and ink paintings for sale wholesale through retail shops and **direct-to-consumer** by way of art fairs, is interested in expanding his portfolio of revenue generating activities via **e-commerce**. He could go "all in" and set up an e-commerce website, develop a new body of work, and build out a new **marketing strategy** – all without doing market testing using an MVP (not advised!). Another option carrying less investment of time and financial risk is to create an MVP perhaps through utilizing a print-on-demand (POD) service by scanning and uploading a limited selection of illustrations to be reproduced on a curated inventory of products. James could then share the link to the POD shop, monitoring potential purchases and web traffic analytics over a set period of time. The information gleaned from the MVP market testing can inform whether or not this is a sustainable opportunity (proof of concept) for moving forward or perhaps learning that this concept is not viable.

Again, when we as makers put ourselves out there in the market, we are risking learning lessons that knock up against assumptions we have. However, it is better to test the market with an MVP and get less than successful results versus investing extensive time, labor, and funds into a product/service the market doesn't need or want.

Closing

While makers are driven by their creative vision and passion, it is critical to be aware of the market environment. Understanding target markets, market segmentation, end-user empathy along with market testing methodologies like MVPs and design thinking are invaluable for designing a creative venture that is attractive and sustainable out in the world.

Mini Case: End-User Empathy at the Sangwari Tribal Self-Help Group by Marie Segares

The Sangwari Tribal Self-Help Group (Sangwari SHG) is a livelihood entrepreneurship community made up of women who collect produce from the Dantewada forest in Chhattisgarh, India, to process and sell to urban customers. The group formed after the divisional forest office conducted an economic development training program to teach women to process Mahua (Bassia Latifolia), a tree with a variety of uses. After the training, 21 women decided to form the Sangwari SHG and received grant funding from the local government for the first three months of startup costs. Later, they funded expansion using low-interest loans from the Ministry of Tribal Affairs earmarked for improving tribal incomes by developing tribal products. The Sangwari SHG **product mix** includes a variety of sweets such as halwa, digestive bars and little millet cookies, and tamarind sauce, all made using Mahua from the forest. Mahua flowers are edible and can be used to sweeten, dried and added to flour, or expressed as an oil which can substitute for or be an additive to ghee. Mahua flowers or the processed bark or expressed oil are also used as a remedy for a variety of ailments. Mahua can also be used to make alcoholic beverages and is intoxicating in large doses. As a result, many of the urban customers who are less familiar with Mahua are fearful of Mahua products or have a negative perception about Mahua as an ingredient in products for children.

End-user empathy informs the Sangwari SHG's approach to customer communications and product design. The founding president of the Sangwari SHG, Malti Kunjam, has a process for training the women how to communicate with prospective customers before going to an event or trade show in an urban community. Many of the women are from extremely rural communities, and some have rarely interacted with people from outside of their families before joining the Sangwari SHG. The women learn how to overcome their fear of meeting new people and public speaking, as well as how to explain that Mahua is similar to dry grapes and that it doesn't cause hallucinations. Additionally, the women are prepared to discuss medicinal benefits and to talk about the important role Mahua has in tribal life and culture. Based on feedback from customers, the Sangwari SHG stopped manufacturing products with high sugar content in response to concerns about the impact on children's health. Additionally, feedback from retailers in the early months of the COVID-19 pandemic encouraged the Sangwari SHG to shift from making perishable products to those with a shelf life of at least six months.

Sources: Agrawal, A. (2022, April). [Unpublished interview with Sangwari Tribal Self-Help Group members conducted in Hindi and translated into English]; Plants for A Future. (n.d.) Bassia latifolia – (J.König ex L.) J.F.Macbr. *Plants for a Future*. https://pfaf.org/user/Plant.aspx?LatinName=Bassia+latifolia; Rakesh, K. (2022, February 25). Scheduled tribes in India. *Government of India Vikaspedia*. https://en.vikaspedia.in/viewcontent/social-welfare/scheduled-tribes-welfare/scheduled-tribes-in-india; Viji. (2024, July 24). Van Dham scheme. *Government of India Vikaspedia*. https://en.vikaspedia.in/viewcontent/social-welfare/scheduled-tribes-welfare/van-dhan-scheme

Activities

Activity 1: Ideal Client Empathy Exercise

Think of your ideal client for your creative venture. Picture them as an actual person. Sometimes it is helpful to even give them a name! You are going to answer the following questions to create a narrative about that ideal client. This helps us create value and communicate in a targeted fashion (remember: talking to everyone is talking to no one!). Also, remember this is an exercise of assumption unless you are embedded within a community of ideal clients, and in that case you may have more intimate knowledge of them.

- *Demographic information.* Consider age, profession, income, education, marital status/children, location.
- *Behavioral information.* Consider hobbies, civic group participation, religious affiliation, media consumption, disposal income spending, shopping habits, and how they spend their free time.
- *Psychographic information.* Consider what you assume to be their core beliefs and value systems, life challenges and joys, life aspirations and fears.

Activity 2: Market Segmentation Activity

If you are so inclined, you can consider your target market of ideal clients and segment them into two to three different personas using the questions above. In this chapter, we looked at an example of market segmentation with a textile artist. Do this exercise thinking of different clients that all share an interest in your work as a creative entrepreneur, but are discrete personality/persona types that have different motivations. This is a helpful exercise in doing groundwork for marketing strategy to reach different ideal clients.

Activity 3: Belonging Framework Activity

Diving further into ideal client empathy, let's return to the chapter's information about the Belonging Framework. It's important to pull back the layers of assumed decision-making to engage with your creative venture and get to foundational motivations of an individual. Considering your ideal client, answer the following (some of this you might have addressed in the psychographics section of the Ideal Client Empathy exercise)

- What do they fear?
- What do they want?
- What do they believe?

Activity 4: Benefits/Features Copywriting

Pick one of your potential products or services to do copywriting on the benefits and features. It is helpful to look at the digital marketing of your **exemplars** or competitors for inspiration as well as e-commerce copy. Typically, copy – the written description of the product or service – starts with the benefit. As a reminder, the benefit solves for pain or provides a gain and is the "why" of the motivation to purchase and engage with the product/service. The features are the "nuts and bolts" of the product/service. Benefits typically come first: as an example, people most likely buy a bike for the joy of riding and/or needing a mode of transportation. Features back up the quality of the product/service, as in we want to be assured that the bike is crafted of quality components.

- Write a benefits description for your product/service. How will this provide a gain or solve a pain for the ideal client?
- Make a list of the features involved in the product/service. Things to note if it is a product: size, materials, color(s), style/aesthetic, weight, product care suggestions, country of origin. If a service, list as appropriate: means of engagement, duration, logistics, and end product resulting from service.

Activity 5: Design Thinking Reflective Writing

Before we move on to the last activity on prototyping and market testing, reflecting on the design thinking questions from the chapter can prepare us to actualize this. Consider the following and do reflective writing on each question prompt:

- How will you employ means of engagement with potential end users and their needs/wants?
- How can you articulate the pains/gains identified through end-user research?
- How will you ideate an abundance of solutions, without editing for practicalities?

- How will you develop prototype(s) representing a selection of solutions?
- How can you design an intentional system to market test, collect data, reflect, and iterate for your venture?

Activity 6: Minimum Viable Product Development and Market Testing Activity

As noted in this chapter, design, development, and testing of an MVP are extremely useful to figure out if your venture value assumptions are correct. Basically, do people want what you are planning to offer? This information can be packaged as a presentation to your peers or in a written document on your own. As with any research, the process starts with a question – what assumption are you testing? Consider the following questions from the chapter to lead you through the process. Remember that if you indeed learn that people are not interested, that is still incredibly helpful information prior to investing your capacity and capital!

- What MVP could you create that is directly related to your UVP that is small in scale, needs little financial investment, and can be readily deployed to a target market?
- What assumptions are being tested? Design, function, aesthetics, price?
- In what context will it be tested? Through actual sales, online engagement, surveys, focus groups, one-on-one conversations?
- How will you collect and measure the data you collect from this experience?
- How will you utilize this information to inform the development of your venture's product(s)/service(s)?

Resources and References

Brown, T. (2009). *Change by design: How design thinking transforms organizations and inspires innovation*. Harper Business.

Clark, T., Osterwalder, A., Pigneur, Y., Hazen, B., & Smith, A. (2022). *Business model you*. John Wiley & Sons.

Osterwalder, A., & Pigneur, Y. (2010). *Business model generation: A handbook for visionaries, game changers, and challengers*. Wiley.

Osterwalder, A., Pigneur, Y., Bernarda, G., & Smith, A. (2014). *Value proposition design: How to create products and services customers want*. Wiley.

Ries, E. (2011). *The lean startup: How constant innovation to creates radically successful businesses*. Portfolio Penguin.

5 Crafting a Brand Identity, Marketing Your Work, and Distribution Channels

Jennifer A. Reis

Introduction

Branding, **marketing**, and **distribution** considerations are key to any entrepreneurial **venture**. You as a creative maker designing and operating a successful **micro-enterprise** in particular need to develop a narrative crafted through images, words, and content, aligned with how you show up for opportunities out in the world. You'll have a brand regardless if it is intentional or not – people will make assumptions about you and your work based on how you communicate about yourself regardless of the platform or context. Branding needs to be an authentic reflection of the maker and their work; it must resonate with their target market/end user and incorporate the venture's **unique value proposition (UVP)**. Along with creating a brand, creative entrepreneurs need to understand marketing basics to reach their **target markets** through concepts such as **positioning maps**, **marketing mix (5 Ps)**, and the **customer decision-making process**. Developing a *marketing strategy* to reach those target markets is a valuable planning opportunity as is understanding the means of distribution for the venture including logistics and potentially *hidden costs*.

Learning Outcomes

- **Define** branding in the context of a creative micro-enterprise
- **Explain** key marketing concepts: the marketing mix (5 Ps), positioning maps, and the customer decision-making process
- **Formulate** a UVP for a creative venture
- **Assess** how well a venture's marketing strategy aligns with its target market
- **Justify** the selection of a specific distribution channel based on a venture's goals

Branding Basics

What is a "brand"? Some consider it as what people think or describe the creative venture and/or maker as to others when they are not in the room. Sometimes the term "branding" can manifest inefficiently in the development of a logo only without consideration of other elements of brand communication. Some makers may see the development and implementation of a brand strategy as overly corporate and inauthentic to their creative journey. However, when the creative entrepreneurial venture is typically tethered to the maker and their presence in the product and/or service, consideration in developing a brand that is aligned with the personal and the business is key to consistent communication.

DOI: 10.4324/9781003588771-5

Simply put, a brand is a bridge between the creative venture and related target market(s). It is the sum "story" of YOU in the entrepreneurial effort through the venture's name, images, copy/communication style, content, hashtags/keywords, logo, online presence (including website and social media), and how one shows up and engages with clients and opportunities.

> Jenna, a furniture maker who crafts Shaker-inspired rustic yet high-end work, has been selected to be in a cohort of regional makers for a creative entrepreneur fellowship program. A significant aspect of the program includes development and resources associated with branding and marketing assets especially important to launching **e-commerce** efforts. This opportunity allows her to reflect on her brand identity and how she wants to communicate that through video and still image photography. She wants to connect herself through styling and clothing as well as the props she uses during the photography sessions. Questions she'll want to ask herself is how she will show up for the session, and what props she will bring to make the furniture "at home" to communicate function to the assumed buyer? What process images will be most valuable – and pragmatic! – to plan for during the time she has with the photographer? Jenna will want to communicate that there is an affinity between her as the furniture maker to the end product: this may be a refined version of herself as a maker, not as she is in the workshop, outfitted to do the work and covered with wood dust, but rather a more polished iteration ready to meet the public.

Reflecting on and developing a brand strategy for the venture as a maker is particularly important as clients and customers are engaging with you as an actual creative individual. Explicitly, a consistent brand with all the components mentioned above working in concert communicates a narrative about the venture's UVP (and the maker!). Implicitly, it communicates the professionalism and intention associated with the creative business.

Developing Brand Guideline and Style Boards

While we are focusing on micro-enterprise and **solopreneurs**, we can learn how larger entrepreneurial ventures manage their brands. Often, they are called **brand guidelines** and *style boards*. Brand guidelines specify colors, fonts, particular phrases, and other visual and copy elements integral to the brand. Style boards can include images that reflect the mood and general venture "vibe." When working with a professional brand expert, a maker could commission a document which includes one or both of these. The resource could include the specific Pantone colors for the entire venture, keywords related to the business's brand, **digital marketing** content suggestions, and even AI-generated images of the maker in brand-appropriate environments and styling. However, you don't need to hire a professional brand "curator" if that's not of interest or in the budget. Reflect on what people have said about you as a maker, and also unifying elements that are consistent in your work and your values. It can be helpful to use online tools like Canva, Photoshop, Illustrator, or InDesign to design a personal brand board for visualization and a reminder when you are developing marketing content, designing/researching new packaging options, or creating (or pivoting) an e-commerce opportunity (Table 5.1).

Brand Assets to consider:

Justin the broom maker is interested in **scaling** up their hobby into a business. They use natural materials and found objects to create their brooms and value **environmental sustainability** and upcycling. Justin should consider these values and motivations when developing the brand strategy as well as reflect on the target market personae of the typical end user. Most likely, the logo and images will reflect a rustic, natural aesthetic, as will any digital marketing including a website and presence on any social media. The brand story should also be consistent in print materials such as business cards and packaging. When Justin shows up at sales opportunities either business-to-consumer (B2C) like an art/craft fair, they may want to "look the part" by wearing natural and casual clothing. If they decide to partner with another creative venture, including retail spaces for wholesale/commission relationships, Justin should consider whether or not the venue is "in brand" and a good fit for their work.

An important element to brand development for a creative venture is to reflect on what we value and do – and what we DO NOT. An artist and their business might value the empowerment of individuals to express themselves creatively and therefore they facilitate artmaking workshops. They also do NOT do "paint parties" or other services where participants mimic an existing image or composition. The creation of a brand is not a superficial marketing scheme – it should be the authentic understanding and communication of the creative entrepreneur and the venture's value in the market. Also you as a creative maker need to consider the long-term implications of the design choices that are made. The following maker story illustrates this.

Andy is a crochet and knitting pattern designer. In the early days of her business, she purchased logo design services from an Etsy shop. After a decade in the yarn industry, Andy was able to achieve one of her dreams: collaborating with a large yarn manufacturer and distributor to develop her own yarn line. Andy is thrilled with the yarn quality and colors, and that she was able to negotiate getting her business name and logo co-branded on the yarn label. After nearly a year in development, the yarn line is scheduled to be released when Andy gets a text message from her friend. The friend says she just saw the image from Andy's logo being used by a beauty supply business. Andy does a reverse image search of the image, planning to share other intellectual property violations with her lawyer. Andy discovers that the image is being used in many logos…because it was an included image in a popular design software. As a result, Andy's image rights to the logo are non-exclusive. Andy contacts the yarn company to explain that she will be changing her logo to an original design that can be registered as a trademark. The company has already printed the labels for the yarn line, and it will cost thousands of dollars to reprint the labels while also delaying the yarn launch. Andy is worried that it may doom her yarn line from the start. Because of her strong relationship and years of collaborating with the company, they agreed to move ahead with the product launch. The added cost and delays due to redesigning and printing labels damaged her image within the company and were likely a factor in the eventual discontinuation of the yarn line.

Table 5.1 Brand Assets

Logos	Primary logo plus secondary logos and/or submarks.
Color palette	Curated set of brand colors, including Pantone numbers.
Typography	Fonts consistently used for headings, subheadings, and body text.
Imagery style	Visual examples of photography, textures, and images that illustrate the brand's aesthetic.
Design elements	Any recurring visual assets to refer to such as icons or motifs that align with brand communication.
Assets in use	Examples of brand assets in use for promotion including print and digital marketing.

Table 5.2 The 5 Ps of Marketing

Product	Creative entrepreneurial efforts need a desirable and competitive offering, the product/service they are putting out in the market.
Pricing	Pricing involves understanding how that product/service's value is appropriately monetized and how it exists within other offerings available. For example, is the offering a high-value object that customers expect an associated costly price? Or is the product/service meant to be more accessible financially and the cost is reflective of that?
Promotion	Promotion is what we typically think of when the term "marketing" is used – the communication about the venture through images, copy, and content through various channels.
Place	Distribution concerns pertain to place. Where – online, in real life (B2C), or through an intermediatory business – will the venture engage with potential clients?
People	The people element in the 5 Ps includes the venture owner, partners and stakeholders, and, of course, identified target market(s).

Understanding Key Marketing Concepts

Once your creative venture has a clear brand concept and related communication assets, the next step is understanding key marketing concepts. Marketing itself is the means of reaching the target markets through **promotion**, sales, and distribution of the venture's product or service to the identified end user. Woven through the marketing message is the communication of the UVP – the value provided to the target market(s). Marketing strategy takes information about the venture's UVP as well as the target market(s), its competitive advantage, appropriate communication channels based on the UVP and end users, defined and ideal **return on investment (ROI)**, and the venture's (often the makers!) capacity in time and resources available for this work. Before addressing **marketing strategy**, it is valuable to address three core marketing concepts: the 5 Ps, the UVP, positioning maps, and the **customer decision-making process**.

The 5 Ps of marketing include the venture's **product** (and/or services), **price**, **promotion**, **place**, and **people** (Table 5.2).

Nat is a fine art painter whose body of work consists of large installation style and brightly hued acrylic paintings focusing on slightly unhinged domestic environments and objects which she sells through high-end retail spaces as well as exhibits in public galleries and museums. Her prices for the medium to large paintings are quite expensive although she had a range of small works that start at $500.00. She promotes her work through digital marketing including her website, social media platforms, and email campaigns. When she is participating in solo or group exhibitions, she is diligent in photographing these shows (including pictures of herself with her work!) and shares them through the digital marketing efforts. She also has a self-published book on her work, printed postcards, and stickers of her pieces. These are helpful to share with people who have purchased one or more of her paintings, especially to tuck into the packaging when shipping her work. As mentioned prior, Nat has opportunities both in-person through exhibitions and online via digital marketing that consist of the place in the 5 Ps. The people in her venture include herself as the painter (and how she shows up online and IRL in relation to her work), partners/stakeholders of curators and gallery owners, and, of course, her target market of collectors interested in contemporary painting that is domestically situated and slightly sinister.

As mentioned in Chapter 4, the UVP includes the specific product/service the venture offers, the value provided (**benefits**), and details about the offering (the **features**). It is the core of the marketing message and a creative entrepreneur needs to be able to communicate the UVP in a clear and compelling manner. The creative venture's UVP does not exist within a vacuum and there are probably **competitors** in the same sector that have a very similar UVP. This is where a **positioning map** is useful. As previously mentioned, identifying and studying competitors prior to a venture's launch is important for business planning. A positioning map is a helpful tool in this effort as it allows for mapping out competitors based on traits identified as important to the creative venture's target market(s), thus illuminating if there is room in the market or if it is an "oversaturated market" in which it will be difficult to thrive. For instance, if the two traits are "cost" and "originality," a positioning map would have an X-axis for cost ranging from

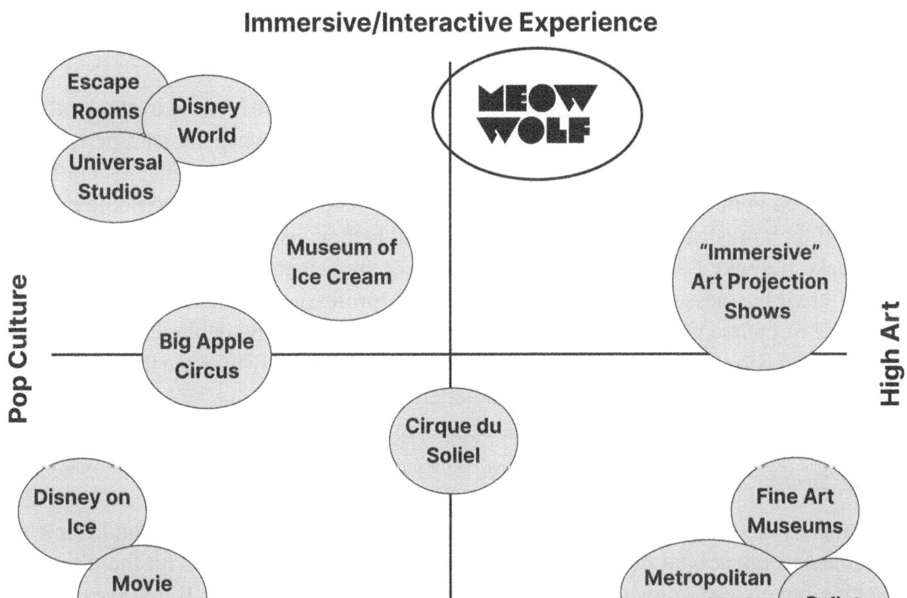

Figure 5.1 Meow Wolf positioning map.

Source: Sara Hartmann

"expensive" to "affordable" and a Y-axis of "one-of-a-kind" to "reproduction." When planning the creative venture, you as the maker can place the different competitors on the map within these parameters to see where there is market opportunity by analyzing where there are open areas to leverage a competitive advantage.

Below is an example of a positioning map using the example of Meow Wolf (meowwolf.com), a multi-site immersive art environment organization. You can see that Meow Wolf is sited within a landscape of competitors ranging from high art to pop art and immersive/interactive to passive experience. Meow Wolf is able to take advantage of a market gap situated in the upper right quadrant (high art) yet it is in close proximity to pop culture making their work extremely accessible to a range of audiences (Figure 5.1).

Finally, consider first the **customer decision-making process**. While some purchases may be impulsive, others – especially for those products/services intended to solve a problem or pain, like buying a gift for a particularly picky individual – might follow a more intentional and purpose-driven path. With the customer decision-making process that businesses can use to inform their marketing and distribution strategies, the interested buyer might go through the following steps and questions to ask yourself:

- **Problem/Need Recognition:** How will your customer discover their problem/need?
- **Information Search:** How will your customer find your creative venture?
- **Evaluation of Alternatives:** How does your UVP stand up to alternatives/competitors in the market?
- **Purchase Decision:** How and when (impulse or intentional purchase?) will your customer decide to buy?
- **Post-Purchase Behavior:** How will your customer share their (hopefully!) positive experience with your product or service? Will you be engaging with them post-purchase?

Alice is a quiltmaker who makes custom t-shirt quilts for people looking to show off concert merchandise that otherwise would sit in the closet. From the customer's perspective, they may first become aware of t-shirt quilts from a friend or social media, generating an interest/need in upcycling things which are currently taking up space into home décor to show off their musical tastes. They look online and in their geographic region for ventures that make bespoke t-shirt quilts. Seeing that there are several in their city, they look at the different businesses and compare quality, cost, professionalism, ease of communication, and of course glowing customer reviews/testimonials if available. Based on this, a purchase decision is made within those parameters and hopefully they are thrilled with the resulting quilt and will happily provide a flattering review.

Marketing Strategy and Assets

Developing a marketing strategy enables a creative entrepreneur to develop and implement a sustainable and intentional plan for communicating about their venture with the ultimate goal of reaching buyers and converting those efforts into business **revenue**. It involves digital and print assets, online communication, **public relations**, merchandise, and **advertising**. Marketing strategy empowers us as creative entrepreneurs to get specific and direct in communicating our UVP to target market(s). Unless a maker is operating solely in the branding and marketing sector, often these efforts are outside of their primary venture's work and can be a distraction at best and an unsustainable chore that drains time and energy at worst. We want to focus on making our work and engaging with potential clientele. Marketing strategy allows us to be smart with our capacity to get the largest ROI without burning out (Figure 5.2).

Figure 5.2 A Crafty Chica-branded merch sticker.

Source: Courtesy of Kathy Cano-Murillo/Crafty Chica

The use of target market(s) in this chapter points to another marketing term – **market segmentation**. As mentioned in Chapter 4, this is the process of considering anyone – a target market – that may be interested in the venture's UVP and has the capacity to pay for the product/service. If a ceramist is starting an art business selling product **business-to-business (B2B)** and B2C as well as teaching pottery classes, they may have several target markets. In market segmentation, we consider the needs, wants, and motivations of each specific target market. With B2B, the ceramicist will be communicating and working with another business owner, perhaps a gallery owner. B2C may include a collector of ceramics who is visiting a craft fair. A workshop participant interested in pottery as a hobby could be another target market. All of these target markets have their own "client avatars"; even though in all cases there is interest in ceramics, they are coming from different points of view and marketing assets should be crafted accordingly.

Digital marketing and related platforms are constantly in evolution. You may be using one efficiently, getting a good ROI that makes the effort worth it in creating interest and of more importance, opportunities that generate revenue. Remember, unless you are intending to be a **content creator**, influencer, or brand developer through your creative venture, you need digital marketing to work for you AND not be a drain on your time and capacity. Additionally, the utility and effectiveness of various digital platforms will evolve as your business as well as the priorities and functionalities of the technology does.

A simple recipe for digital marketing can include the following components with related issues to consider.

- **A home for your work online.** This is commonly a website, but it could also look like an Etsy shop. It is updated regularly, but the point of the online presence is to be more of a portfolio that is outward-facing and typically doesn't prioritize back-and-forth communication other than a means to contact you via email (pro tip: keep your personal email, phone number, and geographic address OFFLINE for security's sake).
    - Ask yourself: What is this for? Is it to showcase a body of work? To sell a production line? To sell a service whether "plug and play" or commission/bespoke? Who is it for – who do you expect will visit the website? These issues will direct the structure, design, and components of the site. What brand assets will you need to create it and how will you insure they are "in brand" with what you do in-person?
- **A relationship-based platform, often via social media**. This is a **para-social** digital marketing effort, where you as the maker are sharing information about you and your work to relation-build with potential and current fans. Unlike the website, this is interactive and takes more capacity daily or weekly.
    - Ask yourself: Where are your people (aka, the target market)? Consider their demographics and media consumption. What platforms do your **exemplars** and competitors engage with? What visual and copy content will you share? If hashtags are used on a specific platform, which ones are right for your work and market? Hint: look at your exemplars and competitors for inspiration!
- **A direct marketing option**, commonly using an online email campaign service to reach people who have either engaged with your venture previously or who opt-in to receive information. It is important to note that with email you own your audience. Social platforms can fall out of favor or ban your account; you could lose your whole audience overnight! However, an email list is an asset that is yours to keep and is portable to other platforms.
    - Ask yourself: Do people want this – have they asked you if you have one and/or do you engage with ideal clients who do not want to be on social media? Which email campaign works for you in ease of use and cost? How many times annually will you send out an email newsletter and what will you feature? What sorts of visual assets will you need? How will you collect the necessary emails from potential subscriptors both online and in-person?

Charli is founder and CEO of a media production company, self-producing her own video and media content as well as working for hire for **for-profit** and **non-profit** entities. Her business's UVP is to shine a light on successful rural entrepreneurs and community and economy development initiatives. When she left a traditional 9–5 job in order to scale up her venture from **side hustle** to full-time business, she contracted with a friend who is a brand editor and marketing strategist. Charlie communicated her UVP to her friend and they did a deep dive into the previous and current work of the venture including the associated marketing efforts. They also brainstormed about how the venture should be branded and arranged for a photo session. They further met to frame out the work needed: a consistent brand style guide with visuals, keywords, and content/concepts to highlight in marketing. From there, Charli had a valuable asset to guide the style pivot of digital media and promotional photography to communicate the value of the business. Now she has a roadmap for a consistent brand and digital marketing strategy which includes a website, compelling social media content, as well as a consistent weekly email newsletter campaign.

While much focus is placed on digital marketing, it is important not to forget the impact of print marketing. Again, looking at examples from competitors and exemplars alike for your venture is a good exercise in ascertaining what might be appropriate for you to do as well. Common options are business cards, postcards, brochures, packaging elements, stickers, and other branded merchandise (merch). There are numerous services to create these assets. Research the quality, price, and process of creating and producing these materials and of course make sure they are in-brand and desired by your target market (ideal client).

Consider these options as you are reviewing your overall marketing strategy (Table 5.3).

Table 5.3 Promotion Options for Creative Businesses by Marie Segares

Promotion Type	*Description*	*Examples*
Advertising	Broadcast media	television or radio ad
	Print media	newspaper, magazine, directory ad, or listing
	Outdoor	billboard, street furniture, mobile billboard, transit media
	Online	banner ads, video ads on websites, or social media
	Brand spiraling	using conventional advertising to drive traffic online, often using a special link
	Native advertising, product placement, and branded entertainment	paid advertising that seamlessly integrates into the publication or media, like a sponsored post written by the blogger in their own style or product used conspicuously in a video by a YouTuber
	Infomercial	long-form video or television ad that resembles programming
	In-store marketing	free samples, point-of-purchase displays, shelf placement, back of receipt ads
	Event marketing	free samples, demonstrations, or "make-and-takes," see also Sponsorship
	Brand ambassadors and influencers	paying and/or providing free or lower cost products to someone who represents your company or product positively; can be a long-term relationship or a single review or post
	Search engine marketing	paid ads to improve visibility in search results

(*Continued*)

Table 5.3 (Continued)

Promotion Type	*Description*	*Examples*
Database and direct marketing	Email newsletter, direct mail, catalog, coupons, telemarketing, text alerts	messaging sent directly to a potential or existing customer using email, mail, phone calls, and/or text
E-commerce	Website with a shopping cart, selling through social media accounts, a storefront on an online marketplace	your own website's store functionality, Pinterest's Shoppable Pins, an Etsy shop
Content marketing	Creating and publishing online content	organic/unpaid social media and blog posts or videos
Retargeting	Pixel-based retargeting	browser cookie follows potential customer who visited your website by displaying ads on social media or in search results
	Email retargeting	email newsletter service automation sends automated emails based on subscriber behavior such as clicking a link or not opening the email
	Abandoned cart recovery	e-commerce tools that track people who abandon their cart on your site and follow up with email and/or website notifications
Buzz marketing	Marketing activities to generate interest and discussion	launch events, user-generated content and reviews, and other activities to generate word-of-mouth interest
Sponsorship	Supporting an event, activity, or individual	offering need-based scholarships for your classes; donating funds to an event in exchange for a booth, signage with logo, or advertising in event materials
Public relations	Building reputation through local, regional, and national media and community relations	sharing press releases about an award you've won, and contributing work to a local non-profit organization
Branded materials	Branded merchandise (also known as "merch" or "promo items")	items such as t-shirts, buttons, stickers, pens, and tote bags, which are branded with logo, company name, and/or colors, can be distributed for free, sold at cost, or priced following your pricing strategy
	Branded displays	store window signs, craft fair booth displays, and other signage and display items that are branded with company name, logo, and/or colors

Understanding and Utilizing Concepts of Distribution Channels Specific to Venture and Target Markets

Along with brand identity and marketing strategy is the important issue of distribution to your target market(s). How do the potential end users decide to buy from your creative venture versus others doing similar work? What logistics including **costs** are related to delivering the venture's UVP to clients whether in-person or online? The following is an introduction to distribution channels followed by an in-depth analysis.

Before jumping into the venture's work, you as the creative maker need to consider your **distribution channels**. You might start with just one, like selling at a local arts market, and gradually scale up by adding wholesale/commission-based relationships with regional retail outlets or adding e-commerce to the revenue generating portfolio. Or, you may map out a distribution strategy that combines selling one-of-a-kind works through a gallery space while offering print-on-demand reproduction products. Regardless of the path you choose to distribute your product/service, you need to be mindful of the logistics and costs involved as well if the particular distribution is a good fit with your target market(s).

If you decide to sell "in real life" whether through a brick and mortar or a temporary opportunity like an art and craft fair or teaching a class, there are issues to consider. What fees or commissions are required to participate? What are the costs of preparation or packaging or framing? Is this an opportunity that necessitates travel and related food costs? Are there time commitments related, whether being in the vendor booth all day (or multiple days), the classroom, or the opening reception? Does the opportunity warrant the involved costs – commonly known as a **cost-benefit analysis?**

> Helen is a sewist who uses upcycled textiles to create one-of-a-kind fashion accessories. She is looking to expand her in-person opportunities regionally and has made a spreadsheet of art and craft shows three hours or less from her home. She has columns for each opportunity that list the event host, communication/adjudication information, show fees, associated travel costs, and focus/theme of the event. If possible, it would be very helpful to visit the event the year prior to participating. When Helen does her reconnaissance, she should be keen to observe the environment, especially the type of work featured, the quality of the event (hopefully well managed!), the density of the potential buyers, who they are buying from, and that event visitors are carrying around shopping bags or items as evidence that people are actually purchasing work rather than using this event as free entertainment. Helen might also want to chat up art and craft vendors – of course when they are not busy – to do **primary market research** on their experiences.

While e-commerce, especially direct to consumer, might seem attractive especially after investigating financial concerns related to commission rates and other costs, as a creative entrepreneur, you will need to do your research on providing an excellent purchasing process for their end users. Are there professional visual and copy assets associated with the product/service? What percentage and/or fees are required with using the Internet platform? With a product-based business, what are the costs and logistics involved with shipping the work to the buyer? Importantly, if you plan on shipping internationally, what current tax issues and trade policies could be a potential impact? If it's a service-based business, is there professional communication about the particulars, especially the purchase price (or price points for different types of services), and is there a seamless way for potential clients to begin the process of working with the venture? Finally, consider what issues are posed by **search engine optimization (SEO)** and algorithms related to the sales and social media platforms utilized.

> Rachel is a contemporary basketmaker living in a rural environment with limited access to markets that have the capacity to afford an appropriate price point for skilled handcrafted work. She is invited to join a cohort of other makers in her region who are interested in setting up shops on a popular art and craft e-commerce platform. In order to get her shop set up, Rachel must first do her research on that particular marketplace – what is selling, for how much, how other similar basketmakers are telling their story on the platform, and

how are they shipping the product (including shipping charges, delivery timing, refund policies, and if shipping out of country, specific international trade policies). After doing this work, Rachel must first decide if this is a good **product-market fit** for her pieces, and if so, must develop her own pricing, shipping and logistics policies, product copy (including benefits and features), visual assets of all the products for sale (including process images) as well as of herself, and a maker's biography written in a style that matches other maker stories on the platform. She also needs to develop a marketing strategy for the e-commerce platform that includes understanding specifics related to SEO, generative engine optimization, and algorithms as well as developing and employing methods of driving traffic to her shop unrelated to the search methodology of the specific platform.

Channel Analysis – A Deeper Dive and Analysis by Sara Hartmann

You were just introduced above to basic concepts of evaluating which **channels** to use for the **promotion** and **distribution** of your products, primarily from the perspective of customer relationships – identifying the best channels to meet your customers where they are and most likely to engage with your products. In this section, we will consider the question of channel analysis from a business operations perspective, asking which channels are best suited to your ventures' operational capacity and revenue goals.

Many creative entrepreneurs strategically use multiple channels to distribute their products to potential customers. For example, a jewelry designer might have a small showroom attached to their studio, sell through their own website, offer some styles on Etsy, sell **wholesale** to boutiques, and participate as a vendor at art markets. Each channel comes with its own unique set of operational challenges, competency requirements, costs, and earning potential. If your business is already active in several channels, we also recommend noting your historic revenue in each channel and factoring that in as a variable during this analysis. In any channel analysis exercise, you will compare all of your current and potential channels side-by-side by asking the following questions about each of them:

- **Channel Reach:** How large is the potential audience this channel exposes you to? Does this channel represent an attractive opportunity to significantly increase your brand awareness and audience size?
- **Time Resources:** How much time does it take to manage this channel on an ongoing basis? This could look like the hours you spend in any given month updating your website and shipping orders, or the hours that go into setting up and running a booth at an art market.
- **Channel-Specific Capabilities:** What specific skills and competencies do you need to possess or hire for to manage this channel effectively? For example, to run a successful and independent e-commerce site, you might need to develop skills in digital marketing and content management, while to effectively manage a wholesale channel, you would need to develop strong networking and sales capabilities.
- **Channel Costs:** What are the **fixed** and **variable costs** associated with selling in this channel? Fixed costs might include things like the booth fee for a market or a design fee paid for a web designer to create or maintain your website. Variable costs per channel can include items like percentage-based seller fees charged by a platform, or the changes to your unit economics from selling at wholesale rather than retail prices.
- **Channel Risks:** What are the reputational, financial, and operational risks associated with this channel? For instance, opening your own retail store to sell your products may carry a higher

degree of financial risk because of the large fixed costs that will need to be covered. Selling on a large platform such as Etsy, while having lower fixed costs, carries its own risks, such as having your merchandise displayed potentially next to offensive products, or having your visibility and effectiveness on this platform disrupted by changes to the platform's policies and algorithms.

- **Anticipated Revenue:** Considering the size of the audience accessible through this channel, the costs associated with selling, and reasonable assumptions about buyer behaviors, how much revenue can you realistically expect to bring in through average performance in this channel?

Channel Analysis Example

Chloe is an artist who sells Risograph prints of her work. She has found some success at local markets and is now exploring other channels to sell her art.

First, let's look at her unit economics. Chloe's most popular items are 11"×17" prints. She sells them for $38 each, with a total product cost of $6 for printing and packaging. This gives her a contribution margin per unit of $32.

Chloe is considering the following channels for selling her work: weekly vendor fairs, Etsy, wholesale to boutiques, and starting her own website (Table 5.4).

Based on these data points and estimates, Chloe has made the following projections for her anticipated monthly revenue from each channel.

Weekly Vendor Fair – At the markets Chloe has done in the past she has sold an average of 20 prints per market. She projects that if she makes some improvements to her display and

Table 5.4 Channel Analysis Example for Risograph Artist

Metric	*Weekly Vendor Fair*	*Etsy*	*Wholesale*	*Own Website*
Channel Reach	10,000 monthly visitors	400 million monthly visitors	Estimate each boutique gets 2,000 visitors per month	Estimate the website will get 3,000 visitors per month
Time Resources	50 hours of labor each month for four markets	12 hours of labor each month to update listings and fulfill orders	Estimate it will take 15 hours each month to manage outreach to wholesale buyers	Estimate it will take 20 hours each month to maintain and market the website
Channel-Specific Competencies	Customer interaction, visual **merchandising**	Platform keyword research, listing optimization	Networking, understanding wholesale terms and practices, sales	Site design best practices, content management
Channel Costs	$100 per market to vend, plus $1,000 initially for a market tent and display	Approximately 9.5% in fees, plus a $0.20 listing fee per item	Selling at a wholesale price (estimated at 50% of retail)	3% of each sale in processing fees, plus a $70 per month subscription
Channel Risk	Low foot traffic on bad weather days; labor-intensive with no guaranteed sales	High competition; fees can add up; platform dependence; algorithm changes can impact visibility	Lower profit margins per unit; difficulty in finding and maintaining partner relationships	No built-in audience; requires significant time and financial investment in marketing to drive traffic; slow to build a following

makes the effort to sell at the market every week she can increase this to an average of 30 prints per market.

> Revenue: (30 prints per market) x (4 markets per month) x ($38 per print) = $4560 per month
> Cost of Goods Sold: ($6 cost per print) x (120 prints sold) = $720
> Channel Costs = ($100 per market) x (4 markets per month) = $400
> Net Monthly Gain: $4,560–$720–$400 = $3,440

Etsy – Chloe has a few of her prints on Etsy, but she puts little effort into the channel and sells an average of four per month. She estimates that if she puts more effort into posting new products and optimizing her listings she can increase her sales to 30 per month.

> Revenue: (30 prints per month) x ($38 per print) = $1,140
> Cost of Goods Sold: (30 prints per month) x ($6 per print) = $180
> Channel Cost: ($1,140 sales per month) x (9.5% platform fees) = $108
> Net Monthly Gains: $1,140–$180–$108 = $852

Wholesale – Chloe doesn't do any wholesale yet, but there are a few local boutiques that have inquired about carrying her prints. If she starts to sell wholesale, she will have to set wholesale prices and a policy on minimum orders. Chloe thinks she can start out selling to three shops at a Wholesale price of $18 per print, with a minimum order of 10 prints.

> Revenue: (3 shops) x (10 prints) x ($18 per print) = $540
> Cost of Goods: (30 prints sold) x ($6 per print) = $180
> Channel Cost: In this case, the channel cost is already worked into the lower price per item. There may be additional costs if Chloe decides to increase her wholesale sales volume by selling on wholesale platforms like Faire.
> Net Monthly Gains: $540–$180= $360

Own Website – Right now, Chloe directs people to check out her Instagram account or her Etsy page when they ask about her online presence, but she's thinking of setting up her own website with an online store. She knows that it will take time and a new skill set to build regular traffic to her website, so she expects monthly sales on her site to be small in the first year.

> Revenue: (6 prints per month) x ($38 per print) = $228
> Cost of Goods:(6 prints sold) x ($6 per print) = $36
> Channel Costs: ($228 sales per month) x (3% processing fee) = $7
> E-commerce platform subscription ($70/month)
> Net Monthly Gains: $228–$36–$7–$70 = $115

Considerations for Digital Channels

Most creative entrepreneurs will consider using digital platforms for promoting or distributing their products. Whether selling on **marketplaces** like Etsy, Amazon, or Faire, creating your own website on an **e-commerce** platform or promoting your work through social media, digital channels offer the opportunity to connect with potential customers all over the globe at a rate that would have been previously impossible. However, there are several key operational considerations to make when deciding which platforms to use.

Audience Acquisition

While most digital platforms offer potential access to millions of users, getting found on each platform takes time and skill. Each platform has its own algorithm and set of criteria that it uses to determine a user's visibility. It's important to remember that mastering the best practices for one platform won't necessarily translate to another. To truly benefit from a platform, you must invest the time in developing the capabilities necessary to succeed on it. While the audiences are large, so are the number of users and brands competing for their attention.

Intellectual Property

For each platform you participate on, take the time to familiarize yourself with its **intellectual property** rules. What policies does the marketplace have in place to protect you from counterfeit versions of your brand being sold? Does the platform have rights to use the content you post for its own purposes? While a deep dive into the terms and conditions of any given platform will likely yield some terms that are not ideal for a small business, most entrepreneurs decide the trade-off is worth it. They participate in the channel because the gains in audience reach and business outweigh the intellectual property concerns, but it is always good to take a look at the fine print before investing time and resources into a platform.

Platform Dependence

One risk that many small businesses fail to consider is what happens when things start to go well on a platform. It's not uncommon for an entrepreneur to grow their business to rely on a single platform for a significant portion of sales. This approach can work as long as things are going well, but it creates a vulnerability for the business in the long run. Changes to the platform or its algorithm can threaten to take away a primary source of revenue.

It's important to remember that these platforms are businesses themselves. Many are publicly traded and have a responsibility to generate profits for their **shareholders**. Decisions to raise fees or to make it more difficult to get organic visibility to drive ad sales are ways these platforms can extract increased value from the entrepreneurs and creative businesses that use them. Being overly reliant on any single platform increases your vulnerability to such changes. While success on a platform is something to celebrate, a good strategy is to be careful never to rely on a single platform for the majority of your business.

Whatever type of distribution channel(s), there will always be hidden costs that a creative entrepreneur is unaware of at the beginning. As they are discovered, the ideal situation is to make note of them to plan and adjust pricing and other business logistics accordingly. If you do the research at the beginning of venture planning, it will reveal many costs as an alternative to discovering them when you are "in the weeds" of doing business.

Closing

Carefully considering your brand, marketing strategy, and distribution channels is invaluable with venture planning. A brand needs to be both authentic to you as a maker and resonate with your target market(s). The scaffolding from your brand to your buyers consists of marketing strategy and distribution channels – it's how you reach your people! Given that, using marketing concepts like the 5 Ps and positioning maps helps you to explore the landscape prior to communicating to a specific strategy in both marketing and distribution.

Mini Case: Building an Environmentally Sustainable Brand at Clochee

Daria Prochenka and Justyna Szuszkiewicz are the founders of Clochee. Justyna is a seasoned cosmetic designer, while Daria is a savvy entrepreneur. Daria encountered a youthful woman with breast cancer when visiting her grandmother in the hospital and could not fathom how such a young person could have cancer. She learned from hospital staff that consumers are continuously exposed to toxins and that women often accumulate these dangerous chemicals in their lymph nodes. Daria and Justyna discussed the many chemicals used in mainstream cosmetics lines. While talking with Justyna, Daria discovered her friend's passion for mixing her own cosmetics. Clochee was created in 2013 after the two explored how they might individually add value to a new company. Justyna was assigned to locating recipes and ingredients, while Daria was tasked with producing tables, datasets, advertisements, and promotional materials.

The business started with six product lines. Clochee specializes in environmentally-friendly, vegan cosmetics for the face, body, and hair. The business aspires to prove that sustainable, environmentally friendly goods can be attractive, fashionable, and popular with customers. The brand strives to offer entirely natural goods and does not use potentially harmful substances; some ingredients that Clochee's products do not contain include silicones, mineral oils, paraffin, parabens, dyes, synthetic fragrances, ethoxylated substances, carbomers, and propylene glycol. Packaging from recyclable, reusable materials validates the brand's commitment to protecting the environment. Clochee was Poland's first business to make this the main emphasis of their product range. Clochee now sells 90 products through 200 channels in Poland and has grown to include a distributor in Taiwan and significant international partners in Canada, the United Arab Emirates, and the United Kingdom.

Remixed with permission from Kelley, J.N. (2021). Daria Prochenka, Justyna Szuszkiewicz. In Gupta, V.K. (Ed.), WE: The inspiring stories of entrepreneurial women from around the world (pp. 41-44). University of Alabama. Additional source: Clochee www.clochee.com/en

Activities

Activity 1: Crafting Your Venture's Brand Vibe

Through reflection writing and designing either a presentation to share with your peers or a digital visual board, you will create a brand overview to access throughout your creative entrepreneurship journey. Think of this as a "brand compass" asset to keep you in alignment with your venture's communication and marketing strategy.

Write

- Return to your UVP and clarify/edit as needed.
- Create a list of brand keywords that are reflective of your venture.
- Develop a list of what your venture IS and what it IS NOT.
- Write a brief statement on the communication style (voice) associated with your venture's brand identity.

Design

- Create a brand style board that reflects your venture's brand identity, includes aesthetics, color, and associated cultural references.
- Develop a collection of visual resources that illustrates how you intend on showing up as THE brand ambassador for your venture.

Activity 2: Employing Marketing Concepts for Your Venture

The marketing concepts activity consists of three exercises noted in this chapter: a positioning map, 5 Ps information, and a reflection on the customer decision-making process (Figure 5.3).

Figure 5.3 Positioning map.

Source: Jennifer A. Reis

- Positioning Map
    - Develop the market environment axis you are interested in exploring.
    - Research direct and indirect competitors within that space.
    - Identify the market gap that your venture could exist.
- 5 Ps
    - Reflect on and clarify information associated with the 5 Ps for your venture.
- Customer Decision-Making Process
    - Consider your ideal client/target market and reflect on what you might assume their decision-making journey would look like.

Activity 3: Mapping Out Your Market Strategy

Create a marketing strategy plan-of-attack. Be empathetic with your end user and consider how to most effectively engage with them. Develop either a presentation to share with your peers or a portfolio to clarify a marketing strategy for your venture that is within your capacity and sustainable over time.

- What is the assumed ROI for your marketing efforts? How will you know (key metrics) that your messaging and assets are converting into the desired result?
- What will your digital marketing consist of and what assets do you need?
- What will your print marketing consist of and what assets do you need?
- How will you push out your marketing efforts and within what timeframe and frequency?

Activity 4: Investigating Distribution Channels

Think about your potential distribution channels and develop related venture offerings associated with your UVP. This can be a personal document or one to share with peers.

- Distribution channels:
    - What is the primary distribution channel you intend to use?
        - What are the opportunities?
        - What are the challenges?
        - List the logistics involved.
        - Note the distribution costs (not of the actual product/service, but associated with the means of distribution).
    - What is the secondary distribution channel you intend to use?
        - What are the opportunities?
        - What are the challenges?
        - List the logistics involved.
        - Note the distribution costs (not of the actual product/service, but associated with the means of distribution).

- Developing additional venture offerings:
  - If you are doing a product-based venture, list three potential services analogous to the product. Don't self-edit! This is only a brainstorming list.
  - If you are doing a service-based venture, list three potential products analogous to the product. Don't self-edit! This is only a brainstorming list.

Resources and References

Ilasco, M. M. (n.d.). *Creative, Inc.* Chronicle Books.
Macneil, N. (2015). *The conquer kit: A creative business planner for women entrepreneurs.* Perigee Books.
Nest. (n.d.). Learning + Community. *Nest.* https://www.buildanest.org/nest-guild
Rochester, S. (2022). *Making a living.* Nicholas Brealey.

6 Money Basics

Cost Analysis and Pricing Strategies

Sara Hartmann

Introduction

There's an unfair but widespread stereotype that creatives are "bad" with money. This notion is untrue; being skilled in one area doesn't magically make you deficient in another, and in reality, many creatives are perfectly capable money managers. What is true, however, is that entrepreneurs of all varieties can sometimes jump into launching a business with passion and enthusiasm to spare, yet neglect the crucial step of developing a solid financial plan. For creatives, it's all too easy to let the excitement of realizing a unique artistic vision overshadow the necessity of financial forecasting and analysis, often leading to the assumption that artistic success will inherently translate into financial viability.

Consider the experience of Lisa, a talented designer specializing in bespoke fashion and accessories. Her part-time business, focused on special occasion wear and handcrafted handbags, demonstrated strong sales performance at temporary events such as trunk shows and pop-up shops. However, her e-commerce website struggled to gain traction within the digital marketplace. Driven by the tangible success of her in-person sales, Lisa made the decisive move to establish a full-time brick-and-mortar **retail** presence. She secured a location that resonated with her aesthetic sensibilities and enthusiastically entered into a five-year lease agreement.

It was around the time of her store's grand opening that Lisa began engaging in formal business education and collaborating with experienced mentors to develop a comprehensive business plan for her new retail operation. This crucial process, however, revealed several critical oversights in her initial planning. Lisa had not yet undertaken a thorough calculation of the **profit margins** on her **products**, leaving her without a clear understanding of the unit-level **costs** associated with their production. Furthermore, she had not conducted a **breakeven analysis** to determine the precise volume of monthly sales required to cover the significant *overhead* of the retail space, including rent, employee salaries, and her own **compensation**.

As Lisa analyzed the financial implications of her new venture, a sobering reality emerged. Based on the substantial cost of rent for her chosen location and the relatively narrow profit margins on her product line, the required **sales volume** to achieve profitability proved to be exceedingly unrealistic given the actual foot traffic in the area. Lisa faced a difficult choice: either significantly reduce her production costs, potentially compromising the quality of her designs, or drastically decrease the overhead associated with her retail space. Unwilling to sacrifice the integrity of her product, Lisa ultimately made the challenging decision to terminate her lease and return to a **business model** centered on online sales and temporary pop-up events, albeit with the future aspiration of reopening in a more financially sustainable location.

While Lisa's business ultimately persisted, the financial repercussions of opening and subsequently closing the retail store were considerable. This scenario underscores a critical question:

DOI: 10.4324/9781003588771-6

what if Lisa had conducted a thorough financial analysis *before* committing to a long-term lease? Had she possessed a clear understanding of the operational costs and the necessary sales volume, she might have deferred signing the lease until a more affordable and visible location became available.

In this chapter and the next, we will delve into the fundamental financial analysis techniques that are indispensable for every entrepreneur, regardless of the scale or nature of their enterprise. By mastering these core concepts, arts entrepreneurs can move beyond intuitive decision-making and navigate the financial landscape with greater clarity, foresight, and ultimately, a higher likelihood of sustainable success.

Learning Outcomes

- **Calculate** a business's unit economics using provided data
- **Prepare** a breakeven analysis for a new product or business
- **Develop** a pricing strategy for a product or business venture

Unit Economics: The Foundation of Financial Understanding

Understanding the **unit economics** of a business serves as the essential first step in comprehending its financial viability. Unit economics measures the direct **revenues** and **costs** associated with a single unit of sale. In simpler terms, consider the fundamental offering of your business: the revenue represents the income generated from selling one instance of that offering, while the cost encompasses the direct expenditures incurred to produce that single unit.

The primary purpose of a unit economics analysis is to illuminate the financial gain or loss resulting from the sale of a single unit. Surprisingly, many business owners neglect this crucial calculation and can inadvertently price their goods or services below their per-unit cost of production, ultimately jeopardizing the sustainability of their venture.

Unit Economics Example for a Product Business

Eugene operates a business that designs and sells handwoven tapestries. For the purpose of unit economics analysis, we will define a "unit" as one tapestry and base our calculations on his average figures. A typical tapestry sells for $600. On average, Eugene spends four hours completing each tapestry and utilizes $50 worth of wool yarn. He values his time at a rate of $50 per hour.

Revenue per Unit: $600
Cost per Unit (Variable Costs): $250 per unit

Labor Cost: 4 hours x $50/hour = $200
\+ Material Cost: $50

= $250

Profit per Unit (Contribution Margin): $350

Revenue per Unit $600
− Cost Per Unit $250

= $350

Unit Economics Example for a Service Business

Joy is a freelance illustrator who works on commission. Her pricing typically operates on a per-image basis, with a sliding scale depending on the client's budget. A typical client engages her for a single project. For the purpose of unit economics, we can define a "unit" as one commissioned illustration project. Let's assume her average project fee is $800, and the direct costs associated with a typical project (materials, specific digital assets) average around $50.

Revenue per Unit (Average Project Fee): $800
– Direct Costs per Unit: $50

Profit per Unit (Contribution Margin): $750

Let us now define each element of a unit economics analysis in detail.

First, the **Unit**. For some businesses, defining a unit is straightforward. If the core offering is a tangible product, then one instance of that product constitutes a unit. For businesses with multiple product lines, an analysis might focus on a best-selling item or a product representing the median price point. However, many artists and creative professionals operate businesses centered on providing creative services or producing events. In these instances, the definition of a "unit" can be more nuanced and is often determined by the prevailing operating norms of the business. A unit could be a specific project, a client under a retainer agreement, a single event produced, or a defined block of service hours.

Next, **Revenue**. Revenue per unit is the income generated from the sale of one defined unit. For businesses selling tangible products with a consistent price, this is readily measurable – the revenue is the established selling price of a single item (as illustrated in Eugene's example). For service-based businesses, estimating revenue per unit is contingent upon the chosen definition of a unit. Consider a business with multiple clients paying a monthly retainer. If a "unit" is defined as one month of service provided to a single client, the revenue per unit would be the agreed-upon monthly retainer fee. Alternatively, for an artist creating custom commissioned work, where engagements are typically project-based, a "unit" might be defined as a single commission, and the revenue per unit would be the average price charged for a typical commission (as seen in Joy's example).

Now, let us define **Cost**. Every business incurs two primary categories of costs: **Variable Costs** (also known as **direct costs**) and **Fixed Costs** (also known as **indirect costs** or overhead). Variable costs are the expenses directly attributable to the production of a single unit of a product or the delivery of a single unit of a service. These costs are termed "variable" because their total amount fluctuates in direct proportion to the volume of sales. Examples of variable costs for a product business include the cost of raw materials and direct labor involved in manufacturing each item. For a service business, variable costs might include the cost of specific materials or software used for each client project or the wages paid to temporary staff or contract workers directly involved in service delivery for a particular unit.

Fixed Costs, on the other hand, encompass all other expenses associated with maintaining and operating the business as a whole. These costs are often referred to as overhead and can include expenses such as rent for a studio or office space, marketing and advertising expenditures, salaries of administrative staff, and fees paid for professional services like legal and accounting counsel. While the total amount of fixed costs can vary from period to period (for instance, utility costs might be higher in certain seasons), they do not change in direct relation to the number of units sold. To illustrate, the cost of heating an art studio may increase during winter months, but this cost is still classified as a fixed cost because it is not a direct component of the labor or materials required to produce a single artwork.

Let's return to the example of Eugene's wall tapestry business.

We have already identified Eugene's **Variable Costs per Unit**:

- Wool Yarn: $50 per tapestry
- Labor: $200 per tapestry

Now let us add up Eugene's **Monthly Fixed Costs**:

- Studio Rent: $400
- General studio supplies: $150
- Wifi & Utilities: $200
- Insurance: $200
- Website and Digital Marketing: $250

As we can see, Eugene has a total monthly Fixed Cost of $1,200. It is crucial to understand that while these fixed costs are essential for operating his business, they are not directly tied to the production of a single tapestry and are therefore not included in the initial unit economics calculation.

Finally, let us consider **Unit Profit**. The profit per unit, also frequently referred to as the **Unit Contribution Margin**, is calculated by subtracting the variable cost per unit from the revenue per unit. This metric is termed "contribution margin" because it reveals how much revenue from each individual transaction contributes towards covering the business's fixed costs and ultimately generating net profit. A positive contribution margin is essential for long-term sustainability, as it indicates that each sale generates more revenue than the direct costs associated with it, providing the necessary funds to cover overhead and contribute to the bottom line. This is distinct from **gross margin**, which is calculated as total revenue minus the cost of goods sold, before any other expenses are subtracted. For a small creative business, the unit contribution margin and gross margin often refer to the same thing, but it's important to understand the technical distinction as you grow.

Breakeven Analysis

A breakeven analysis stands as one of the most fundamental calculations an entrepreneur must master. Fortunately, once you've completed a unit economics analysis, you possess all the necessary components to conduct a thorough breakeven analysis.

This crucial calculation reveals the sales volume at which a business will precisely cover its fixed expenses and subsequently begin to generate a profit, based on the figures derived from your unit economics analysis.

The Formula:

Breakeven Point (in Units) = (Fixed Expenses to be Covered)/(Contribution Margin per Unit)

In other words, we begin by identifying the total fixed expenses that need to be covered and then divide this by the contribution margin generated by each unit sold. The result of this calculation indicates the number of 'units' you need to sell to fully cover your fixed expenses and achieve profitability.

Let's revisit our ongoing example with Eugene. We know that Eugene incurs monthly fixed costs totaling $1,200. Furthermore, we've established that Eugene's Unit Contribution Margin is $350 per tapestry. A breakeven analysis can precisely determine how many tapestries Eugene must sell each month to cover his fixed expenses and break even.

$$\$1200\left(\text{Monthly Fixed Costs}\right)/\$350\left(\text{Unit Contribution Margin}\right) = 3.4 \text{ Tapestries}$$

Naturally, Eugene is unlikely to sell four-tenths of a tapestry. Therefore, in practical terms, this calculation tells us that once Eugene sells his fourth tapestry within a month, he will have fully covered his monthly fixed costs and, in fact, will have generated a profit.

For instance, selling 4 tapestries yields:

$$4 \times \$350 = \$1,400$$

Subtracting his monthly overhead:

$$\$1,400 - \$1,200\left(\text{Monthly Overhead}\right) = \$200 \text{ Profit}$$

The utility of breakeven analysis extends far beyond simply calculating a monthly breakeven point. This versatile calculation can be applied to estimate the sales volume required to break even on the initial startup costs of launching a new business.

For example, let's imagine Eugene invested $6,000 in supplies and equipment to initiate his business. How many tapestries would he need to sell to recoup this initial investment?

$$\$6,000\left(\text{Initial Investment}\right)/\$350\left(\text{Unit Contribution Margin}\right) = 17.14 \text{ Tapestries}$$

Additionally, performing a breakeven analysis is an excellent practice when evaluating the financial viability of a potential new project.

Consider a scenario where Eugene is contemplating selling his artwork at an out-of-town art market, which comes with a significant participation cost. While this market is prestigious and attracts high-end clientele, it carries a $2,000 booth fee, and Eugene anticipates spending an additional $1,500 on travel. This brings his total cost of participation to $3,500.

$$\$3,500\left(\text{Cost to Participate in Art Market}\right)/\$350\left(\text{Unit Contribution Margin}\right) = 10 \text{ Tapestries}$$

So, how should Eugene leverage this information to inform his decision about attending the market? The primary consideration is the likelihood of selling this many tapestries. He might choose to consult with other vendors who have participated in previous years to gauge their typical sales figures. If the breakeven point for this market appears high relative to the event's normal sales, Eugene might decide to forgo participation. Conversely, if most vendors report sales significantly higher than the breakeven point, this market likely represents a sound investment.

It's also important to acknowledge that there might be other compelling reasons to attend, even if Eugene doesn't anticipate breaking even financially. Perhaps this market presents a crucial networking opportunity that could lead to future sales or other valuable prospects down the road. In such cases, Eugene might be willing to incur some financial loss on this particular market in order to cultivate new connections and build his professional network.

Pricing Your Products and Services

One of the most common questions creative entrepreneurs grapple with is, "How do I price my work?" When it comes to **pricing**, it's crucial to understand that there isn't a single, universally "right" answer or a magic number you need to discover. The customer's willingness to pay for a product or service is influenced by a multitude of factors, some quantitative and others qualitative. Even large firms that employ entire teams of MBAs and PhDs to study and recommend ideal prices often adjust their prices multiple times before arriving at what they consider to be an optimal price range. Rather than striving to find a singular magic number to assign to the work you're selling, think about pricing as a quest to understand the various factors that affect your customers' price sensitivity and, from that understanding, determine a range of acceptable prices for your product or service.

Debunking Oversimplified Formulas and Focusing on Perceived Value

If you've spent time online researching pricing strategies and formulas, you've likely come across some overly simplified calculations, such as "cost times two" or "cost times four equals price." While these formulas may provide adequate answers in very limited circumstances, it is generally not advisable to set your prices using such a simplistic **cost-plus** approach. The most important variable you need to understand in order to effectively set your prices is the customer's **perceived value** of what you are selling. It could very easily be that a customer would value your work at a significantly higher price than a simple cost-plus formula would suggest. Selling to them at the lower, formula-derived price leaves money on the table and sells you short as an entrepreneur.

For example, let's say you make glass ornaments with a variable cost of $10 per piece. Using a "cost times two" formula would suggest these pieces should be priced at $20, while a "cost times four" formula would suggest a price of $40. But let's also assume that customers absolutely love these pieces and they sell easily at a retail price of $60. In this scenario, rigidly using a cost-plus formula to determine the price would cause the artist to sell their work for substantially less than what customers are actually willing to pay, thereby missing out on significant potential revenue and undervaluing their creative output.

Pricing Objectives

When setting your own prices, it's natural and often beneficial to research what other businesses, both large and small, might be charging for goods or services in the same or similar categories. However, when surveying the current market landscape, it's important to recognize that companies may be using different objectives to set their prices, and not every company's objectives will align with your own goals for your small business. Here are some of the most common objectives companies may use to set their prices:

- **Survival Pricing:** This objective is employed when a business is setting prices primarily to **liquidate** their **inventory** and bring in cash during a period of severe financial hardship or emergency. With survival pricing, the objective to turn a profit is temporarily set aside in the interest of generating enough **cash flow** to navigate a period of downturn and simply keep the business afloat.
- **Profit Maximization:** This is generally the recommended pricing objective for small businesses. In part, this is because a small business typically has a relatively limited capacity to produce goods or services, making it crucial to maximize the gains on the work that the business is able to produce. This objective focuses on finding the price point that yields the highest overall profit.
- **Penetration Pricing:** This is a strategic pricing objective typically utilized by larger businesses with substantial financial resources. With penetration pricing, a business sets its prices lower than competitors, or sometimes even sells at a loss, in order to rapidly gain new customers and capture a larger share of the market. The expectation is that eventually, after customers are acquired and market share is established, prices can be increased to achieve greater profit margins.
- **Price Skimming:** This is another objective and strategy often used by larger businesses with more substantial resources. Price skimming typically involves a company introducing a cutting-edge new technology or product for which they anticipate there will be an audience of people eager to pay premium prices to be the first adopters. Price skimming then involves introducing a new product at a very high initial price to establish perceptions of quality and prestige and to capitalize on people willing to pay an early adopter premium, before eventually introducing more affordable versions to the market. For example, the original iPhone was introduced at a very high price at the time, a strategy companies like Apple routinely use when launching new products.

Understanding Price Positioning: The Interplay of Pricing and Branding

Now that we have established that perceived value is one of the most important elements in pricing, we must ask: what factors affect our perceptions of value? Many people are surprised to learn that pricing is just as much a **branding** question as it is a financial one. The ways and places that a brand chooses to communicate information about prices profoundly affect the customer's perceptions about value. This means that how you present your prices is as critical as the price itself in shaping customer expectations and willingness to pay.

Transactional vs. Relational Pricing Signals

Broadly, the signals we receive about pricing can be placed into two categories: **transactional** and **relational**.

- **Transactional signals** emphasize the direct exchange of money for a good or service. They highlight that the customer is getting a good deal for their money, often focusing on discounts, low prices, or bargains. Transactional signals appeal to customers who are highly price-conscious and primarily looking to meet a need without overspending. Transactional customers are most pleased when they feel they are securing a bargain for their money.
- **Relational signals**, conversely, emphasize that the brand deeply understands the customer's needs and will deliver on meeting those needs in satisfying ways. In this approach, the money

changing hands is deemphasized. Relational customers are seeking a purchase that will meet their specific desires to a high degree of satisfaction, and the price being paid is a secondary consideration relative to their overall satisfaction from the purchase.

There isn't a "right" or "wrong" way to position your pricing; depending on what you're selling, it is equally valid to pursue transactional positioning for your product or relational positioning. However, many small creative businesses that are working from a profit maximization objective often find that relational positioning is better suited to their business strategy.

The Peril of Mixed Signals

Businesses often run into trouble with pricing when they send mixed signals by using tactics associated with transactional pricing alongside those of relational pricing. This inconsistency can confuse customers and undermine their perceived value of your offering. To be effective in your pricing communications and to establish clear price positioning, it's a good idea to revisit your prior research from earlier chapters about your target customer's needs, wants, and beliefs. The fundamental basis of effective relational price communication is to demonstrate that you deeply and truly understand your customer.

Touchpoints That Shape Price Perception

Every aspect of the customer's interaction with your business plays a role in shaping their expectations and perception of your pricing. Here are a few examples to consider:

Price Displays: When physical products are being sold, the placement and size of the font used in pricing information send distinct signals to customers about what to expect. Transactional brands are more likely to display prices prominently and in large, bold fonts. They may

Figure 6.1 A transactional price display for food items. Note the large font and messages emphasizing low prices.

Source: itkannan4u via Pixabay

Figure 6.2 A relational price display for food items. Note the small font and artful presentation.

Source: Farhad Ibrahimzade via Unsplash

also heavily feature prices in their display advertising. Relational brands, on the other hand, are more likely to display prices discreetly and in smaller fonts, and they rarely feature prices in their advertisements.This distinction also extends to the denomination in which prices are listed. Transactional brands often list the price down to the exact cent, which implies they are trying to give the consumer the best possible deal for their money, right down to the last possible penny. A relational brand, however, will rarely price down to the cent and may even forgo the decimal entirely, showing the price only in whole dollars, euros, or pounds.

It's important to note that the distinction between transactional and relational pricing presentation is not always a simple one between discount brands and luxury brands. For example, when purchasing airfare or selecting a hotel room on a booking engine, it's not uncommon to see the prices of luxury hotels listed down to the exact cent. This is because someone using that platform to select a hotel room is likely to be more price-sensitive about value per dollar than a customer who is going directly to the luxury hotel's website to make their booking. Consider the competitive landscape between Starbucks and Dunkin' Donuts in the United States, both of whom compete aggressively for market share in the coffee and specialty drinks-to-go category. Dunkin' Donuts employs a transactional pricing strategy, often displaying their prices in very large fonts directly in their advertisements. Starbucks, in contrast, never displays prices in their advertisements and even in-store displays prices in a very small font.

Transaction Setting: The venue where a transaction takes place also significantly impacts customer perception of the value being offered. A painting displayed in a formal art gallery, for instance, will command a higher price expectation than the same painting displayed at an outdoor art market. Spend some time visiting multiple retail stores, and you'll notice that stores employing a transactional strategy are more likely to have bright lights and vibrant colors in their interiors, while stores using a relational strategy are more likely to feature muted tones and soft surfaces. The effect of place extends beyond the retail industry; suppose you are a creative freelancer. A client who meets with you in your professional studio space may assign a higher perceived value to your services than they would if you met with them in a casual neighborhood coffee shop.

Figure 6.3 A vendor selling at an outdoor art market.

Source: Photo by Melissa Ostrow. Courtesy of Massachusetts College of Art and Design

Pricing Challenges for Creative Businesses in Transaction Settings

One common challenge that many creative small businesses face is that they are often not in full control of the setting where the transaction is occurring. For many, art markets and pop-up vendor shows are an important form of **distribution** in the early days of their business. While there are many wonderful aspects to these types of events, one downside is that multi-vendor events can foster an expectation of discounts or the ability to bargain among some shoppers. Having a customer attempt to haggle with you over the price of your work is a common and often frustrating experience for many creative entrepreneurs.

When selling in settings like this, it's important to think about how you can use your price displays and communications to subtly counteract the expectation that you are there to be bargained with. In many cases, simply having a price list or price tags that are professionally printed rather than handwritten can go a long way towards achieving this. Handwritten tags, no matter how lovely your penmanship, can inadvertently be seen as a signal that your prices are not fixed but rather an opening for negotiation. Similarly, if you offer a creative service, having a price list presented in a fixed PDF document to share with prospective clients can significantly enhance your perceived value, as opposed to going back and forth about prices in an email.

It can be a helpful exercise to think about all the touchpoints a prospective customer encounters in a transaction with you and ask yourself: are your communication strategies and materials for each of these touchpoints sending relational or transactional signals? It's likely that if this is your first time conducting such an audit, you'll find that you are sending mixed signals. It's important then to consider how you can adjust your price communications to send a more consistent and aligned message that supports your desired price positioning.

Understanding Price Sensitivity

Price sensitivity refers to the degree to which a customer's purchasing decision is influenced by the price of a good or service. Customers who are more price sensitive will be more reluctant to pay higher prices for items, seeking out better deals or alternatives. Conversely, customers with lower price sensitivity will be more willing to pay a higher price, often prioritizing other factors like quality, convenience, or brand loyalty over cost. Understanding this spectrum of sensitivity is crucial for any business, especially for creative entrepreneurs looking to establish sustainable pricing.

Price sensitivity varies significantly and is impacted by a number of factors. Recognizing these can help you anticipate how your target customers might react to your pricing:

- **Relative Size of the Purchase:** How large is the purchase relative to the customer's disposable income or budget? If the cost represents a significant portion of their available funds, they will generally be more price sensitive.
- **Access to Alternatives and Information:** How much access does the customer have to information about alternative products or services? In markets where comparisons are easy and substitutes are plentiful, price sensitivity tends to be higher.
- **Perceived Value or Prestige:** How much prestige, perceived value, or unique benefit is associated with the product or service? Offerings with higher perceived value or unique qualities often command less price sensitivity.
- **Add-on to a Previously Purchased Asset:** Customers may be less price sensitive if they are purchasing a good or service as an add-on to something they've already committed to. For example, a client buying a photo album as an add-on to their wedding photography package might be less price sensitive than if they were buying the album independently.
- **Third-Party Payment:** If a third party is footing the bill for the transaction, the customer making the purchasing decision may exhibit lower price sensitivity. For instance, if you're a graphic designer securing client work, the person making the purchasing decision at a larger firm (who is using their employer's budget) may be less price sensitive than a small business owner paying out of pocket.
- **Repair or Upgrade to an Existing Asset:** Customers may also be less price sensitive when paying for a repair or upgrade to a previously purchased asset, such as having a custom suit they already own altered to fit them perfectly.

Measuring Price Sensitivity: The Van Westendorp Analysis

When a large firm with substantial resources aims to understand price sensitivity to inform the pricing of a new product or service, they will sometimes undertake what is known as a **Van Westendorp analysis**. This robust survey-based technique asks a large group of target consumers four specific questions to determine price sensitivity and identify a range of acceptable prices for a product or service. These questions are:

- **At what price would you consider the product to be so expensive that you would not consider purchasing it?** (This identifies the "Too Expensive" price point.)
- **At what price would you consider the product to be expensive, but still a good deal or worth buying?** (This identifies the "Expensive/Good Value" price point.)
- **At what price would you consider the product to be a bargain?** (This identifies the "Bargain" price point.)
- **At what price would you consider the product to be so cheap that you would question its quality and not consider purchasing it?** (This identifies the "Too Cheap" price point.)

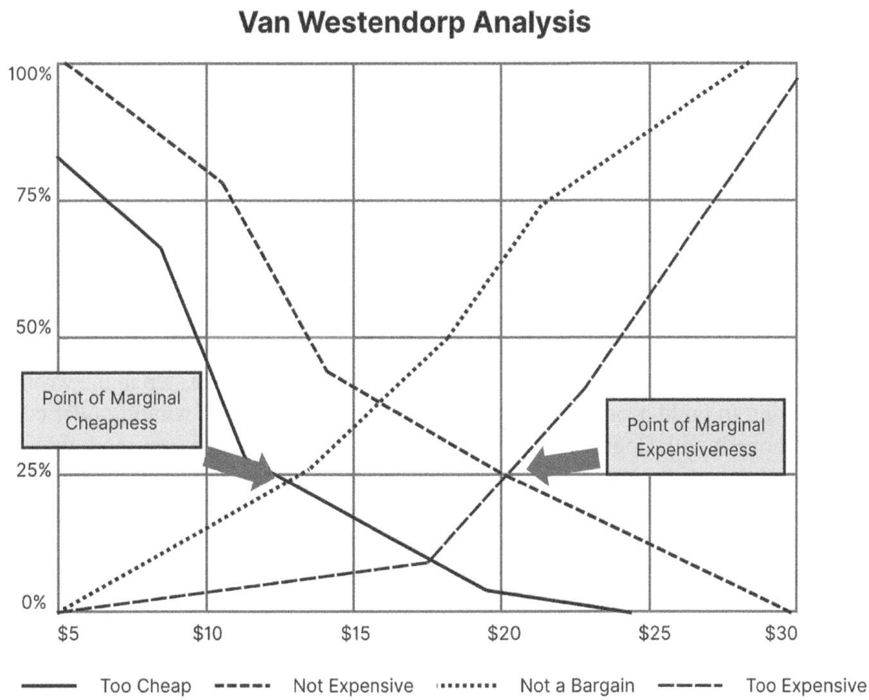

Figure 6.4 The Van Westendorp Analysis can be used to determine the range of acceptable prices.

Source: Sara Hartmann

When customer responses to these four price points are mapped on a grid (as seen in Figure 6.4), we can visually identify the range of acceptable prices. This range typically falls between two key points:

- **The Point of Marginal Cheapness:** This is the point where an equal number of customers say that the price point is "too cheap to be of any good" and that the price point is "starting to become expensive and no longer a bargain." If a business prices their goods anywhere below this point, they risk alienating customers rather than attracting them, by sending negative signals about product quality and value.
- **The Point of Marginal Expensiveness:** At the other end, this is the point where an equal number of customers say that a product is either "too expensive to be considered" or "a good deal." Raising the price beyond this point also deters more customers than it attracts.

For a large company with the resources to conduct such an analysis at scale, the points between the point of marginal cheapness and the point of marginal expensiveness represent the **range of acceptable prices**, where prices are attracting more customers than they are deterring. Most businesses will choose a price that falls within the upper end of this range of acceptable prices. In some cases, such as with luxury goods, limited edition products, or for small businesses with inherently limited production capacity, brands may even price above the point of marginal expensiveness if sufficient customers exist to purchase the limited quantities of goods or services available at this higher price point. If you are not planning to produce large volumes of a product, there's no need to price to attract a mass market.

Approximating Price Sensitivity for Creative Entrepreneurs

As a creative entrepreneur, you likely don't have the resources to engage a market research firm to conduct a study like the Van Westendorp analysis at a scale where the data would be statistically relevant. However, you can effectively approximate the range of acceptable prices by conducting comparative **market research**. Customers' ideas about the range of acceptable prices are partially formed by prices they've already been exposed to in the market. By identifying as many products or services currently for sale that might inform your customers' perception of value and typical prices for your offering, you can sketch out a rough idea of what the range of acceptable prices might look like to your customer.

It is most important to note and understand your product's **point of marginal cheapness**. Many entrepreneurs are tempted to resort to cutting prices and offering discounts during periods of slow sales or uncertainty. However, simply lowering prices is often a step in the wrong direction when trying to build a sustainable business and may not even be winning over customers the way you hope it will. Cognitive Surplus, profiled in Case 10.3, does not work with liquidators, and lowers prices on slower moving products by selling "mystery boxes," offering limited sales as exclusives for newsletter subscribers, or donating items to charitable organizations. Understanding what the point of marginal cheapness is for the work you produce is an important guardrail against pricing yourself out of business and inadvertently signaling low quality.

Anchoring in Pricing

Once you have a good sense of your target customers' rough range of acceptable prices, the natural next question becomes: how can you guide customers towards the upper end of that price range? In addition to auditing your price signals and brand assets to ensure they consistently present a high-value, relational price position, the next strategic step is to think about how you can effectively anchor your customers' price expectations. **Anchoring** is a particularly effective strategy here. Anchoring bias refers to a well-documented cognitive bias that causes people to "anchor" their price expectations and subsequent judgments around the first piece of numerical information they are given. This initial number, even if it's not directly related to the item they are considering, sets a powerful benchmark that influences their perception of value and fairness for other prices they encounter.

How to Leverage Anchoring in Your Pricing Strategy

The principle behind anchoring is that by showcasing attention-grabbing, higher-priced offerings that are significantly more expensive than your intended bestsellers, you can help frame customer expectations towards the upper end of the price spectrum. This, in turn, makes your core products or services seem more accessibly priced and a better value in the process.

Consider these classic examples:

- The "Luxury" item on display: As the saying goes, the best way to sell a $2,000 watch is to place it next to a $10,000 watch. The higher-priced item serves as the anchor, making the $2,000 watch appear much more reasonable and attainable by comparison.
- Restaurant Wine Lists: Think about restaurants that feature an expensive wine list. The higher-priced bottles make the more moderately priced glasses of wine, or even slightly less expensive bottles, look like a perfectly reasonable and appealing option when placed side-by-side.

For many artists and creative entrepreneurs who regularly participate in live shows, pop-up markets, or even online portfolios, this strategy can be directly applied. You might consider bringing a few of your most eye-catching, one-of-a-kind, or larger-scale pieces that command a significantly higher price. These pieces serve to grab people's attention and, more importantly, anchor their price expectations at a higher level. This elevated anchor can then subtly influence their perception of your more popular, core items, making those pieces seem like an excellent value within the established (higher) price context. By strategically introducing a high anchor, you can gently nudge customers towards recognizing the full value of your work and being more willing to pay a premium for it.

Pricing and Distribution Channels

The **distribution channels** you choose to utilize – the paths your products or services take to reach your consumers – will significantly impact the prices you charge for them. While considerations for analyzing and selecting distribution channels were explored in greater detail in Chapter 5, it's crucial to understand that each distribution channel comes with its own built-in costs that must factor into your pricing decisions. Below are some major types of distribution channels and key pricing considerations for each.

Direct to Consumer

If you are selling your goods or services directly to consumers (direct to consumer [**DTC**]), whether through your own website, your personal brick-and-mortar space, or at markets and events, you will generally have the most straightforward pricing formula. In this model, you retain the entire retail price. Your pricing equation is simply:

Retail Price - Variable Cost = Contribution Margin

This direct approach allows you to maximize your per-unit profit, as there are no intermediaries taking a cut of the sale.

Third-Party Platforms

When you sell your goods or services through a third-party platform like Amazon, Etsy, or a similar online marketplace, the platform will typically take a fee. This fee is usually a percentage of your sale. These fees can vary significantly by platform, so it's essential to conduct thorough due diligence during your platform selection process. At the time of this publication, these fees can range anywhere from 3% to 25% or more, depending on the platform and category. These fees directly affect your margins, and your price equation becomes:

Retail Price - Platform Fees - Variable Cost = Contribution Margin

You must account for these platform fees to ensure your profitability.

Wholesale

If you are selling your products to retailers or other businesses who will then sell these products to consumers, your pricing formula will change substantially. Generally speaking, a retailer will expect to sell a product for at least double the **wholesale** price, if not more, to cover their own operational costs and achieve their desired profit margins. Large businesses with more significant buyer power may even expect wholesale prices to be as low as 25% of the suggested retail price. Your formula for wholesale pricing is going to be:

Retail Price - Retailer Margin = Wholesale Price

Wholesale Price - Variable Cost = Contribution Margin

As you can see, your contribution margin per unit may be much lower when selling wholesale. However, the increase in sales volume that often comes with wholesale partnerships will typically more than make up for the lower profit per unit.

Galleries

If you are selling editions or one-of-a-kind work through a gallery, they will generally take a **commission** on any sales of your work. A 50% commission is a common rate, though this may vary depending on the influence and reputation of the gallery. Galleries do not typically purchase any work upfront; rather, they sell on **consignment**. A good gallery will be a valuable partner in pricing your work, as they should be well-versed in the current market rates for artists like yourself and have a deep understanding of their own consumer base.

Consistency Across Channels

Finally, it's critically important to consider consistency across channels when setting your prices. While your margins on a per-unit basis may be lower if you are selling wholesale to a retailer or through a gallery, it is essential not to undersell your own distribution partners by listing the same works or products for less through your own DTC channels. Doing so risks alienating key business partners and burning bridges within the industry. Many retail partners will expect you to adhere to an agreed-upon **Minimum Advertised Price** to protect their own margins and the perceived value of your brand.

It is, however, an acceptable practice to charge somewhat higher rates when listing on third-party platforms like Amazon or Etsy than you would list for on your own website or direct channels. This slight price difference helps you absorb part of the cost of the platform fees, allowing you to maintain healthy margins while still leveraging the platform's reach.

Conclusion

Financial planning is not a barrier to creativity; it is a prerequisite for sustainable success. The stories of entrepreneurs who failed to understand their unit economics or perform a breakeven analysis serve as cautionary tales, reminding us that passion alone is not enough. By using these fundamental tools, you can accurately assess your business's financial viability, avoid costly mistakes, and make informed decisions about pricing and growth plans. This financial foresight ensures that your business can not only survive but thrive, allowing your creative work to reach its full potential in the marketplace without being derailed by unforeseen costs.

Mini Case: Pricing at Hertunba by Marie Segares

Florentina Agu has been entrepreneurial from a young age, selling in local markets with her brother as a child and then funding her schooling through an event planning business. A former model with a passion for textiles and creative expression and the desire to create positive impact, Florentina founded Hertunba in Lagos, Nigeria in 2020. Her designs honor her Nigerian heritage as well as the time she spent living in Benin and celebrate the strength and diversity of African women while merging high-end fashion with sustainability. In addition to Akwete cloth, a textile handwoven with traditional Igbo processes, Hertunba uses ethically sourced materials and upcycles 90% of their textile waste into interior decor products or "wearable art pieces." Florentina also aims for social impact with Hertunba. She is committed to providing fair wages to local artisan contractors as well as to Hertunba's in-house tailors.

Figure 6.5 Selections from Hertunba's Catharsis collection.

Source: Courtesy of Hertunba

In the first five years of Hertunba, Florentina created 15 collections including The Women Before Us which was inspired by "powerful Edo matriarchs, their stories and what they'd wear if they lived in today's world." Her designs have received acclaim and have been worn by celebrities including actress Meagan Good and beauty YouTuber Jackie Aina. In 2024, Florentina was awarded the Veuve Clicquot Bold Future Award which honors women entrepreneurs who have owned the business for less than five years. In "recognition of her trailblazing work in sustainable fashion and cultural preservation," she received a 2024 XTANT Leadership Program Scholarship in collaboration with Guzangs, a platform that highlights African fashion designers and artisans.

While many brands with sustainable and social impact goals use only profit maximization pricing objectives, Florentina ensures that "every collection has an entry level piece the average woman can afford." Hertunba sells direct-to-consumer through its website and brick-and-mortar store, as well as through various retail outlets. Several collections include garments at multiple price points with a range of $300 between the lowest and highest priced items. Price sorting on the Hertunba website defaults to bestselling and indicates that both lowest priced and highest priced options are bestsellers in different collections.

Sources: Afrique Noire. (2024, October 28). Founder's story with Hertunba. Afrique Noire. https://afriquenoirmagazine.com/founders-story-with-hertunba/; Belinda B. (2025, April 14). From tradition to trendsetting: Florentina Agu leads a cultural movement with Hertunba. *Shine My Crown*. https://shinemycrown.com/from-tradition-to-trendsetting-florentina-agu-leads-a-cultural-movement-with-hertunba/; Guardian Life. (2024, October 5). Veuve Clicquot: Bold Women merging heritage with vision. *The Guardian*. https://guardian.ng/life/veuve-clicquot-bold-women-merging-heritage-with-vision/; Guzangs https://guzangs.com/; Hertunba https://www.hertunba.com/; Laide, I. (2025, March 26). The visionary behind Hertunba: How Florentyna turns African craft into global statements. *Crest Africa*. https://crestafrica.com/the-visionary-behind-hertunba-how-florentyna-turns-african-craft-into-global-statements/; Owoh, O. (2025, August 6). Florentina Agu ushers in a cultural renaissance with Hertunba. *Essence*. https://www.essence.com/fashion/designer-spotlight-florentina-agu-hertunba/; Suleiman, Y. (2021, August 11). Meet Florentyna Agu the creative mind behind the eco-friendly brand 'Hertunba.' *Allure*. https://allure.vanguardngr.com/2021/08/meet-florentyna-agu-the-creative-mind-behind-the-eco-friendly-brand-hertunba/

Activities

Activity 1: Do Your Own Unit Economics Analysis

This exercise will guide you through calculating the unit economics for your own creative business or an idea for a business you'd like to start. This is a crucial first step in understanding if your business model is financially viable.

1 List all of your business costs: Begin by making a comprehensive list of every single cost associated with your business. Think about all expenses, from materials and labor to rent and marketing costs.
2 Sort costs into Fixed vs. Variable based on the definitions described in this chapter.
3 Define what a single "unit" of your work is, such as one item, a single project, or an hour of service. Then, calculate your total variable cost per unit using the list you made in step 2.
4 Determine your revenue per unit by defining the price you will charge for a single unit of your product or service.
5 Calculate your contribution margin per unit by subtracting your variable cost per unit from your revenue per unit. This figure shows how much each sale contributes to covering your fixed costs.

Activity 2: Breakeven Analysis

Now that you have your contribution margin per unit, run a breakeven analysis on a few different scenarios to understand how your costs and new projects impact the sales volume you need to become profitable.

1 Breakeven on Fixed Costs: Using the fixed costs you outlined in Activity 1 and your contribution margin per unit, calculate how many units you need to sell in order to cover your fixed costs.
2 Impact of Variable Cost Reduction: Imagine you reduce your variable costs by 10%. Calculate your new contribution margin per unit, and then determine how many fewer units you would need to sell to break even on the fixed costs from Activity 1.
3 Project-based Breakeven: Imagine you're taking on an exciting new, high-cost project (like an ad campaign, a pop-up shop, or an event). Estimate the fixed costs of this project. Now, using your original contribution margin per unit, calculate how many units you would need to sell to break even on this specific new project.

Activity 3: Studying Price Signals

This exercise helps you recognize how businesses use both obvious and subtle cues to communicate their pricing strategy to consumers.

1 Explore and Document: Go to a commercial area like a mall, downtown street, or shopping center. Take a notebook and/or a camera and visit a variety of different businesses, paying attention to how they communicate their pricing. Make sure to visit a mix of stores that target both luxury and bargain-conscious customers.
2 Document Your Observations: For each business, document the following:

    - Price Display: How and where are the prices displayed? Are they prominent and in large, bold fonts, or are they discreet and in small print?
    - Store Design and Atmosphere: How does the design of the space reinforce the price strategy? Think about lighting, music, colors, and the general feeling of the store. Does it feel bright and bustling, or calm and exclusive? How is the merchandise presented?
    - Advertising: What kind of promotional language is used in their windows or advertisements? Do they emphasize "deals," "sales," and "bargains," or "quality," "craftsmanship," and "experience"?

3 Analyze and Reflect:

    - What are the biggest differences you observed between the transactional and relational businesses you documented?
    - Did you see any businesses doing something particularly clever to reinforce their price position? Describe the method and explain why it was effective.
    - Did you notice any businesses sending mixed signals? What would you recommend they change to be more consistent and reinforce their intended price position?

Resources and References

Kotler, P. (1999). *Marketing management: Analysis, planning, implementation, and control* (9th ed.). Prentice Hall.

Van Westendorp, P. (1976). NSS price sensitivity meter (PSM): A new approach to study consumer-perception of prices [Conference session]. *Proceedings of the 29th ESOMAR Congress*, Venice, Italy.

Williamson, O. E. (1985). *The economic institutions of capitalism: Firms, markets, relational contracting*. Free Press.

7 Business Funding and Financial Statements

Sara Hartmann

Introduction

Now that you know how to conduct a **breakeven analysis**, you're already ahead of the curve. The most important building blocks of financial management are a clear understanding of the **unit economics** of a business – the **costs** and *revenues* associated with each individual item you produce. While the previous chapter focused on this granular, unit-level perspective, this chapter will build on that foundation by discussing money at the **enterprise** level. We will address the perennial entrepreneurial question of how to get money to start or grow a business, and we will learn about the key financial documents a business uses to track its money once it's up and running.

For many first-time business owners, both of these topics can feel intimidating. The process of getting the resources you need to launch a business can feel like an impossible task, and when you are new to them, **financial statements** can look like overwhelming lists of numbers. However, this chapter is designed to help you move past that intimidation and master your business's numbers. By using the building blocks you gained in the last chapter, you will learn how to understand the information contained in financial documents, enabling you to read and interpret the stories hidden within your business's records. This chapter will equip you with the information and language you need to make confident financial decisions.

Learning Outcomes

- **Explain** the concept of effective cash flow management
- **Compare and contrast** various funding sources to determine which is most suitable for a given business
- **Interpret** the financial health of a business by reading its financial statements

Getting Funding for Your Business

If you are just starting out or are in the early planning stages of your creative venture, one of the most common and pressing questions is: "Where can I get money to launch and grow my business?" It's important to know that while many **funding sources** exist for both small and large businesses, most new **ventures** begin small, without any major infusions of outside financial resources.

The funding landscape for entrepreneurs typically involves a combination of both formal and informal sources. Formal sources include funding from institutional investors and traditional

DOI: 10.4324/9781003588771-7

business loans, while informal sources encompass bootstrapping (self-funding), and contributions from friends and family.

Informal Funding Sources

- **Self-Funding:** This is any funding provided directly from the entrepreneur's own personal accounts. This may include personal savings, or personal loans that they have taken out in their own name. Self-funding through personal savings is the most common source of funding for new venture creation. Formal sources, such as banks and investors, tend to want to see that a business owner has some "skin in the game" and experience or a successful track record already running a business before they will commit their own funds. Therefore, even businesses that eventually seek larger infusions of **capital** from formal sources are likely to have started out as self-funded ventures in the beginning.
- **Friends and Family:** This refers to money provided through personal contacts within the entrepreneur's existing network. This may include both personal loans from friends, family members, and associates, or equity investments from the founder's personal network.
- **Grants:** Grants are one-time infusions of cash that do not need to be repaid and do not require the founder to give up equity in their business. In many cases, creative entrepreneurs may be eligible for both artist grants (focused on artistic development or specific projects) and for small business grants (focused on economic development or innovation). Aaliyah Taylor, the owner of Exalting in Beauty (profiled in Case 10.4), has successfully obtained grants for creative entrepreneurs, for small businesses, and for business owners of color through local and national organizations including the Nest's Makers Future Fund, the Tory Burch Foundation Fund, and the Fearless Fund.
- **Crowdfunding:** Many creative entrepreneurs use platforms like Kickstarter or Patreon to fund new product launches or projects. Crowdfunding allows **founders** a platform to raise money in the form of many small donations or pledges from their audience and community. It should be noted that running a successful **crowdfunding campaign** can be a major project in and of itself, and most successful crowdfunding campaigns require a robust **marketing plan**. Entrepreneurs should carefully consider the size of their audience and network when setting a crowdfunding goal. Crowdfunding campaigns tend to be more successful when they are preselling a tangible product, funding a community-based business or event with a strong physical presence, or if the entrepreneur has a substantial online following.

Formal Funding Sources

Equity Funding

In **equity funding**, an **investor** provides an entrepreneur with an agreed-upon amount of money in exchange for a percentage of ownership in the business. In this transaction, the founder (entrepreneur) and the investor are making an agreement about the business's implied value. For example, if an investor gives an entrepreneur $100,000 in exchange for a 10% ownership stake in the company, this implies that the company is worth $1 million (because 10% of $1 million is $100,000). This process of determining the value of a business for the purpose of selling an equity stake is known as **valuation**. There is not a single, universally applied formula for valuation; rather, values are often based on the investor's belief in a business's future earning potential, not necessarily on its current revenue, existing *assets*, or an entrepreneur's past **sunk costs**.

Types of Investor Funding

- **Seed Funding:** If a founder has a high-potential idea in a high-growth industry, they may be able to raise an early round of investment known as seed funding to pursue this idea and cover the initial expenses associated with developing a proof of concept. Seed funding investments can vary in size and range from the tens of thousands of dollars to several million dollars.
- **Angel Funding: Angel investors** are individuals or investor groups who invest in early-stage businesses. Angel investors are willing to take a risk on early-stage companies that they believe have strong growth potential in the future. Some angel investors may also focus on funding businesses that are aligned with a specific mission, like supporting green technology or investing in female founders. Like seed funding, Angel investors also make investments that vary in size from the tens of thousands of dollars to several million dollars.
- **Venture Capital (VC) Funding:** VC firms make substantial investments, often in the tens of millions of dollars or higher, in companies that have progressed beyond the early-stage startup phase. VCs seek out more established companies with a proven track record and strong potential for rapid, scalable growth.

Considerations for Investor Funding

While "investors" loom large in the popular imagination, institutional investor funding plays a role in the funding of only a small percentage of entrepreneurial ventures. This is due in part to the fact that investors are looking to see a substantial return on their investment in exchange for taking a risk on backing a new venture. Investors expect that entrepreneurs will have a clear plan to grow a business aggressively and then return value to investors in a major **exit event**. Exit events are when founders and early investors "cash out" their investment. Common exit events may include selling the company to a larger firm (an **acquisition**) or listing shares of the company on the stock market (an **Initial Public Offering, or IPO**).

Taking money from investors also leads to **equity dilution**, meaning the founder of the company owns smaller percentages of the company as ownership shares are sold to investors. If a founder owns less than 51% of the company, they can potentially be fired by the company's board or pushed out by other investors. Investors can be a valuable asset for a founder who is focused on prioritizing aggressive growth of the company and who is comfortable with the eventual sale of the company. An investor has a vested interest in seeing the company succeed, and many investors can help make crucial connections and open doors that a founder might not be able to on their own.

It's important to note, however, that creative industries tend to attract less interest from institutional investors than high-growth industries like technology and life sciences. Investors who are active in arts and culture ventures tend to look at businesses that are more established, with an engaged customer base and clear paths to **scalability**. Furthermore, many investors will expect founders to prioritize financial returns and aggressive growth over creative vision or artistic integrity. Elizabeth Caven, profiled in Case 10.5, received seed funding through pitch competitions and VC funding for KITE, which was later acquired by a major retailer to manufacture the first commercially available sewing pattern projector. Her case highlights the possibilities and challenges for creative businesses seeking investors.

Debt Funding

Debt funding is a more common source of growth capital in many creative sectors than investor funding. Debt funding includes short-term loans, long-term loans, and lines of credit made available directly to businesses. It's important to note that this does not include personal loans taken out by the entrepreneur. While it's not uncommon for entrepreneurs to take on personal debt to fund a new venture, this debt belongs to the individual entrepreneur, not the business itself. This is a critical distinction because if the business fails and defaults on its debts, in most cases of business debt, the business owner is not personally liable for the money owed (assuming the business is structured as a separate legal entity, like a limited liability company or corporation).

Many commercial banks perceive a new business as highly risky and may therefore make higher interest loans to these new ventures, or they may choose to lend only to businesses that can show two or more years of positive cash flow. Establishing a business bank account that is separate from your personal bank account from the very beginning will help you to establish a verifiable financial history for your business, which can help you secure business loans down the road. Take some time to compare options when selecting a bank; local institutions, credit unions, mutual banks, and banks with a B Corporation certification may offer more favorable terms for small businesses.

Some countries also have government offices that underwrite or provide guarantees for small business loans to stimulate the economy by reducing a bank's risk in lending to small businesses. For example, the **Small Business Administration (SBA)** in the United States works with banks around the country to help small business owners access capital by providing guarantees for a significant portion of the loan. Geoff and Kristen Zephyrus, the founders of Cognitive Surplus, profiled in Case 10.3 used an SBA loan to purchase a 36,000-square-foot warehouse after outgrowing several rented warehouse spaces.

Bootstrapping Your Business

You may have heard the term **bootstrapping** used in business to describe a way of funding a venture. Bootstrapping means launching and growing a business with limited resources, relying primarily on internally generated revenue rather than external funding. In other words, launching with low **overhead**, prioritizing decisions that will bring money in quickly, and reinvesting **profits** to support business growth. Interestingly, the phrase is borrowed from the idiom, "pull yourself up by your bootstraps" – a term originally used sarcastically to describe a physically impossible task.

In reality, many creative entrepreneurs bootstrap their businesses without even realizing there is a term for what they are doing. Artists, more than most, are skilled at making something out of nothing, and building a business is no exception. Many of the case studies you'll explore in Chapter 10 are great examples of bootstrapped businesses. This approach leads to a crucial question: how exactly do you find the resources to launch and grow your venture?

Mapping Your Resources

Sarasvathy's theory of **effectuation** offers a useful framework for bootstrapping. This theory suggests that entrepreneurs should be "means-driven" rather than "ends-driven." In other words, instead of starting with a grand plan and then searching for the resources to achieve it, you should begin with a detailed inventory of the assets you already possess. This includes not just financial assets but also your skills, relationships, existing equipment, and facilities. Once you've mapped these resources, you can ideate on ways to leverage them to build your new venture.

This theory also encourages entrepreneurs to consider their **acceptable loss**. This means defining the resources you are comfortable risking and potentially losing in the pursuit of a business idea. Having a clear boundary on what you are willing to risk helps manage risk and makes it easier to be flexible and pivot when faced with new information. Defining this acceptable loss in advance also makes you less susceptible to the **sunk cost fallacy**, where you might be tempted to throw good resources after bad.

Bootstrapped-Friendly Operating Decisions

In the next chapter, you will learn more about business **operations**. Certain decisions you make about how you operate your business and the types of products or services you offer can have a significant impact on your ability to bootstrap effectively.

In many cases (though certainly not all, as the circumstances of each business are unique), **service-based businesses** reach break-even and achieve profitability faster than **product-based businesses**. This is primarily because service businesses do not usually have to invest in the cost of *inventory* upfront. For example, imagine you are a clothing designer interested in starting a business. If you were to launch a line of ready-to-wear dresses, you might have to invest thousands of dollars upfront in the cost of fabric, materials, and labor to make your first run of dresses before making your first sale. However, if you were to launch a business that produces made-to-order bridal or special occasion dresses on commission, you could start with a much smaller investment in studio materials and potentially break even when you book your first client.

Some artists who have a physical product concept can also explore **licensing agreements**, where another business handles the production and sales of their products, and they receive a commission or licensing fee, as is the case with Crafty Chica (profiled in Case 10.1) and The Punny Quilter (profiled in Case 10.2). This allows them to generate income from their creative work without the financial risk of inventory.

The Operating Cycle and Its Impact on Bootstrapping

In the next section of this chapter, we will explore the **operating cycle** from an **accounting** point of view. The operating cycle measures how long a period is between when a business invests money in the creation of a product or service and when it receives money in return for the completion of that product or service. Long operating cycles can make it harder to bootstrap a business, as your limited cash resources can be tied up for a long time waiting for the completion of a sale.

Thinking creatively about your operating decisions can help you keep your operating cycle shorter. Short operating cycles make it much easier to bootstrap your business, as they allow cash to flow back into your business quickly, which you can then reinvest in materials, marketing, or other growth-oriented activities.

The Basic Financial Statements

In Chapter 6, we covered the fundamental building blocks of breakeven analysis and unit economics. Now, let's transition to the crucial skill of reading and understanding financial statements. There are three primary types of financial statements that businesses, regardless of their size, utilize to measure and communicate distinct aspects of their financial position. Each of these three financial statements narrates a different part of the comprehensive story of a business's financial health. While financial statements may initially appear as an overwhelming and somewhat Byzantine collection of jargon and numbers, once you acquire the ability to decode them, you can comprehend the narratives these statements convey and leverage these insights to profoundly enhance your understanding of the business.

One highly effective way to familiarize yourself with financial statements is to actively practice reading those of other companies. Large corporations that are **publicly traded** on stock exchanges, such as the New York Stock Exchange or the London Stock Exchange, are legally obligated to publish their financial statements on both an annual and quarterly basis. We encourage you to seek out the financial statements of a large company that genuinely interests you and read through their financial disclosures side-by-side with this section.

The Income Statement

The **Income Statement**, sometimes referred to as a Profit and Loss statement, is specifically designed to tell a story about how profitable a business was during a designated period of time. This reporting period could be a full year, a fiscal quarter, or, as is common for many small businesses, it may be tracked on a monthly basis. The income statement begins by listing the company's revenue for the specified period at the very top. From this revenue, it then systematically subtracts both the company's variable costs and its fixed costs, ultimately revealing the net profitability at the bottom.

In other words, the income statement uses this basic equation:

Revenue - Costs = Profit

Income statements provide a clear narrative about how effective a business is at generating profit through the normal course of its operational activities. It's important to recognize when you are examining an income statement that the profitability shown pertains exclusively to a fixed period. Therefore, it is crucial to consider what the specific period is that you are analyzing. It is entirely normal for many businesses to experience a seasonal flow to their profitability, with certain times of the year generating substantial profits, while other, slower periods may predictably result in losses. Consequently, it is normal for a business to have some periods that are quieter and not profitable. Seeing an income statement that displays a loss is not inherently concerning for the overall health of the business. When reading an income statement, consider the broader context of the business's story. For example, if we are analyzing the income statement for a retail boutique, it would be entirely normal to observe very large profits during the bustling December holiday season, followed by lower profits or even losses during the relatively quieter winter months that typically follow.

Reading an Income Statement

When reading an income statement, you will likely encounter the following terms.

- **Revenue:** This is all the money a business brings in from selling its products or services. It's important to note that in our Unit Economics Analysis revenue referred to the money brought in from the sale of a single unit. On the income statement, it refers to the money brought in from all sales during a period.
- **Cost of Goods Sold (or Cost of Goods):** This is the direct cost of making the products or providing the services that were sold. This is also known as variable cost, as covered in the prior section on Unit Economics.
- **Gross Margin:** This is the money left over after you've paid for the direct (variable) costs of making your products or services. It shows how much profit you made from just selling your main things, before subtracting your fixed business costs.
- **Operating Costs:** These are the regular expenses a business has to pay to keep its doors open and run day-to-day, even if they aren't directly related to making a product. These are also known as fixed costs, as discussed in the prior section on Unit Economics. There are two main types of operating costs you are likely to encounter on an income statement:
    - **Selling, General, Administrative:** This covers most types of operating costs including:
        - Selling: Money spent to sell the product (like advertising or sales commissions).
        - General: Everyday costs to run the business (like office supplies, phone bills, or utilities).
        - Administrative: Money spent on managing the business (like salaries for office staff or legal fees).
    - **Research & Development (R&D):** This is money spent by a company to discover new things, create new products, or improve existing ones. It's investing in future ideas.
- **Earnings Before Interest, Taxes, Depreciation, and Amortization (EBITDA):** This is a way to look at how much money a business is making from its core activities before subtracting some of the more complex costs like interest payments and depreciation.
- **Taxes:** This is the money a business has to pay to the government based on the profit it makes.
- **Interest:** This is the money a business pays when it borrows money, like from a bank loan. It's the "fee" for using someone else's money.
- **Depreciation:** This is a way to spread out the cost of expensive things (like buildings, machines, or big equipment) over the many years they are used. Instead of counting the whole cost in one year, you count a little bit of the cost each year as the item gets older or wears out.
- **Net Income:** This is the *final* profit a business has left after paying *all* of its expenses, including costs of goods, operating costs, interest, and taxes. This is often called the **bottom line** because it's at the very bottom of the income statement.

The Balance Sheet

The **Balance Sheet** is the financial statement that tells a story about what a business owns and what it owes at any given moment in time.

The balance sheet uses this basic equation:

Assets = Debt + Equity

The balance sheet shows us what assets a business possesses and how much of those assets are owned outright versus being financed by debt. This statement can provide us with a crucial understanding of the business's overall financial health and its risk profile. A business whose assets are highly financed by debt may be in a riskier financial position than a business with less debt. As a small business owner, you will likely not spend a great deal of time thinking about your own balance sheet on a day-to-day basis, but its importance will become evident if you seek external funding to grow your business. If you plan to secure a small **business loan** or obtain funding from an investor, you will almost certainly be required to present a balance sheet both before and after securing the funding.

Reading a Balance Sheet

When reading a balance sheet, you are likely to encounter the following terms:

Assets: These are all the things a business owns that have value. Think of them as everything the business *has*.

Current Assets: These are assets that a business expects to turn into cash, or use up, within one year. They are things that are easily available or will be used soon. Current assets may include:

- **Cash:** The actual money the business has, either in a bank account or as physical money. This is the most **liquid** (easiest to use) asset.
- **Inventory:** These are the products a business has ready to sell, or the materials it has to make products. It's the "stuff" waiting to become a sale.
- **Accounts Receivable:** This is money that customers owe the business for products or services they've already received but haven't paid for yet. It's like an I Owe You (IOU) from a customer.

Non-Current Assets: These are assets that a business expects to keep and use for more than one year. They are usually bigger, longer-lasting things and may include:

- **Property, Plant, and Equipment:** This is a specific type of non-current asset. It includes land, buildings, machinery, and vehicles that the business uses to operate. These are the physical things that help the business produce.
- **Investments:** These are assets like stocks, bonds, or ownership in other companies that a business plans to hold for more than one year, hoping they will grow in value or provide income. It's like putting money aside for a long-term goal.

Liabilities: These are all the things a business *owes* to others. Think of them as the business's debts.

Current Liabilities: These are debts that a business needs to pay back within one year. They are short-term debts and may include:

- **Accounts Payable:** This is money the business owes to its suppliers for things it has bought on credit but hasn't paid for yet.
- **Short-Term Debt:** Money borrowed that must be paid back within one year.

Non-Current Liabilities: These are debts that a business does not have to pay back within one year. They are long-term debts.

Equity: This is the portion of the business that the owners or shareholders own free of debt. It represents what the net value of the business would be if assets were used to pay off all outstanding debts. Equity includes:

Owner Contributions: This may also be referred to as paid-in capital. This is the money or value that the owner or shareholders paid into the business to get it started or to fund growth.

Retained Earnings: This is the total amount of profit that the business has made that has not been paid out to the owner or shareholders in the form of dividends or owners withdrawals.

Figure 7.1 Bowls made and sold by a ceramics business.

Source: Photo by Melissa Ostrow. Courtesy of Massachusetts College of Art and Design

Morgan is a ceramic artist who runs a thriving small business that generates significant revenue by balancing artistic creation with smart distribution. Morgan sells their ceramics through a dual-channel approach: direct online sales and strategic placement in multiple boutiques and galleries.

To manage production volume, Morgan employs two part-time studio assistants. The business operates out of a rented studio space, and its main fixed assets are two large kilns valued at $12,000, which were purchased three years ago and financed with a bank loan. This structure – high sales, staff, and long-term debt – makes Morgan's business an ideal case study for understanding the three core financial statements (Table 7.1).

Table 7.1 Sample Income Statement and Balance Sheet
Income Statement for Year Ending Dec 31, 2025

		Explanation
Revenue	$220,000	The total money earned from sales of ceramics, generated through online sales and multiple retail partners/galleries.
Cost of Goods Sold	$75,000	The direct costs of production for all sold pieces. This includes the cost of bulk raw materials and the hourly wages paid to production assistants.
Gross Margin	$145,000	Revenue – COGS. This large margin indicates high efficiency and strong profitability on the core product before accounting for overhead costs.
Operating Costs		
Selling, General, and Administrative Expenses	$110,000	The fixed overhead costs, which include the owner's administrative salary, plus costs for studio rent, insurance, and marketing/website maintenance.
Research and Development	$1,000	Money spent on creative exploration, such as advanced material sourcing or prototyping new products.
Operating Income	$34,000	Gross Margin – SG&A – R&D. This figure shows the profit generated by the core operations *after* covering the owner's salary and all business overhead.
EBITDA	$36,400	Operating Income + Depreciation. This is the cash generated by the business operations, excluding the tax, financing, and non-cash depreciation decisions.
Interest	$500	The cost of borrowing money, such as interest paid on an operating line of credit or a loan used for equipment.
Depreciation	$2,400	The estimated wear-and-tear (loss of value) on the two kilns ($12,000 total initial cost) for this year. This is a consistent annual non-cash expense.
Taxes	$6,200	The calculated tax owed to the government based on net income.
Net Income	$27,300	The final profit remaining after all expenses have been paid. This money is transferred to Retained Earnings on the Balance Sheet.
Balance Sheet on Dec 31, 2025		
Total Assets	$53,000	Current Assets + Non-Current Assets. The sum of everything the business owns that has economic value.
Current Assets	$47,400	Assets that are expected to be converted into cash, sold, or used up within one year.
Cash	$29,400	This is the current cash balance in the business's checking/savings accounts.
Inventory	$10,000	The cost of all unsold items, including finished ceramics, raw materials (clay, glaze powders), and works-in-progress still in the studio.
Accounts Receivable	$8,000	Money owed to the business by retail partners or galleries for ceramics you have already delivered and invoiced, but for which payment has not yet been received.

(Continued)

Table 7.1 (Continued)

		Explanation
Non-Current Assets	$5,600	Assets that are expected to be used or owned for more than one year.
Property Plant and Equipment	$5,600	The two kilns and other long-term equipment, shown at their original cost ($12,000) minus the accumulated depreciation (the total wear and tear recognized so far, which we assume is $6,400).
Total Liabilities	$10,000	Current + Non-Current Liabilities. The sum of all the business's debts.
Current Liabilities	$7,000	Total debts that are payable in the next 12 months.
Accounts Payable	$3,000	Outstanding bills owed to suppliers for purchases of clay, glaze, or services bought on credit.
Short-term Debt	$4,000	The portion of any business loan that must be repaid within the next 12 months.
Non-Current Liabilities	$3,000	The portion of any business loan that is due after the next 12 months. This represents the long-term commitment to repaying assets like the kilns.
Total Equity	$43,000	The owner's residual claim on the assets after all debts has been paid (Total Assets – Total Liabilities).
Owner Contributions	$7,300	The total initial cash or asset investment the owner put into the business.
Retained Earnings	$35,700	The accumulated net profits of the company since it started have been reinvested in the business rather than paid out to the owner.
* Owner's Draw	($10,000)	Morgan took $10,000 of the business's retained earnings as an owner's draw this year.

The Statement of Cash Flows

The **Statement of Cash Flows** narrates the story of how cash moved both into and out of a business during a specific period of time. This might initially sound like the same information provided by an income statement, but it is, in fact, a distinct and complementary piece of the financial story. While the income statement is limited to measuring the revenue that comes into a company and the costs that go out during the normal course of its operations, a statement of cash flows meticulously measures *all* of the money that flows through the business during the same period.

The Statement of Cash Flows follows this basic equation:

Cash on Hand at the Beginning of the Period
+ Cash received during the period
- Cash spent during the period
= Cash on Hand at the End of the Period

For many small businesses, the statement of cash flows will look largely interchangeable with their business checking **account ledger**. Multiple sources of cash may enter a business that are not direct revenue from operations; this can include money contributed by investors, cash received from a business loan, or other similar inflows. Consequently, there can sometimes be a very significant difference between a business's **cash flow** and its reported profit. Understanding how to read both sides of this financial story is absolutely necessary to comprehend the complete picture.

Reading a Statement of Cash Flows

When reading a statement of cash flows, you are likely to encounter the following terms:

Cash Flow from Operating Activities: This shows how much cash a business made or spent from its normal day-to-day operations – like selling products, paying employees, or buying supplies. It's the cash that comes and goes from the main work of the business.

Cash Flow from Investing Activities: This shows how much cash a business made or spent on buying or selling long-term assets, like property, machinery, or equipment. It's about how the business invests in its future.

Cash Flow from Financing Activities: This shows how much cash a business made or spent from borrowing money, paying back loans, or getting money from investors (or giving money back to them). It's about how the business gets and uses money to fund itself.

Cash vs.Profit: Understanding the Difference

It is possible for a business to record a loss on its income statement and simultaneously report a gain in cash on its cash flow statement during the exact same period. Conversely, it's just as possible for a business to show a profit for a period of time while experiencing a shortage of cash. How can it be possible for two different financial statements to tell such seemingly divergent stories about the same period of time?

Here are a few common points of departure between the income statement and the cash flow statement that small business owners are likely to encounter:

Inventory

For businesses that deal with physical products, the cost of inventory is frequently a major expense. In this context, "inventory" also encompasses purchases of the raw materials that are used to create the final product; these materials would be considered **Work in Progress (WIP) Inventory**. As a business owner, you would record the cash outflow for the inventory you purchase on the Statement of Cash Flows at the precise moment that the cash to pay for this purchase leaves your account. However, this same inventory is recorded on the Income Statement only when it is sold, appearing under **Cost of Goods Sold**. So, to illustrate, if you spend $500 to purchase fabric to make silk scarves in July, and then sell the scarves you create in December, the $500 cost would be recorded on the Statement of Cash Flows in July as an inventory purchase, but it would only be recorded on the Income Statement in December as Cost of Goods Sold.

Because cash invested in inventory is not recorded as an expense on the income statement until that inventory is actually sold, it is entirely possible for a business to report a profit for a given period on their income statement while, in fact, their cash reserves are largely tied up in unsold inventory.

Capital Expenditures

Another significant area where expenses are treated differently between the two statements involves **capital expenditures**. Capital expenditures are larger purchases of **durable assets**, such as equipment, that a business owner reasonably expects to have a useful life spanning several years. Many countries or jurisdictions will have specific guidelines regarding when a purchase should be classified as a capital expenditure, and it is always advisable to consult with an accountant if you are considering the purchase of major equipment for your business.

Let's imagine, for example, that you are a photographer and you decide to buy a $4,000 new professional-grade camera for your business. On the Statement of Cash Flows, you would record the full $4,000 outflow at the time the purchase was made. However, on your Income Statement, you would spread this cost over a period of several years.

This systematic process is called **depreciation**, and it's always best to collaborate with your accountant to determine the appropriate depreciation schedule for any major purchases you make. In the case of the camera, you might reasonably estimate that the useful life of this equipment is five years. Therefore, on the income statement, rather than showing the entire $4,000 cost in the period where it occurred, you would show an $800 depreciation expense each year for the next five years. In the short term, this can be frustrating for business owners because you are not able to deduct the full amount of your investment from your profit for the purpose of calculating taxes in the year the investment was made. However, in the remaining periods of the depreciation schedule, this does provide you with an extra $800 deduction that can reduce your tax liability in future years.

Figure 7.2 A professional grade camera could be considered a depreciable asset for a photography business.

Source: NoName_13 via Pixabay

Operating Cycle

The operating cycle refers to the total amount of time it takes a company to acquire materials, transform those materials into a finished product or service, sell the product or service to a customer, and finally, receive payment for the good or service. This duration can be very short for some businesses and considerably long for others, significantly impacting cash flow and profitability.

Short Operating Cycle

For example, let's say you have a side business doing face painting at live events. Imagine that you spend $100 on materials five days before an event. At this event, you earn $500 in revenue for your face painting services. Your customers pay you cash at the festival, so all of the money is received at the same time that your services are rendered. In this case, you would have an operating cycle of five days, because it took five days between when you first invested money in supplies and when you received payment for your completed services.

In this specific case, because the operating cycle is so short, the $100 invested in inventory (supplies) would likely be reflected as a cost on both your income statement and your statement of cash flows in the same period. Similarly, the $500 payment for these services would be reflected as revenue on your income statement and as operating cash flows on your statement of cash flows, also within the same period.

Long Operating Cycle

Now, let's consider the same face painting business with a longer operating cycle. Imagine you get a contract to do face painting for a corporate event. You spend $100 on materials five days before the event, just as you did before. However, the corporate client pays you by invoice, and their payment terms are net 60, meaning they will send payment 60 days after the invoice is submitted. Your operating cycle for this project would be 65 days, which is the sum of the five days it took to acquire materials plus the 60 days it took to receive the payment. In this case, while your income statement might reflect the revenue and expenses in the same month, your cash flow statement would show a very different picture, with the initial cash outflow for supplies occurring well before the corresponding cash inflow from the client's payment. This delay highlights how a longer operating cycle can strain your cash flow, even when a project is ultimately profitable.

Using Your Financial Statements

Beyond merely tracking past transactions, the true power of financial statements lies in their ability to provide actionable insights into your business's performance and stability. Understanding your finances gives you the ability to analyze your business's performance, plan more effectively for the future, and raise outside capital when needed.

To Analyze Your Performance

Once you understand how to read financial statements, the next crucial step is to leverage this knowledge to effectively manage your own business. As a small business owner, you will routinely use your income statement to track profitability on a monthly, quarterly, or annual basis. However, the utility of these statements extends far beyond simple tracking. Financial statements can also be powerful tools for identifying potential risks and vulnerabilities within your business operations. For instance, Figure 7.2 illustrates common **performance ratios** and **metrics** that you can calculate, along with explanations of what these results signify for your business. Periodically calculating and reviewing these ratios can provide a crucial financial check-up for your business, enabling you to track progress and continuously improve your financial performance over time (Table 7.2).

To Plan for the Future

Financial statements are not limited to merely recording transactions that have occurred in the past. They also serve as a vital tool for future planning. You can create **pro forma financial**

Table 7.2 Performance Metrics

Performance Metric	*How to Calculate*	*What It Tells You*
Gross Margin	(Revenue - Cost of Goods Sold) ÷ Revenue	This tells you what percentage of sales is available to cover your fixed costs and yield a profit. A higher percentage is better.
Net Profit Margin	Net Income ÷ Revenue	Tells you what percentage of sales you retain in the form of profits. A higher percentage is better.
Current Ratio	Current Assets ÷ Current Liabilities	Shows how able your business is to pay debts due within the next year using assets that can be converted to cash in the near term. A higher ratio is better; a ratio below 1 is a sign of liquidity problems.
Debt to Assets	Total Debt ÷ Total Assets	Shows the extent to which your company's operations are financed by borrowed funds. Lower ratios are better.
Inventory Turnover	Cost of Goods Sold ÷ Average Inventory During the Period	Measures the number of times your inventory turns over during a given period. (Usually a year) Higher numbers are better.

statements that outline your estimates for financial performance in the future. While the accuracy of these predictions generally improves with more historical financial data, it is crucial to remember that the objective is to make reasonable estimates, as complete accuracy in predicting the future is unattainable. Preparing a pro forma financial forecast can be instrumental in helping you estimate the potential financial benefits of future projects or strategic initiatives for your business.

To Raise Money

At various stages of your business's growth, you may decide to raise additional capital. This could take several forms, including grants, small business loans, or investor equity. In all three scenarios, it is common, and often a requirement, to present both historical and pro forma financial statements as part of your application. Lenders, investors, and **grantmakers** alike will examine the financial health and projected performance of your business before committing their own financial resources to it.

A Final Note on Accounting Methods

It's important to note that there are primarily two types of **accounting methods** that small businesses may choose to employ: cash accounting and accrual accounting. **Cash accounting** records transactions precisely when cash changes hands – for example, when a bill is actually paid or when money is received. **Accrual accounting**, conversely, tracks revenues when they are earned and expenses when they are incurred, regardless of when the cash transaction actually takes place. Many small businesses prefer cash basis accounting due to its simplicity and ease of management. However, many large businesses in the United States are legally required to use accrual basis accounting because it is a prerequisite for compliance with **Generally Accepted Accounting Principles**. Most readers of this text will likely utilize cash basis accounting, but it is always worthwhile to have a detailed conversation with your accountant about the specific nature of your business and your growth objectives to determine which accounting method is most appropriate for you.

Conclusion

Navigating the financial side of a creative business is a critical task for any entrepreneur. While the practice of managing ledgers and analyzing reports may not be the primary motivation for a creative venture, mastering these skills is what enables a business to thrive. By understanding how to read and interpret your financial statements, you can proactively manage cash flow, make informed decisions about funding, and confidently plan for future growth. Ultimately, this financial skillset transforms a creative pursuit into a sustainable, resilient, and enduring enterprise.

Mini Case: Funding at Tickle Tots by Marie Segares

Tickle Tots was founded in 2012 by Sophia Ferguson on her kitchen table in Shropshire, England. While on maternity leave, she experimented on her sewing machine to find an ideal design for a reusable nappy that would be more environmentally friendly than using disposables. After becoming confident in her designs, Sophia decided to expand Tickle Tots and obtained a business loan through Virgin Start Up, a not-for-profit founded by Sir Richard Branson which offers fixed interest rate loans from £500 through £25,000 in addition to mentorship and accelerator programs. By 2015, Sophia had identified a manufacturer in China to produce the nappies using bamboo fabric printed with surface designs made from her illustrations. In an effort to further expand Tickle Tots, in 2018, Sophia appeared on the popular reality show Dragons' Den, where entrepreneurs pitch their business concepts to a panel of prospective investors. Sophia asked for a £50,000 investment in exchange for 20% equity. Touker Suleyman countered, offering her the same amount in exchange for 50% equity. After deliberating in the hallway, Sophia agreed, but before the show aired, the investment "'fell through.'"

Sophia continued on without the investment and has since guided Tickle Tots expansion. Their commitment to sustainability has moved beyond simply creating a reusable product using a sustainable fiber. Now, the fabric used in the nappies meets Oeko-tex Standard 100 for fabric certified as chemically safe and "harmless to human health." Tickle Tots products use materials from China and are also manufactured there, limiting their carbon footprint. Tickle Tots has also expanded their product mix to include reusable nappies and wet bags, reusable menstrual pads, and reusable straws.

Sources: Dragons' Den. (2019, November 25). Dragons "Torn" Between Entrepreneur And The Business | Dragons' Den [Video]. YouTube. https://youtu.be/om2rburFZrM; Ferguson, S. (2018, February 16). Tickle Tots - Behind the brand, Sophia Ferguson. *Babipur Blog*. https://www.ethicalshoppingforbabies.co.uk/reusable-nappies/tickle-tots-behind-brand-sophia-ferguson/; Oeko-Tex www.oeko-tex.com/en; Tickle Tots www.tickle-tots.com; Trigg, K. (2018, February 21). From a Shropshire kitchen to Dragons' Den: Nappy firm earns £50k but deal collapses. *Shropshire Star*. https://www.shropshirestar.com/news/2018/02/20/from-a-shropshire-kitchen-to-dragons-den-nappy-firm-earns-50k-but-deal-collapses/; Virgin StartUp www.virginstartup.org

Activities

1 Select a publicly traded company that you find interesting – perhaps one that aligns with your creative interests. Navigate to their "investor relations" section on their official website to download their most recent annual report, which will contain their financial statements. Alternatively, you can search for the company's "10-K filing" on the US Securities and Exchange Commission website, or you can look up the company's financial statements on a financial reporting site like Yahoo finance or MarketWatch.

Instructions

- Locate and identify the Income Statement, Balance Sheet, and Statement of Cash Flows within the report.
- As you read through each statement, find the financial terms discussed in this chapter (Revenue, Cost of Goods Sold, Net Income, Assets, Liabilities, Equity, etc.). Highlight or note where they appear.
- What story do these statements tell you about the company's financial health? For example, are its profits growing? Is it taking on more debt? Is its cash flow positive?
- Compare the company's revenue and costs over the past two years. Is its revenue increasing or decreasing? How do its fixed costs compare to its variable costs as a percentage of sales?

2 Using the financial statements from the company you chose in Activity 1 (or your own business if you have the historical financial data), calculate the five performance ratios listed in Exhibit 7.2 Performance Metrics.

  - Calculate the Gross Margin, Net Profit Margin, Current Ratio, Debt to Assets Ratio, and Inventory Turnover for the company's most recent fiscal year.
  - Based on your calculations, how would you describe the company's financial strength?
    - Which ratio do you think provides the most insightful information about the company's health, and why?
    - Where does the company have the most room for financial improvement?

3 Financial statements are not just historical documents, they're also tools for future planning. Let's create a simple pro forma (projected) income statement for your chosen company or for your own business.

  - Look at the income statement for the last two years.
  - Based on the company's recent performance and any external factors you know about create a projected income statement for the upcoming year.
  - For each line item, provide an estimate and a brief explanation for your choice.
    - Will revenue go up or down? Why?
    - Do you expect costs to increase or decrease relative to revenue?
    - Will the company be profitable? Justify your prediction.

Resources and Further Reading

Additional resources and information can be found in Appendix C Tax Considerations for Your Business.

Cole, H. (2025). *Taxes for humans: Simplify your taxes and change the world when you're self-employed.* Wiley.

Michalowicz, M. (2017). *Profit first: Transform your business from a cash-eating monster to a money-making machine.* Portfolio.

Tycho Press. (2015). *Accounting for small business owners.* Tycho Press.

References

Financial Accounting Standards Board. (n.d.). *FASB Accounting Standards Codification.* Retrieved from https://asc.fasb.org

Sarasvathy, S. D. (2001). Causation and effectuation: Toward a theoretical shift from economic inevitability to entrepreneurial contingency. *Academy of Management Review, 26*(2), 243–263.

8 Operations

Making Business Work

Sara Hartmann

Introduction: What Is Operations Management?

Operations refers to all the decisions, actions, and systems that take place behind the scenes, day-to-day, to make a business actually run. Most large businesses dedicate considerable energy to assessing their operations and managing them for peak **efficiency** and **productivity**, all with the aim of maximizing **profits**. However, for the **creative entrepreneur**, it can often feel like there's a natural tension between the organic flow of the creative process and the structured demands of an optimized process. There's a valid concern that treating your creative work too much like a factory might diminish the joy and spontaneity that are central to the work itself.

Yet, when approached strategically, **process optimization** can actually create more room for creative freedom. Any business owner will tell you that their to-do list can feel impossibly long; a good operational **strategy** can help an entrepreneur find systems and resources to manage the myriad of tasks they are responsible for, while freeing up more time for creative work. The key lies in finding the right balance between structured processes that enable efficiency and the flexibility needed for genuine creative exploration and **innovation**. This chapter will explore how thoughtful operational management can streamline your business, reduce friction, and ultimately free up more time and mental space for what you do best: creating.

Learning Outcomes

- **Analyze** the trade-off between efficiency and effectiveness for a creative business
- **Evaluate** a value chain to find opportunities for optimization
- **Formulate** optimization strategies to develop a plan for improving a business's operations
- **Assess** the sustainability impact of a business's processes and propose alternatives

Understanding Operations Management: Efficiency vs. Effectiveness

Operations management is fundamentally about designing, analyzing, and improving the systems and processes that enable a business to run smoothly and effectively. When evaluating these processes, there are two key, and sometimes opposing, qualities that are measured and analyzed: **effectiveness** and **efficiency**.

> **Effectiveness** measures how well a company delivers on its promise and creates value for its customers and audience. A process that is fully optimized for effectiveness might spare no expense or resource in the pursuit of delivering the greatest possible value for the customer, ensuring their needs are met comprehensively and to the highest standard. This intense focus on value delivery, if unchecked by efficiency considerations, can lead to increased costs and potentially result in the business losing money.

DOI: 10.4324/9781003588771-8

Efficiency measures how well a process creates value or profit for the company and its **stakeholders**. A process that is fully optimized for efficiency might prioritize cost-saving and resource minimization, potentially at the risk of failing to deliver the promised value or desired experience for customers.

In practice, it is generally not advisable to completely maximize processes for efficiency while neglecting effectiveness, nor is it advisable to completely optimize processes for effectiveness while neglecting efficiency. Entrepreneurs who over-emphasize efficiency risk losing a vital piece of their business's creative vision, while it is also very common for creative entrepreneurs to under-consider efficiency and subsequently struggle to become profitable.

A strategic entrepreneur will make careful decisions around how to manage these sometimes competing priorities. The key lies in finding the right balance between structured processes that enable efficiency and the flexibility needed for genuine creative exploration and innovation. In earlier chapters, you developed a **unique value proposition** for your business. In this chapter, you will think about how to develop realistic and manageable systems that will help you execute on and ultimately deliver this core business promise to your customers.

The first essential step to doing this is to conduct a thorough audit of all the systems, processes, and tasks that are required in the day-to-day operation of your business.

The Porter's Value Chain Analysis

Porter's **Value Chain Analysis** is a framework used for systematically assessing all of the activities a company engages in to create value for its customers. By breaking down the business into its individual components, this framework helps identify opportunities for improvement, cost reduction, and differentiation. The value chain divides a company's activities into two major categories: primary activities and support activities. **Primary Activities** are those directly involved in the creation, sale, and distribution of the good or service being sold to customers. In contrast, **Support Activities** encompass all the necessary functions a business engages in that are not directly tied to the *production* of the company's **goods** and **services**, but which enable the primary activities to function effectively (Figure 8.1).

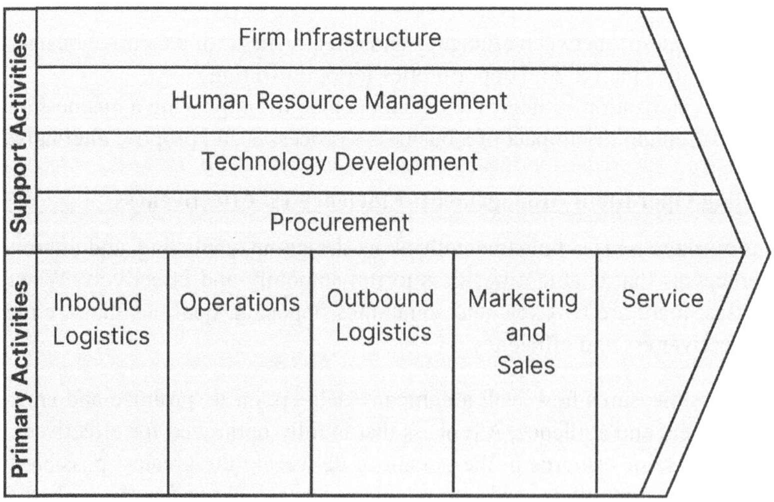

Figure 8.1 Porter's Value Chain framework.

Source: Sara Hartmann

Primary Activities

Primary activities are the core functions that directly contribute to the creation and delivery of your product or service to the customer.

- **Inbound Logistics:** These are the tasks that involve receiving, managing, and storing all of the raw inputs and resources necessary to create your work. For a creative entrepreneur, this can include:
  - Sourcing and receiving physical supplies like clay, paint, fabric, specialized tools, or raw materials for jewelry.
  - Managing digital assets, such as stock photos, fonts, sound libraries, or client-provided files, and ensuring their secure storage and accessibility.
  - Organizing and maintaining your studio space for efficient material flow.
- **Operations**: This is the actual creation process where you transform your inputs and materials into outputs (your finished products or services). This includes:
  - The physical act of sculpting, painting, sewing, designing, writing, or composing.
  - Digital processes like coding, video editing, graphic design, or 3D rendering.
  - The time spent on conceptualization, sketching, prototyping, and refining your creative output.
- **Outbound Logistics:** These are the processes that involve distributing your finished goods and services to customers. This can include:
  - Careful packaging of physical products to ensure safe transit.
  - Shipping and delivery arrangements.
  - Digital file transfers for online products, designs, or commissioned digital art.
  - The final installation of large-scale artworks, custom pieces, or immersive experiences.
- **Marketing & Sales:** These are all the activities involved in promoting and selling your work and acquiring customers. This might include:
  - Managing your social media presence and content creation.
  - Participating in arts shows, trade events, or pop-up markets.
  - Designing brand assets, websites, and promotional materials.
  - Direct outreach to potential clients, writing proposals, and negotiating contracts.
  - Running advertising campaigns, both online and offline.
- **Service:** This refers to any post-sales support that you provide to customers. This is crucial for building loyalty and reputation, and may look like:
  - Customer support, addressing inquiries, feedback, or issues.
  - Handling returns, exchanges, or warranty claims.
  - Providing ongoing consultation or revisions for commissioned work.
  - Offering maintenance or repair services for physical products.

Support Activities

Support activities are essential functions that enable the primary activities to operate efficiently and effectively, even if they don't directly create the product or service.

- **Firm Infrastructure:** These encompass all the general management and administrative tasks required to run your business. This can include:
    - Filing your taxes and managing financial records.
    - Managing your business insurance policies.
    - Paying employees or contractors.
    - Engaging in strategic planning and goal setting.
    - Meeting with mentors, advisors, or business coaches.
    - Legal compliance and intellectual property protection (e.g., copyright registration).
- **Human Resources (HR) Management:** These are tasks involved with recruiting, training, and managing employees. Even if you are a solo entrepreneur or a "company of one," HR activities include any time and resources that you invest into your own professional development, skill acquisition, and well-being, as you are your most critical human resource. For businesses with staff, it includes payroll, benefits, and performance management.
- **Technology Development:** Technology development can include *research and development* and the implementation of **automation**. You don't have to be a tech company to have a technology development component to your activities. For the small creative business, this can simply include:
    - Taking time to stay up-to-date on new advancements in creative software, digital tools, or equipment relevant to your craft.
    - Researching and implementing new digital platforms for sales or communication.
    - Automating routine tasks like scheduling, invoicing, or email marketing.
- **Procurement:** This is the process of sourcing and purchasing the inputs and raw materials you need to do your work. It also includes the process of sourcing and vetting any outside vendors or suppliers who may assist you in your operations processes. Examples include:
    - Finding the best suppliers for your art materials, fabric, or digital assets.
    - Negotiating terms with printers, manufacturers, or web hosting services.
    - Vetting and hiring freelancers or contractors for specialized tasks.

Using the Value Chain Framework for Your Business

Now that you understand the components of Porter's Value Chain, the next step is to apply this framework to your own creative business. Begin by conducting an exhaustive audit of all the activities you engage in, listing every single task, process, and decision under its appropriate primary or support activity category. Be as detailed as possible, from the moment you source materials to your post-sale customer interactions, and every administrative task in between. Once you have this comprehensive list, critically examine each activity by asking yourself the following questions:

- *Which activities do you spend the most time on?* Quantify this if possible, perhaps by estimating how many hours per week or per month you dedicate to each activity.
- *Which activities are most closely tied to the successful delivery of your unique value proposition?* These are often where your "magic" happens. You've spent time articulating what it is you do that is unique to you and you alone – what are the key activities you need to excel at in order to fulfill your value proposition effectively?

- *Where is your personal touch most critical to maintaining* **quality** *and value?* Identify tasks that absolutely require your unique creative input or expertise. These are the tasks that would be the most difficult to outsource or delegate effectively without compromising your core offering.
- *Which activities are you least satisfied with and feel there is significant room for improvement?* These are potential **pain points** or **bottlenecks** in your **workflow**. Are there tasks that always seem to take up more time and energy than they should? These might be activities you avoid because they are unpleasant to perform, or ones where you are frequently unsatisfied with the results.
- *Which activities could be delegated or outsourced to free up more of your time for more important matters, particularly those more closely tied to your value proposition?* Consider tasks that are necessary for your business to function but don't require your specific creative genius. What would be the easiest tasks to take off your plate?
- *Which activities could be performed more efficiently or effectively with better resources, knowledge, or support?* Think about new tools, training, or external expertise that could enhance these areas. Sometimes making significant process improvements requires investing in the development of new capabilities for yourself or your business.

Once your audit is complete and you've thoroughly considered your answers to each of these questions, you will likely have a decent-sized list of ways to improve your business's processes and systems. It's important to note that updating or improving a business's operational plan is not a simple, one-time overhaul. Operations management should be approached as an ongoing series of projects to help you manage your business more efficiently and effectively, rather than a one-time checklist that you complete and then move on from.

We suggest you look at the list of possible improvements you have identified from your initial audit and pick a handful that you think can be reasonably implemented at this time, saving the others to revisit at a future date. You may also find it helpful to refer back to your **Growth-Share Matrix** from Chapter 3. Focusing on creating optimized and standard processes around your **cash cow** activities can be an excellent starting point for many businesses, as these are often reliable income generators that benefit significantly from increased efficiency.

Most operational improvements will generally fall under the following broad categories: **Outsourcing, Internal Process Refinement,** and **Capacity Building**.

Outsourcing and Delegation

For the purpose of this text, we will consider **outsourcing** to be any tasks that are not directly performed by you, the entrepreneur. This broad definition includes outsourcing in the traditional sense (hiring an external firm or company to perform specific tasks) and also encompasses **delegation** (assigning tasks to other individuals who may be working full- or part-time within your own company). In the early days of many creative small ventures, it's not uncommon to feel that cash is your most constrained resource, leading to the temptation to try and do everything yourself in the name of saving money. However, the pitfalls of this approach are significant: you may not be valuing your own time effectively, you could be setting yourself up for burnout and exhaustion, and you might be overlooking the fact that there are others with different skill sets who could perform certain tasks more efficiently and effectively than you could yourself (Figure 8.2).

Figure 8.2 Delegating work to a studio assistant can free you up for more interesting or complex tasks.
Source: Photo by Melissa Ostrow. Courtesy of Massachusetts College of Art and Design

Objectives of Outsourcing

The strategic objectives behind outsourcing are typically multifaceted, aiming to enhance various aspects of your business:

1 **Free Up Your Time:** Making more strategic use of your time as an entrepreneur is paramount. This objective includes preventing burnout, right-sizing your overall workload, and allowing you to focus on the most creatively important work – the tasks that only you can do or that directly contribute to your unique value proposition.
2 **Reduce Costs:** In some cases, outsourcing specific tasks to specialized providers can actually reduce the overall costs associated with completing those tasks, especially if the external provider benefits from **economies of scale** or specialized equipment you don't possess.
3 **Enable Growth:** As an individual, you have a limited capacity to produce. Outsourcing tasks to others can significantly increase your business's total production capacity, allowing it to take on more projects, serve more customers, and ultimately grow beyond your individual limitations.
4 **Access Specialized Expertise:** Outsourcing allows you to tap into skills and knowledge that you or your immediate team may lack, without the commitment of a full-time hire.

Types of Outsourcing

Outsourcing can take various forms, depending on the nature of the task and the relationship with the external party:

> *Manufacturers*: Entrepreneurs producing physical products may consider manufacturers as a key part of their outsourcing strategy. For some, this may look like having some of their most popular products wholly produced by a manufacturer rather than in-house in their own studio. For others, they might have certain components of their work produced by manufacturers while keeping part of the final assembly or artistic finishing in-house. This allows for **scalability** and consistent production.

Service Providers: Service providers are outside firms or agencies that are hired to perform specialized tasks for a business. This could include everything from the accountant who prepares your taxes, to a graphic design agency that helps develop your logo, a digital marketing agency that manages your social media advertising, or **third-party logistics** and **fulfillment** centers that handle **warehousing**, packaging, and shipping of your products. Service providers can be contracted for a finite project or on an ongoing basis to perform a recurring task. They typically possess specialized expertise or physical resources that allow them to perform the tasks they are contracted for with much greater efficiency and effectiveness than the entrepreneur could bring to the tasks if performing them in-house.

Contractors: Contractors are individuals who perform limited, task-based work for your business on a freelance basis; they are not your direct employees. Contractors can include highly skilled fractional workers. For example, some growing small businesses will contract a fractional CFO (Chief Financial Officer) who will spend a few hours each month reviewing the company's finances and advising the founder on future financial plans. Fractional workers are a great way to access highly skilled expertise without the cost and commitment of a full-time employee. Many small businesses will also hire a bookkeeper as a contractor to spend a few hours each month updating and maintaining their receipts and financial records.

Employees: Employees are individuals who work directly in your company on an ongoing basis; they can be full-time or part-time. Depending on the country and region, employers are subject to varying tax reporting and legal obligations. Small businesses hiring employees for the first time should carefully consider the specific activities you will be delegating to them and what skills are required. Some employees will be hired because they possess a complementary skill set that you lack, and the activities they are delegated should focus on that area. Others may possess similar skills to you or fewer skills but are there to be delegated less complex tasks to free up your time or to assist you in key areas that will increase your capacity, such as an administrative assistant for support tasks or a studio assistant to support primary operations.

Considerations and Potential Pitfalls of Outsourcing

While outsourcing offers numerous benefits, it's crucial for creative entrepreneurs to be aware of potential challenges and manage them proactively:

Loss of Control and Quality Consistency: When you outsource, you relinquish some direct control over how a task is performed. This can sometimes lead to inconsistencies in quality or a deviation from your specific vision. Clear communication, detailed briefs, and regular check ins are essential to mitigate this risk.

Communication Challenges: Misunderstandings can easily arise, especially with external parties who may not be fully immersed in your brand's culture or specific creative language. Time zone differences, language barriers, and a lack of immediate feedback can all contribute to communication breakdowns.

Hidden Costs and Scope Creep: While outsourcing can reduce costs, unexpected fees, revisions, or project creep (when the scope of work expands beyond the initial agreement) can quickly inflate expenses. It's vital to have clear contracts and scope definitions.

Over-Reliance and Vendor Lock-in: Becoming overly reliant on a single external provider can create vulnerability. If that provider experiences issues, raises prices, or ceases operations, your business could be significantly impacted.

Internal Process Refinement

In your value chain analysis, you've likely identified multiple processes or key activities that you prefer to keep in-house and under your direct control, rather than delegating or outsourcing. These are often the processes where your unique touch, specialized skills, and creative vision are essential for the effective delivery of your value proposition. Even these critical activities can be managed for greater efficiency and effectiveness by carefully analyzing them and identifying opportunities for improvement.

Process Mapping: Visualizing Your Workflow

Process mapping is a powerful tool that can help you document and visualize all the steps and inputs necessary to complete a task, making it easier to identify areas for improvement. When engaging in process mapping, it's helpful to focus on a specific, well-defined task or activity, rather than attempting to map vaguely defined or broader activities. It also makes sense to concentrate on tasks that are repeated regularly, rather than trying to map processes around open-ended creative ideation. In other words, if you completed a Growth-Share Matrix for your **offerings**, it's a good idea to think about process improvements connected to your "Cash Cow" activities, as these are often repeatable and benefit significantly from optimization, rather than doing a detailed process analysis around your **Question Marks**.

To create a process map, you will draw a *flowchart* that visually documents the steps involved in completing a specific task. Figure 8.3 contains some standard icons and their meanings used in the creation of flowcharts. Focus first on creating a flowchart that documents the process you *actually* currently use to complete this activity, rather than immediately trying to create an idealized version of the process.

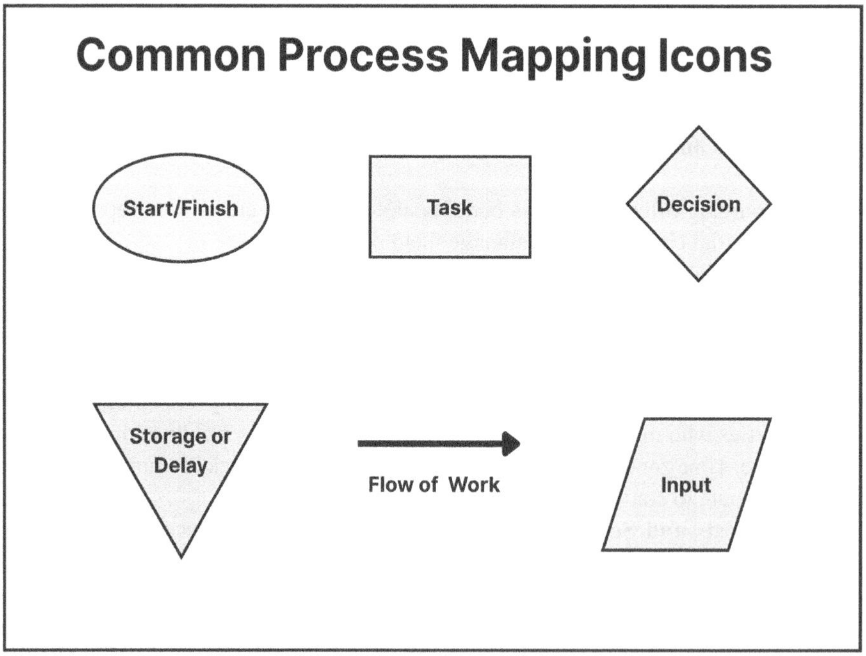

Figure 8.3 Common icons used in process mapping.

Source: Sara Hartmann

If you are mapping a simple process where each step must be completed before the next can begin, this is known as a **sequential process.** However, if you are mapping a more complex process, you may identify **parallel tasks** – steps that can be done independently of each other or at the same time, all leading to a subsequent step (Figure 8.4).

Once you have created a process map, note next to each step how much time is involved in its completion. Add up all the times for all the steps in this process to calculate your **throughput time**, which is the total time it takes to complete a process from start to finish (Figure 8.5).

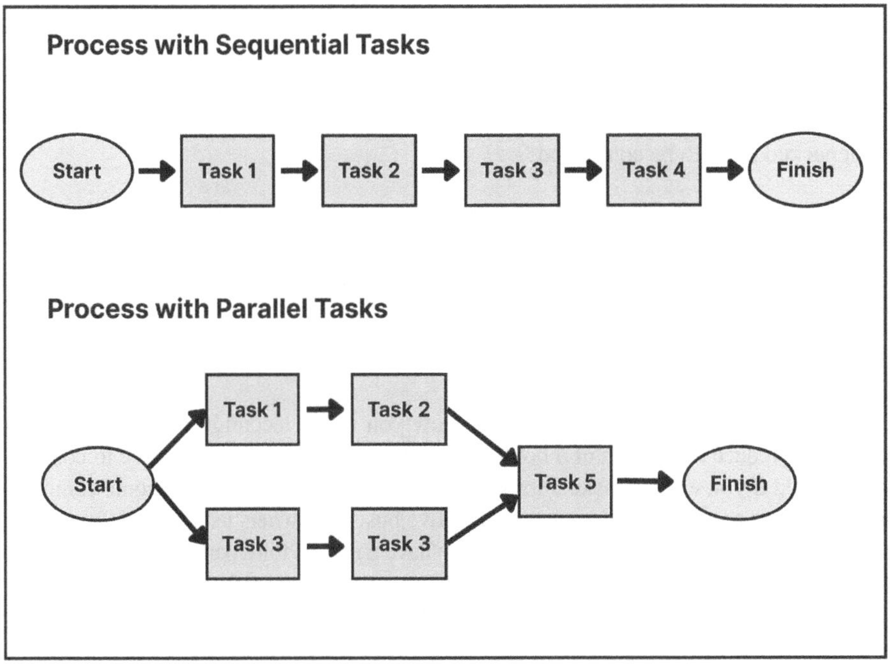

Figure 8.4 Processes maps for sequential and parallel tasks.

Source: Sara Hartmann

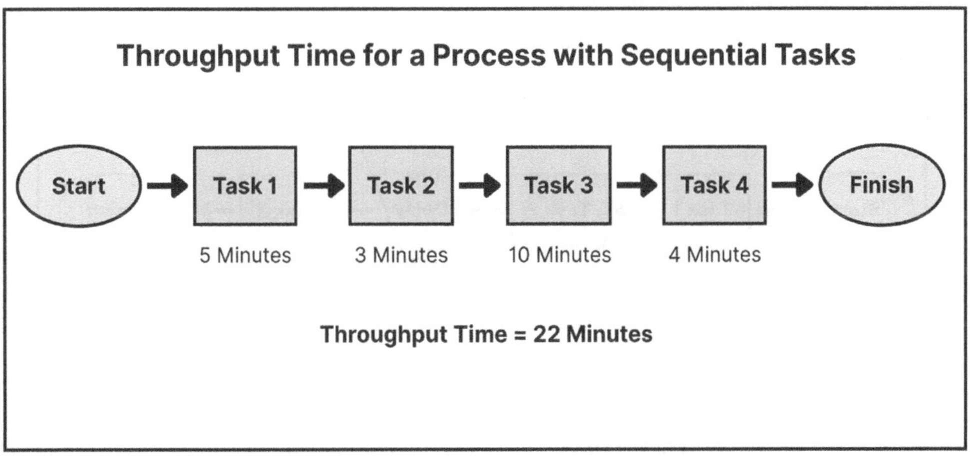

Figure 8.5 A process map with throughput time estimates.

Source: Sara Hartmann

Identifying Inefficiencies: Bottlenecks, Starved, and Blocked Tasks

Now, examine your flowchart to see if you can spot any inefficiencies. Imagine, for the sake of explanation, a factory where each task is performed at its own workstation:

- **Bottlenecks:** A bottleneck is a constraint within your operational process that slows down the entire workflow, reducing your overall capacity. This often looks like the slowest task within your process, and a place where "work in process" inventory (unfinished items or tasks) tends to pile up.
- **Starved Tasks:** A starved task is typically found *after* a bottleneck. This is a task or "workstation" that is sitting idle, waiting for inputs to come off the bottlenecked task.
- **Blocked Tasks:** Blocked tasks in a process flow are usually tasks that are stopped or unable to continue because **work-in-progress inventory** is piling up at their station, waiting for the bottlenecked tasks to be completed.

It's more likely that you are doing all these processes yourself in your own studio rather than in a factory on an assembly line, but it is highly probable that you have bottlenecks in your own processes, and tasks that become starved or blocked because of the slowdowns these bottlenecks create (Figure 8.6).

Common Areas for Process Improvement

Once you've identified inefficiencies, imagine how you might reconfigure your processes in different ways to reduce the impact of a bottleneck. How could the throughput time to complete this task be reduced if you were to make improvements to your process? Here are some common areas for opportunity in process improvement that creative business owners tend to find. In completing a process map analysis exercise, it's often helpful to have a neutral third party – perhaps another artist or creative who works in a similar medium – to talk your process through. There are often many inefficiencies built into a process simply out of habit, and having an outside observer examine a process as you work through it can help you see it fresh and identify opportunities for improvement.

- **Changes to Set-Up Time: Set-up time** refers to the amount of time it takes to prepare a workstation to complete a task, while **process time** is the time it takes to actually complete the task. We often make subconscious trade-offs between the amount of time we spend preparing for

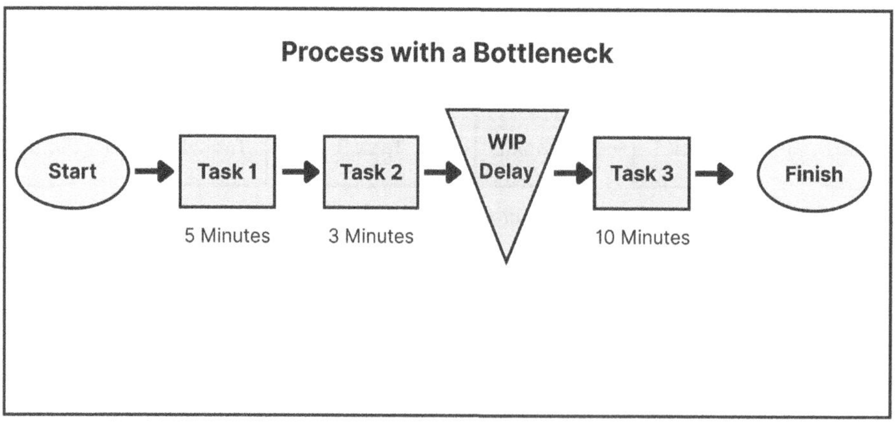

Figure 8.6 Bottlenecks can cause delays as Work-in-Progress inventory piles up.

Source: Sara Hartmann

a task versus completing the task itself. If you're running your business from home without a dedicated studio space, you might spend significant time preparing your space to work and then cleaning up when you are done. Or, if you have a small studio space with a varied process, you may spend significant time setting up workstations between steps. For example, if you are a fashion designer or textile artist working with a single sewing machine, every time you have to re-thread your machine to switch thread colors would be considered set-up time. Think about how much time in the typical completion of a process goes into the set up for each task. Could your workspace be adapted or redesigned, or your process reordered, to reduce the amount of time that you spend setting up?
- **Reevaluate Task Order:** Do your tasks need to be completed in the exact order you process them now, or are there efficiencies that could be gained by reordering your process? Are you treating processes as sequential that could, in fact, be completed in parallel?
- **Studio Help on Parallel Tasks:** If there are parallel tasks involved in your processes, could a studio assistant or additional set of hands help you complete these faster and reduce your overall throughput time?
- **Partial Outsourcing:** Are there specific steps in your process that you could outsource while keeping the most important parts of the process in-house? For example, some entrepreneurs with textile-based products might outsource the cutting of fabrics to factories with digital cutting systems but will sew the products from this cut fabric in-house.
- **Standardized Components:** The larger the variety of materials and components that you work with, the more it tends to increase complexity and slow things down in the workroom, potentially leading to less organized storage and increased set-up times. Are there opportunities to standardize more of the materials that you work with without compromising the uniqueness or creative vision of your product?

Capacity Building

You likely have ambitious plans for your business and a clear vision for where you'd like it to go, perhaps having identified specific areas for expansion during an Ansoff Matrix exercise. Analyzing your business's operations is a critical part of planning and preparing for this growth, because even the best growth plans must align with a business's operational capacity.

Capacity can be defined as the maximum output that a process or an entire business can achieve given its current resources and systems. Based on your current throughput times to complete key activities and the amount of time you spend tied up in support activities, what is the maximum output your business can realistically support? Imagine there was endless demand for what you were selling; how much could you reasonably produce given your current systems and practices to meet this demand?

While this might sound like a problem many entrepreneurs would love to have, it's not uncommon for businesses' operational practices to be set up in a way that makes the founders feel their business is operationally incompatible with growth. Analyzing and optimizing a business's operations isn't simply about pursuing efficiency for efficiency's sake; it's about aligning resources and practices to support a business's growth goals and to give you the room to reach your full potential. Capacity building ensures that your operational capabilities can meet your strategic ambitions.

Sustainability and Operations Management

Like many artists, you're likely driven by a desire to create a positive impact on the world, and this holistic perspective may extend to your business practices. By making choices that align with your values, you can contribute to a more sustainable future for your community and the world at large. Integrating sustainable practices into your operations allows you to build a business that not only reflects your artistic vision but also your commitment to responsible stewardship. As your business expands, so will the complexity of its operational footprint. A growing business means a larger **supply chain**, increased production, and a wider network of stakeholders. Navigating these complexities with sustainability in mind becomes crucial for maintaining alignment with your values and minimizing your environmental impact. The following are areas you may consider when formulating your business's sustainability plans.

Human Rights in Outsourcing

For many artists, the act of making is deeply personal. This often translates to a strong sense of empathy for those involved in the production of their goods. As your business grows and outsourcing becomes necessary, maintaining ethical labor practices and ensuring fair wages is paramount. You can prioritize transparency in your supply chain, seek out **fair trade** partnerships, and conduct regular audits to ensure your values are upheld throughout the production process. If you can't conduct your own audits, looking for certifications like Fair Trade, Nest's Ethical Handcraft Certification, or SA8000, exploring local and regional production facilities, and referencing guidelines from the Fair Labor Association can help you make responsible choices.

Eco-Friendly Sourcing

Eco-friendly **sourcing** is highly dependent on the specific materials you use. However, regardless of your medium, it's important to approach sourcing with the realistic goal of continuous improvement, rather than perfection. Start by examining your current material usage and identifying areas for more sustainable options. For example, if you're a painter who relies on cadmium-based paints for a signature look, you might not be able to fully eliminate them but could offset the impact by making other improvements. Resources like the Cradle to Cradle Certified Products Program can provide a helpful framework for evaluating materials. Even if some materials must be less sustainable, try to counteract this by choosing sustainable options whenever possible and applying improvements where you can.

Sustainable Packaging

Packaging is a major contributor to consumer waste (making up over 80 million tons of waste in the United States alone in 2018), but it's also a key part of your **brand**'s storytelling. You should strive for a balance between minimizing packaging and maintaining your brand's aesthetic. Consider using recycled or biodegradable materials, minimizing package size, and exploring innovative options like mushroom packaging. For shipping, which can have a significant carbon footprint, research carbon-neutral options and consider offering customers the choice to offset their shipment's emissions. Remember, even small changes can make a big difference.

Waste Reduction

Waste reduction is crucial for a sustainable creative practice. Consider using scrap materials in new designs, offering repair or upcycling services, and implementing closed-loop systems. In fashion and textiles, explore zero-waste cutting techniques or using remnant fabrics. For glasswork, recycled glass or cold-working techniques can reduce waste. In ceramics, consider locally sourced clay or low-fire glazes. And for printmaking, water-based inks and solvents are more eco-friendly.

Remember, sustainable options exist for almost every medium. Research how other artists in your field are implementing these practices for inspiration. Exploring innovative ways to reduce waste can be an exciting challenge that sparks creativity and leads to unique artistic solutions.

Conclusion

Navigating the day-to-day work of a creative business can feel overwhelming, but by mastering operational management, you can transform your creative pursuit into a sustainable, resilient, and enduring enterprise. This chapter has shown you that an optimized process doesn't stifle creativity; it supports it by freeing up your most valuable resource – your time. Ultimately, strategic operations are what allow you to move beyond simply creating art and build a business that thrives.

Mini Cases: To Manufacture or to License? by Marie Segares

Kathy Cano-Murillo, the designer behind the Crafty Chica (profiled in Case 10.1), decided early on that manufacturing wasn't the right route for her business. She explains,

> There is the path of making it yourself and having a garage or a warehouse full of your widgets that you designed and made. Or, there is the path of partnering with a manufacturer and getting a commission off of all of the pieces that are sold, and maybe an advance.

The second option is known as intellectual property licensing, wherein the designer or creator is the licensor and the company manufacturing products with that intellectual property is the licensee. Kathy prefers the licensing option for several reasons. "I am the type of person where I cannot just commit to one product line. That's not the life experience that I want to have. I like having variety." Kathy has licensing agreements for products as diverse as quilting fabric, stationery and planners, greeting cards, blank ceramics, die cutting sets, and stencils. Additionally, Kathy says,

> I don't want to manufacture myself. That's where capital comes in, business loans, a fulfillment center, the warehouse, people to load it and unload it. Especially when you work with big box retailers, you have to follow their guidelines so precisely, or you get fined. I don't want to deal with that. I would rather design multiple items, partner with wonderful manufacturers, and they do all of that for me.

Geoff and Kristen Zephyrus from Cognitive Surplus (profiled in Case 10.3) prefer to manufacture their own products instead. They enjoy having greater control over product quality, marketing, and product end-of-life. Additionally, profit margins per unit are higher. Which option is the right one for your creative venture?

Mini Case: Sustainability and Environmental Impact at Cuimer

Aya Laraki is the founder of the Morocco-based startup, Cuimer. She started Cuimer in 2016 to address environmental waste. The company transforms discarded fish skins into high-quality marine leather, offering the fashion industry a sustainable alternative to exotic reptile leathers. Cuimer's approach challenges traditional fashion industry norms, demonstrating that sustainability and style can coexist. Aya believes that by embracing innovative materials like fish leather, the fashion industry can take a major step toward ethical consumption and environmental responsibility. Among the company's achievements are recycling over 40 tons of fish skins, transforming potential waste into a sustainable, high-quality material; offering an eco-friendly alternative to exotic leathers, reducing the demand for reptile skins in fashion, and collaborating with local fisheries to source fish skins responsibly, ensuring the supply chain supports sustainable practices. "We have the power to shift the narrative and inspire others to adopt solutions that prioritize the planet," Aya says. Through Cuimer, Aya is proving that fashion can drive meaningful change while promoting a healthier world.

Remixed with permission from Global Entrepreneurship Monitor (GEM) from Elam, A., Hughes, K.D., & Samsami, M. (2024). Global Entrepreneurship Monitor 2023/24 Women's entrepreneurship report. *Global Entrepreneurship Monitor.* https://www.gemconsortium.org/reports/womens-entrepreneurship

Activities

Activity 1: Value Chain Analysis

Using the framework from this chapter, map out the value chain for your own creative work.

1 Create a list of every task, process, and decision you make. Organize these under the primary and support categories outlined in the value chain framework. Be specific and detailed.
2 Review your list and estimate how much time you spend on each activity. This could be measured in hours per week or per month.
3 Based on your time audit, answer the following questions:

- Which activities are taking up the most time?
- Which activities are most critical to your unique creative vision and must be performed by you?
- Which activities are you least satisfied with, and why?
- Which activities could you delegate, outsource, or improve to free up more of your time for creative work?

Activity 2: Process Mapping and Optimization

Choose a repeatable process from your Value Chain Analysis in Activity 1 and create a process map to visualize it.

1 Map the Process: Draw a flowchart documenting the steps involved in completing one specific task. Note the time it takes to complete each step.
2 Identify Bottlenecks: Analyze your flowchart. Where are the bottlenecks? Are there any starved or blocked tasks that result from this bottleneck?
3 Propose Improvements: Suggest at least two ways you could improve this process. Your ideas might involve:

- Reordering tasks
- Investing in new tools or technology

- Outsourcing a specific step to someone else
- Altering your workspace to reduce set-up time

4 Calculate Throughput Time**:** Re-calculate the throughput time for your improved process. How much time did your proposed changes save?

Activity 3: Sustainability Audit

Reflect on a specific aspect of your creative business and identify opportunities to make this area more sustainable.

1 Analyze Your Practices: Choose one area of your operations (e.g., your sourcing of materials, your waste management, or your product packaging).
2 Research the costs and benefits of a specific sustainable alternatives:

   a Cost Analysis: What is the cost of your current practice per unit or per month? What would be the cost of the sustainable alternative? Calculate the difference. Is it a higher or lower cost?
   b Impact Analysis: Use a quantifiable metric to measure sustainability improvement. For example, if you're changing packaging, you could measure the reduction in plastic waste in grams or kilograms per month. If you're changing a material, you could find data on the reduction in water usage or carbon emissions associated with the new material's production.

3 Formulate Your Action Plan: Create a brief action plan that includes your findings.

   c Financials: Based on your cost analysis, explain the financial implications of the change. Is there a greater upfront investment with long-term savings? Or does the new practice simply cost more, and if so, is it worth the added cost for the environmental benefit?
   d Sustainability Impact: Clearly state the quantitative improvement you expect to achieve. This could be something like "reduce plastic waste by 5 kg per month" or "decrease carbon footprint by 10%."

Resources and References

Drucker, P. F. (1963). Managing for business effectiveness. *Harvard Business Review*, *41*(3), 53–60.
Goldratt, E. M., & Cox, J. (2004). *The goal: A process of ongoing improvement*. North River Press.
McDonough, W., & Braungart, M. (2002). *Cradle to cradle: Remaking the way we make things*. North Point Press.
Porter, M. E. (1985). *Competitive advantage: Creating and sustaining superior performance*. Free Press.
Shapiro, R. D. (2013) *Operations management reading: Process analysis*. Harvard Business Publishing.

9 Action and Business Planning

Marie Segares

Introduction

In this chapter, we will look at how **creative entrepreneurs** plan and implement short- and long-term business **objectives** and **goals**, as well as how they can evaluate if their planning worked! While many creative entrepreneurs seek out different experiences and creative opportunities based on internal factors, from a business perspective, it is important to consider the **external environment**, too. We will also pull together what you've learned from the previous chapters as you plan for the future and explore how you can gather support and feedback from other people and organizations during your planning process.

When your business is just starting, you may develop extremely short-term plans, frequently evaluate how your business is doing, and make changes often. Many emerging creative entrepreneurs find that planning on an annual basis is sufficient. Over time, you may find that creating a longer term, multi-year **strategic plan** is important, especially if you have personal or family income requirements to sustain, a building or machinery to maintain, or staff to support.

Learning Outcomes

- **Apply** a PESTLE analysis to identify the external forces impacting your business
- **Evaluate** feedback from collaborators to refine business strategy and planning
- **Conduct** a threats, opportunities, weaknesses, and strengths (TOWS) or strengths, opportunities, aspirations, and results (SOAR) analysis to develop goals for your business
- **Develop** short-term objectives using the SMART framework

The External Environment and Your Business

As an artist or **maker**, you are likely creatively inspired from within yourself, but as an entrepreneur, it is helpful to explore the external environment – the conditions, events, and factors outside of you and your business – because it can have a strong impact on your business. We will consider both the **PESTLE analysis** and **trend** watching as ways to examine the external environment.

PESTLE Analysis

A PESTLE analysis is a tool many businesses use to provide a structured approach to understanding and analyzing the external environment. PESTLE is an acronym which stands for Political, Economic, Social, Technological, Legal, and Environmental. Let's explore how you can use the PESTLE to analyze external factors related to your creative venture through Table 9.1.

DOI: 10.4324/9781003588771-9

Table 9.1 Using PESTLE Analysis in Your Business

Analysis Type	*How This Might Impact Your Business*
Political analysis examines national or international policy issues, such as wars and other violent conflicts, or fiscal policy such as corporate taxation or tariffs.	You may lose access to materials from a country experiencing political sanctions from your home country. You may consider changing your business's legal structure if your locality is raising corporate taxes. You may need alternative approaches to recruiting employees if immigration policies change.
Economic analysis explores how large-scale economic issues in your region, country, or the world will impact customer spending as well as your business's ability to raise, spend, or save money.	You may need to increase your budget for materials if inflation is high. You may need to create lower-priced products if levels of disposable income decrease among your customers. You may want to avoid or minimize using business loans, lines of credit, or credit cards if interest rates are high.
Social analysis looks at changes or conventions in society, such as demographics, social or religious values, public opinion, and education levels.	You may want to accentuate your size in your marketing materials if consumers value small businesses over larger companies. You may want to change your practices or packaging to minimize environmental harm or pursue a third-party certification to highlight your sustainable products if public opinion shifts toward more environmentally-friendly practices.
Technological analysis considers the impacts of technology.	You may be able to develop new products that incorporate tech such as augmented or virtual reality if consumers are more rapidly adopting technology. You may be able to affordably upgrade tools for your business if the price of communication technology lowers or its availability increases.
Legal analysis investigates the impact of laws such as employment and consumer protection laws and industry-specific regulations.	You may need to update your labels if your region introduces industry- or product-specific regulations related to packaging. You will need to notify your employees, as well as potentially adjust your practices, if employment laws change.
Environmental analysis probes the physical environment including weather and climate in the geographic locations where you make and sell your products, climate change, and epidemics and pandemics.	You may need to consider relocation, flood insurance, or upgraded facilities to avoid loss if there is frequent flooding in the area where you store your materials or inventory. Consumers may avoid certain ingredients even months or years after a major foodborne outbreak.

To generate ideas for a PESTLE analysis, you will need to be relatively informed about the external environment, as well as how changes or continuity in that environment can impact your business. If you aren't very familiar with the external environment, consider:

- **Organizational membership**. Local business networks, arts, **economic development**, and **entrepreneur support organizations** frequently update their members about political, economic, technological, and legal issues, and often survey consumers and members about social matters. Organizations rooted in the communities where you work and sell your products often provide insights into changing or ongoing issues in the external environment.

- **Trade shows and industry events. Trade shows** are industry exhibitions which frequently include classes and speakers, trend updates, **networking** opportunities, and booths displaying new and continuing products. These events are for professionals and business owners and usually require an application and verification process to attend. Examples include AIGA Design Conference, Creativation by NAMTA, DesignerCon, h + h cologne and h + h americas, Impressions Expo, JCK, Nashville Needlework Market, and Texworld (Figure 9.1).
- **Regularly reading, listening to, or watching business publications, podcasts, or videos.** News media often share insights into the PESTLE analysis factors and how they might impact businesses and consumers.
- **Networking with creative entrepreneurs at different stages of development.** Connecting with people with newer, same-age, and older businesses than yours will give you a broader perspective on the external environment and how other creative people are adapting to changes.

Trend Watching

Trends are patterns that ebb and flow and may influence the creation (and dissolution) of **products** and **services**. Trends are often visible in popular culture, entertainment, fashion, and the arts, but they can also be seen in politics, society, and business. While trends are generally influenced by or related to factors you would consider in a PESTLE analysis, you can examine trends separately. If you don't feel ready to conduct a full PESTLE analysis, trend watching is another way to explore the external environment (Figure 9.2).

You may observe trends on your own, or you can use trend watching tools to help you for business planning. Some examples include Etsy Trending Now, Glimpse Top Trends, Google Trends, and Pinterest Trends. Paid tools like Buzzsumo and Semrush Trends are also available for tracking social media and online trends. Pantone's Color of the Year influences the palettes of color in fashion, home decor, and more, while their semiannual Fashion Color Trend Report focuses more specifically on the fashion industry. As with other external factors, you may find

Figure 9.1 A speaker at a Schoolhouse Session workshop at the International Quilt Market introduces a new product.

Source: Marie Segares

Figure 9.2 Speakers at an event hosted by HGTV Magazine discuss trends in color and surface design.
Source: Marie Segares

that organizational membership, news media, and networking are helpful tools for identifying trends and considering how they might apply to your creative endeavors.

Bringing in Your Network

Many creative folks have a do-it-yourself ethos and are tempted to do everything within their business and to control all aspects of their organization. There are many situations where collaborating with others will lead to better outcomes while also freeing your time up for more important work. We recommend consulting with experts like accountants and lawyers periodically to support your business. As part of your annual planning process, you may want to talk with a financial planner or fractional CFO about your goals, develop bookkeeping practices or select financial management software in consultation with an accountant, or meet with a lawyer to discuss your **business structure**, **intellectual property**, or contracts.

Additionally, there are many organizations that provide free or low-cost services for creative entrepreneurs. You may be able to participate in training, meet one-on-one with consultants, or be part of a small accountability group of fellow entrepreneurs. Appendix B includes a list of organizations that we have worked with, as well as those recommended by the creative entrepreneurs we interviewed for this book, along with tips for identifying local organizations including economic development and arts organizations, entrepreneurship and tourism support organizations, **Chambers of Commerce**, nearby CreativeMornings chapters, and colleges and universities to find more ways to expand your network and get support for planning. And, don't forget professional associations which highlight specific creative fields.

Situational Analysis: Where Is Your Business Today and Where Should It Be Going in the Future?

After you've analyzed the external environment using a PESTLE or trend analysis, you'll want to explore your own business to facilitate developing goals for the future. This process is often called a **situational analysis**. Three common approaches to a situational analysis are the SWOT, TOWS, and SOAR analyses.

In this section, we'll use Etsy–an **e-commerce** *marketplace that highlights handmade and vintage goods from over 8 million sellers in over 60 countries – as our example. Keep in mind that Etsy is not a typical creative business. It is currently a* **publicly traded** *company based in Brooklyn, New York with over 2,000 employees.*

SWOT is an acronym for strengths, weaknesses, opportunities, and threats. The strengths and weaknesses refer to internal aspects of your business, while the opportunities and threats refer to issues identified through your PESTLE from the external environment.

Your business's strengths are your existing and accessible resources and capacities, as well as your **unique value proposition** (see Chapter 2), your **competitive advantage** (see Chapter 3), and aspects of the **business model** you use for your business (see Chapter 2), while your weaknesses are your missing or limited resources and capabilities. As you consider your strengths and weaknesses, here are some aspects of your business to evaluate:

- **Brand** identity and reputation (see Chapter 5),
- Customer loyalty (see Chapter 5),
- **Distribution channels** (see Chapters 5 and 8),
- Equipment, facilities, technology, and tools (see Chapter 8),
- Financial situation, such as **operating costs**, **cash flow**, and **debt** (see Chapter 7),
- Location(s),
- **Marketing** practices (see Chapters 2 and 4),
- Operational **processes** and procedures (see Chapter 8),
- Organizational culture and staffing (if you have employees),
- Packaging,
- Partnerships, and
- **Supply chain** (see Chapter 8).

Table 9.2 shows a sample SWOT for Etsy.

While the SWOT is a helpful first step, it doesn't suggest actions to take. For this reason, many folks prefer to use the TOWS analysis.

Table 9.2 Strengths, Weaknesses, Opportunities, and Threats (SWOT) Situational Analysis for Etsy in 2025

Strengths	**Weaknesses**
• Recognized brand identity • Large customer base with over 95 million active shoppers • Easy-to-use platform for sellers and buyers • Lower operating costs than a comparable brick-and-mortar business • Over 8 million sellers in over 60 countries	• Increasing seller dissatisfaction, including seller strike in 2022 and boycott in 2025 • Stock prices dropping • Shrinking web traffic • Inconsistent customer experience • Difficulties preventing/removing counterfeit and mass-produced items from marketplace
Opportunities	**Threats**
• Growth in consumer sentiment to "shop small" and "shop local" • Advances in geolocation technologies to strengthen search and customer targeting • Increased access to affordable communication technology for buyers and sellers • Partnerships with brands, maker collectives, and **retailers** • Possibility of expanding into additional international markets	• Increased competition from e-commerce marketplaces and retailers including Amazon Handmade, eBay, Michaels Makerplace, Redbubble, and Walmart Marketplace • Fluctuating exchange rates impact sellers and buyers • International conflicts, including Ukraine-Russia and Gaza-Israel, impacting sellers and buyers • Growing risk of cyberattack or cybercrime • Increased regulation of technology industry including varied guidelines across countries

TOWS is an acronym for threats, opportunities, weaknesses, and strengths. Note that these are the same categories you used for the SWOT, but arranged differently. As with the SWOT, strengths and weaknesses are internal and threats and opportunities are sourced from the external environment. The TOWS suggests formulating actions based on four different configurations.

- **SO (Strengths-Opportunities)** actions focus on leveraging strengths to matched opportunities. For example, if your business has substantial cash reserves (a strength), you might consider purchasing a new but expensive technology that could improve your **process time** (an opportunity).
- **ST (Strengths-Threats)** actions focus on using your strengths to minimize potential threats. For example, if you have an established customer base (a strength), you may want to launch a loyalty program if there is increasing competition (a threat).
- **WO (Weaknesses-Opportunities)** actions focus on minimizing a weakness to take advantage of an opportunity. For example, during the early months of the COVID pandemic, many creative entrepreneurs had limited distribution channels (a weakness) because vending events were canceled and retail shops were closed. At the same time, consumers were online more (an opportunity), and many of these creatives chose to establish an e-commerce presence for the first time.
- **WT (Weaknesses-Threats)** actions focus on addressing your weaknesses to avert threats. For example, if your company has high supply costs (a weakness) and there are signs of an impending recession (a threat), you could explore ways to lower costs by finding different suppliers or developing more efficient processes.

Table 9.3 shows a sample TOWS for Etsy.

While the TOWS analysis delves deeper into **strategy** than the SWOT, some entrepreneurs find that it focuses too much on "fixing" weaknesses and not enough on boosting strengths. If you feel the same, you may want to consider the SOAR analysis.

SOAR is an acronym for strengths, opportunities, aspirations, and results. As with the SWOT and TOWS analyses, you'll start by identifying the strengths of your business. Like the SO actions in the TOWS analysis, you'll then consider opportunities identified from your PESTLE or trend analysis that your strengths could build upon. Through your planning process, you will also identify aspirations for your business, or goals that are aligned with your vision of the future. Finally, you will identify measurable results that you can use to evaluate your progress toward your goals.

Table 9.3 Threats, Opportunities, Weaknesses, and Strengths (TOWS) Situational Analysis for Etsy in 2025

	Opportunities	*Threats*
Strengths	**Strengths-Opportunities (SO)** • Leverage brand identity and capitalize on consumer sentiment with "shop small" and "shop local" marketing campaigns in targeted markets using geolocation	**Strengths-Threats (ST)** • Develop alternative payment options to expand international sellers in countries not served by competitor marketplaces
Weaknesses	**Weaknesses-Opportunities (WO)** • Use increased access to affordable communication technology to provide customer service training for sellers to minimize inconsistent customer experience	**Weaknesses-Threats (WT)** • Focus on preventing/removing counterfeit and mass-produced items to further differentiate Etsy from competitor marketplaces

Table 9.4 Strengths, Opportunities, Aspirations, and Results (SOAR) Situational Analysis for Etsy in 2025

Strengths	**Opportunities**
• Recognized brand identity • Large customer base with over 95 million active shoppers • Easy-to-use platform for sellers and buyers • Lower operating costs than a comparable brick-and-mortar business • Over 8 million sellers in over 60 countries	• Growth in consumer sentiment to "shop small" and "shop local" • Advances in geolocation technologies to strengthen search and customer targeting • Increased access to affordable communication technology for buyers and sellers • Partnerships with brands, maker collectives, and retailers • Possibility of expanding into additional international markets
Aspirations	**Results**
• To be recognized as the best marketplace for our sellers • To be the top online destination for consumers who want to "shop small" and "shop local" • To develop unique collections with partners that spotlight artisan traditions in a fresh way	• Increase seller retention by 10% • Enhance geolocation search and increase total revenue by 15% • Develop two new collections in collaboration with international partners and sellers

To create goals and refine your strategy using SOAR, ask these questions about your business.

- **Strengths**. What are we good at? What are we proud of? What do we do that is unique?
- **Opportunities**. What possibilities exist for us? What are the top three we should focus on? How are we different from our competitors? Are there customers, markets, products, services, or products that may be possible for us to engage with? What skills should we develop for the future? How can we best meet the needs of our customers, employees, owners, and community?
- **Aspirations.** What are our dreams for the future? What is important to us?
- **Results**. What results are meaningful to us? Which measures would let us know we are on track, if we are successful, or if we are making a difference?

SOAR is meant to be an inclusive process, so if you have employees you should discuss these questions together.

Table 9.4 shows a sample SOAR for Etsy.

While critics suggest that the SOAR deemphasizes weaknesses too much, a major benefit of the SOAR analysis is that it is action-oriented and explicitly reminds you to consider results and measurement from the start of your planning process.

Choosing What to Focus On

Every business, even creative or artistic ones, has three main components: **accounting** and **finance** (see Chapters 6 and 7), marketing (see Chapters 2, 4, and 5), and **operations** (see Chapter 8). While some businesses choose to focus on all three components in their business planning, if your business is new, you may want to take it slow. Ask yourself if there is one component of your business that needs more attention in the coming year, or if there is one component that is very strong and doesn't need much care to continue moving forward. The answers to these questions may help you determine a direction for your business planning.

If you've done your PESTLE or trend analyses, mapped out your business strengths, decided on using a SWOT or TOWS or SOAR, and are still not sure what type of opportunities or aspirations to focus on in the following year, you may find it helpful to review your **artist statement** (if you have one), your unique value proposition (as discussed in Chapter 2), and your approach to strategy (as discussed in Chapter 3). We recommend reviewing these at least annually for guidance on where to direct your energies in your planning process. You may also find that these are too outdated to reflect your business in its current state and you need to make updates.

Identifying Your Focus for the Year

Many entrepreneurs we interviewed for this book make separate financial and creative goals for their businesses. Others include personal goals, too. Here are some examples of how creative entrepreneurs choose what to focus on during their planning processes.

- Kathy Cano-Murillo of Crafty Chica (profiled in Case 10.1) asks herself, "'What are the life experiences I want to have?'" and chooses three as she plans for the following year.
- Aaliyah Taylor of Exalting in Beauty (profiled in Case 10.4) is focusing on stretch goals right now. She wants "to be more intentional" about applying for **grants**, as well as to "do the scary things and put myself out there" as she plans for an **entrepreneurial pivot** into a slow-fashion clothing line.
- Zaire Miles-Moultrie of That Zaire (profiled in Case 10.8) makes five-year plans including personal, creative, and economic goals, such as completing college, making a certain number of pieces and exhibiting in particular venues, and meeting a monthly target of art-related income.
- David Larson from Larson Wood Designs (profiled in Case 10.10) has a target "number in my head" for his annual **revenue** goal. As an emerging entrepreneur, he is also focused on "building my reputation," which includes applying to juried shows and vending events.

Don't Forget the Competitive Environment

Some creative entrepreneurs find themselves too focused on macro issues in the external environment or on their own creative or personal goals, and forget to consider the **competitiveness** in their local community, industry, or the general market. Using a strategic tool like a **five forces analysis** or an approach like **blue ocean strategy** (both described in Chapter 3) are ways to make sure you think about competition during your planning process. As Nina Shaw of The Punny Quilter (profiled in Case 10.2) explains,

> When I look at designing a new product, I look to see if something else like it already exists. If it does, then I won't do it because I only have so much cash flow. To tie up my cash flow in a duplicate product for something that already exists out there automatically puts me in a position of competition. When I'm coming up with unique, brand new ideas, now I have no competitors. That puts me in a better position for success.

Business Planning: Getting Ready for Action

Now that you have an idea of where your business stands, how the external and competitive environment might impact you, and some broad areas of focus, let's talk about how to put this all together and plan for action. Here are some suggestions for getting started.

- **Generate ideas with a brain dump**. Brain dumps are unedited, unorganized lists of ideas. A brain dump is a way of getting everything out of your mind without considering which ideas are infeasible (or impossible), which you are disinterested in, or which you are afraid of doing. Start with a timer and write down or type in everything you can think of as a potential goal or project for your business in the coming year. Some folks find that they generate more ideas when walking or in the shower. If this sounds like you, use voice memos on your phone or a small recorder to create your brain dump list instead.
- **Sort through and categorize your ideas**. Once you have a large list, go through and choose ideas which you want to study further or prioritize for action in the coming year. You may also want to start and maintain a "someday" list of ideas that you aren't ready for now, but which you'd like to return to in the future. For example, Leslie Pearson of Curate Essentials (profiled in Case 10.9) had a long-term plan for offering classes. Three years after launching, she was ready to interview teachers and develop a class schedule.
- **Investigate**. Some ideas will require preliminary research. For example, you might be interested in buying a plotter or a longarm quilting machine or renting studio space outside of your home. Through brief investigation you can get a general idea of the space or budget required and determine whether these ideas are feasible for action in the coming year.
- **Envision with a mood board**. Many creative people find **mood boards** to be helpful tools for thinking through ideas, organizing inspiration, or considering different actions. A mood board is a visual representation of a concept. It can be digital (for example, through a dedicated Pinterest board or using Canva or Miro mood board creators) or physical (for example, on a cork board or in a journal). Mood boards can include words, images, materials, samples, and collages. For example, Kathy Cano-Murillo of Crafty Chica (profiled in Case 10.1) uses Pinterest boards to curate the vibe or color story for new collections.

Goals and Objectives: What's the Difference?

You may have heard the terms goals and objectives used interchangeably, but they actually have different meanings in strategic planning. Goals are higher level, broader, and may take a longer time – even several years – to achieve. Goals should be aligned with your overall values and aspirations for your business. Examples of goals are to increase revenue, to become recognized in your creative field, or to establish an iconic brand. Your goals may be about outcomes (such as increasing sales volume), performance (such as improving **quality**), or processes (such as establishing stronger recordkeeping practices).

Objectives help to outline and direct the activities you'll need to make progress on to meet your goals. Objectives have shorter time frames – typically one year or less – and are easier to evaluate because they have components that are measurable and specific. The SMART approach to developing objectives for businesses is outlined below.

Using SMART Objectives and Backward Planning

Two related processes to help you plan out and then implement actions are SMART objectives and backward planning. **SMART objectives** are those developed when you follow an acronym that stands for **Specific**, **Measurable**, **Achievable**, **Relevant**, and **Timebound**, while **backward planning** is a way to schedule tasks and checkpoints to achieve objectives when working in reverse chronological order from an end date.

Setting SMART Objectives

It's one thing to know the acronym, but how do you go about setting a SMART objective? Let's say that one of the aspirational goals you set using SOAR is "to enhance your reputation as an artisan by vending at the most popular and prestigious holiday market in your local area."

- **Is it Specific?** Yes, you have identified a particular market. Even if you have a slightly broader expectation – such as to participate in your first craft fair, or any juried market, or any venue outside of your hometown – it is still specific. Alternatively, maybe you aspire to make a certain amount of money, or sell a particular number of pieces at the holiday market. These are also specific.
- **Is it Measurable?** If you've met the criteria for being specific, it usually (but not always) indicates that your objective is measurable. In this example, you can determine that you've vended at the market, sold the number of products, or made the amount of money through record-keeping. Being measurable is about having the ability to know whether this objective was achieved when you look back at your progress in the future. Some things that are very important – like improving product quality – can be difficult to measure. That doesn't mean we shouldn't have goals or develop objectives about those more elusive concepts. Instead, it means we should determine how we will measure those concepts during our planning period. (See the **Key Performance Indicators (KPIs)** section for more information on measuring success.)
- **Is it Achievable?** Your situational analysis and the preliminary research you did while you were setting goals and getting ready for action should help you to understand if a particular objective is achievable. For example, if you learn this holiday market is only for artists who are members of an organization that you are not eligible to join, it is not achievable for you. Don't be afraid to include goals that are a stretch for you – goals that *might* be achievable with extra effort but may still be out of reach – because that's how you will develop and grow as an entrepreneur. At the same time, set yourself up for success by not creating so many stretch objectives that you are unable to complete any and feel deflated.
- **Is it Relevant?** Thinking about relevancy is one way to avoid getting pulled in too many directions in your business. If you are creating the type of tangible products that could be sold at a holiday market and want to sell directly to consumers, then this is a relevant objective. Conversely, if your business is service-oriented where you primarily do freelance **business-to-business** services or teach, or if you prefer to **wholesale** or sell products through a **distributor**, you may find vending at a holiday market is not relevant to your business.
- **Is it Timebound?** As the objective is currently written, it isn't timebound. So, what can we do to change that? We can add an end date (such as by June 30), a timeframe (such as within six months), or a cycle (such as monthly) to make any objective that meets the rest of the criteria timebound.

Our updated SMART objective is "to vend at the most popular and prestigious holiday market in my local area by December 25 [or the date of the market]." Once you have the SMART objectives you want to achieve in your planning period, start thinking about the detailed steps you'll need to get there. See Figure 9.3 for a checklist of many of the smaller steps you might need to take to make a holiday market successful for your business.

If your business is well established, you may be able to outline the required steps to complete your objectives with accurate time estimates for each step. If you are an emerging entrepreneur or expanding into a new area of business, you may need to talk to your network or reach out to mentors or experts to get a more detailed breakdown of the necessary steps, or to estimate the times required for each.

Moving From Smart Objectives to Backward Planning

Backward planning will help you to schedule the various activities that are necessary to complete any one of your SMART objectives. In our example, if you've vended elsewhere with similar products, you may already have a clear idea of what is involved and how long it takes you to pack and set up. If you're bringing a new product, you may not yet know how long it takes to make one unit.

- [ ] Apply to be a vendor
- [ ] Make deposit or pay vendor fees
- [ ] Apply for/obtain a sales tax certificate (if required)
- [ ] Research typical customers that attend and their preferred price points
- [ ] Decide which products to sell
- [ ] Create/purchase sufficient inventory for event
- [ ] Rent/buy tent for outdoor venue
- [ ] Decide how to display products
- [ ] Make/borrow/rent/buy display items (shelving, baskets, mannequins, etc.)
- [ ] Get business cards, postcards, or other promotional items printed
- [ ] Activate/confirm account with online payment system to accept card payments
- [ ] Invite someone to manage booth while you take breaks; provide training
- [ ] Get cash in multiple denominations to use for change; set up system for securing cash at event
- [ ] Pack inventory, display materials, and promotional items
- [ ] Transport items to event
- [ ] Set up/break down booth display on day of event
- [ ] Transport remaining inventory back (or make plans to donate it or have it picked up by a retailer)

Figure 9.3 Holiday market vending checklist.

Source: Developed by Marie Segares using thegoodocs.com

Since all of your SMART objectives will be timebound, you can use backward planning to set up milestones or target dates for completing different tasks. Continuing with the example of vending at the prestigious market, let's assume that applications are due three months before the event date. You would add deadlines or time periods for each step you listed starting about three months before the date of the event.

With backward planning, some tasks will have a specific deadline, such as if applications are due on September 15. Other tasks will take place during a period of time, such as if you conduct your venue research during July and August as you attend a series of events and talk with other creative entrepreneurs that have vended there in the past.

An important part of backward planning is to include a **time cushion**, or some flexibility to account for unforeseen events or delays. As an example, if September 15 is the application deadline for this market, you may want to establish your own deadline to submit your application as September 8. If you miss your internal deadline, the time cushion will still provide you with an opportunity to apply. Additionally, don't forget to include time for eating, sleeping, and breaks in your backward planning. For example, if you make your own products by hand, and it takes one hour to produce one unit of your best-selling product, you can't make 24 in a day!

If your business is new and you aren't quite sure about times, or if you are launching with new products and services, be sure to build in extra time for experimenting in your backward planning.

There are many tools out there for tracking dates for backward planning, including task tracking, list management, and project management software. You can also rely on tools you are already comfortable with and use regularly, such as digital calendars or paper planners, task alerts in your email, or alerts on your phone.

Evaluating Outcomes: How Do You Know If You've Achieved Your Objectives?

After your SMART objective has passed its time horizon, you'll want to be able to assess whether you achieved it. Identifying KPIs and documentation will allow you to evaluate your progress and your results.

Identifying Key Performance Indicators

KPIs are **metrics** that you use, and they are part of the measurability aspect of your SMART objective. When available, we recommend using standard key indicators. This simplifies the planning and evaluation processes because you'll spend less time considering and developing metrics, figuring out how to document and measure them, and explaining your achievements or roadblocks to others. Many financial metrics – such as **net income**, **gross margin**, per unit **cost**, and breakeven point – are or can be standardized, so with good record keeping you should be able to determine if you've achieved your objective.

But, what if your objectives center around more intangible or difficult to measure concepts like product quality, business reputation, or customer satisfaction? Start by reaching out to your network or to entrepreneur support organizations to see if other people are using KPIs you can adapt. Whether you use someone else's or create your own metric, be sure to document how you define the metric and how you will assess it. Let's say you want to measure your product quality. Here are some options for you to consider.

- **Inspection**. You could develop a checklist used to inspect each product (or a percentage of products) before sale. To pass the inspection, the checklist must have a certain score; a higher score could indicate the product was high quality. For your quality KPI, you could use the average checklist score, or the total number of inspected products that were at or above your "high-quality" score.

- **Reviews and ratings**. If you sell products on an e-commerce marketplace like Etsy, you could use your customer ratings as a proxy metric for quality. If you teach classes, you can use anonymous evaluation form reviews to measure quality.
- **Acceptance rate**. You could use acceptances to highly-regarded juried shows or markets as proxy metrics of quality.

Each of these quality metrics is developed using different assumptions, and the effort to track each also varies. For a larger business with multiple employees or using **outsourced manufacturing**, the inspection checklist is likely a better metric, while the acceptance rate might be the most appropriate KPI for an emerging business that relies on shows and markets to generate business.

In all cases, the KPIs should be established in advance so you can measure them periodically or at the end of the timeline for that objective.

If you plan to measure an objective that includes a qualifier – such as an increase or decrease, or expanding or maintaining – you will need a **baseline measurement**. A baseline measurement is a starting point to use for comparison. Let's say you want to increase your revenue next year. This year's revenue would be your baseline. Many creative businesses also use baseline measurements for other purposes, including to track year-over-year changes.

Documentation for Evaluation

Once you've identified your metrics, you'll need to establish systems for or use existing documentation to track your progress. There is a saying: "garbage in, garbage out." It refers to the idea that if you put in flawed or poor quality data, your reports will also be flawed or poor quality. Set yourself up for success by choosing documentation methods that you can keep up with and that you can get accurate information from. Unsorted stacks of paper or your entire email inbox are hard to pull information from, but spreadsheets, organized folders, and completed checklists are much easier to get information from. When possible, use existing documentation methods that you are familiar with and feel confident using, or software that is designed for task tracking or project management, like Trello, Asana, or AirTable. One of your goals could also be to establish a record-keeping system or to set up bookkeeping or cash management software for your business!

Creating a Process for Business Planning and Evaluation

It's easy to get overwhelmed by business planning or evaluation, but if you build it into a regular schedule it becomes manageable. Use your calendar or notifications in email or on your phone to remind you to enter information, check progress, and determine if you need to course correct on a regular basis. Depending on whether your business is full time or part time, in its early stages or more established, and on your other life commitments, you might consider monthly, quarterly, or semiannual check ins on your progress. Many businesses begin annual planning in the third or fourth quarter of the previous year, while multi-year planning may start at any point in the year, with three or five year cycles being most common.

Getting Feedback

No matter which tool or tools you use for business planning, you may want to get feedback from your network. Consider:

- **Consulting with experts**. Accountants, lawyers, and business advisors can help you decide which metrics to use for the goals you selected. They often have a lot of information about the external environment. Additionally, they can help you set up systems and recommend tools and resources.
- **Talking to your customers**. Your customers can tell you about your strengths or weaknesses, and share their thoughts about new product ideas.
- **Joining or forming an accountability group**. You may find that an in-person or virtual group with other creative entrepreneurs is a helpful sounding board when you are planning, but also a place where you can check in regularly on your progress or troubleshoot when you feel stalled.

Before you settle on your goals and objectives for the coming year or years, you may find that you go through several versions of your plan, updating it after getting feedback. It's OK to make adjustments while planning, or even during the year as conditions change.

Conclusion: Bringing It All Together

As you read through this book, you likely hit upon chapters that challenged you, overwhelmed you, and excited you. As you set about planning for your business's future, don't forget the ideas that intrigued you, the areas you were concerned about, and the parts that you wanted to go back to and get a better understanding of. Each chapter addresses an important aspect of your business, and one that could be part of a goal for the future.

Mini Cases: Trend Watching at Crafty Chica and Fake Cakery

Some creative businesses are more responsive to trends than others. Crafty Chica (highlighted in Case 10.1) creates craft projects and tutorials that put a Mexican-American cultural spin on trends. Conchas are a traditional Mexican pastry that are shell-shaped and brightly colored. Kathy Cano-Murillo, the artist behind Crafty Chica explains,

> One year, everyone was doing all these things with conchas, and then I noticed in the general market, people were using edible glitter on cakes. So I combined the two and I did 'how to make glittered conchas.' People went nuts for that! Or, the little disco mirrors that were on trend. I took a Mexican sacred heart and I covered that with the little disco mirrors, and people loved it because it's like celebrating tradition combined with contemporary things.

Similarly, Julie Nguyen, the founder of Fake Cakery (highlighted in Case 10.6) launched her business after observing a trend in fake cakes on Instagram (Figure 9.4). Her background working in a bakery gave her experience with making real and display cakes, while her growing interest in working with polymer clay, resins, and acrylic paints as an art school student allowed her to explore different media for making fake cakes.

Figure 9.4 Julie Nguyen, founder of Fake Cakery, sells functional and decorative products including ashtrays, cannabis grinders, card deck boxes, keychains, jewelry boxes, lighter cases, magnets, and sculptures.

Source: Courtesy of Julie Nguyen/Fake Cakery

Activities

1 Develop a PESTLE analysis relevant to your creative business. Talk to someone in your network to get their feedback on any issues in the external environment you are concerned with or need more information about.
2 Search for local business networks and arts, economic development, and entrepreneur support organizations in your community. What type of services do they offer? Are there costs associated with joining or participating? Are there any organizations that would be a good fit for your business in the coming year?
3 Using the trend-watching tools shared in this chapter Resources below and other resources that you know about, develop a list of at least five trends that might be relevant to your business in the next six months. What ideas do you have for new products, product updates or discontinuations, or services based on these trends?
4 Generate a list of the strengths and weaknesses of your creative business today.

   a Make SWOT, TOWS, and SOAR analyses based on your strengths and weaknesses and your PESTLE analysis or trend list.
   b Decide if the SWOT, TOWS, or SOAR analysis is the best option for your business.
   c Based on your SWOT, TOWS, or SOAR, make at least two goals for your business.
   d With the SMART framework, create at least one objective that addresses one of your goals.
   e Using backward planning, set up a checklist or action list with deadlines for the activities you'll need to do to achieve your SMART objective.

5 Choose one area of your business to examine and set up a baseline measurement. Set a target for changing or maintaining that measurement in the next 12 months and determine how you would track it.

Resources

Trend Watching Tools

- Etsy Trends https://www.etsy.com/trends
- Glimpse Trends https://meetglimpse.com/trends/
- Google Trends https://trends.google.com/trends/
- Pantone Color of the Year https://www.pantone.com/color-of-the-year/
- Pinterest Trends https://trends.pinterest.com/
- TikTok Creative Center https://ads.tiktok.com/business/creativecenter/
- You can also watch trends by exploring trending hashtags or topics on social media platforms.

Mood Board Tools

- Canva Mood Board Creator https://www.canva.com/create/mood-boards/
- Milanote https://milanote.com/product/moodboarding
- Miro Mood Board Maker https://miro.com/moodboard/
- Pinterest https://www.pinterest.com/

Productivity, Project Management, and Tracking Tools

- AirTable https://www.airtable.com/
- Asana https://asana.com/
- Google Drive https://drive.google.com/
- LibreOffice https://www.libreoffice.org/
- Trello https://trello.com/

Additional Reading

Adobe Experience Cloud Team. (2025, April 14). Top KPIs and metrics creative teams should track. *Adobe for Business*. https://business.adobe.com/blog/basics/kpis-for-creative-teams

Coquillette, C. (2021, July 28). Trend forecasting for visual creatives. *CatCoq*. https://catcoq.com/blog/trend-forecasting-for-visual-creatives

Forsey, C. (2024, August 2). SWOT analysis: How to do one [with template & examples]. *HubSpot*. https://blog.hubspot.com/marketing/swot-analysis

Hayden, D. (2025, March 21). PESTLE analysis. *Chartered Institute of Personnel and Development*. https://www.cipd.org/en/knowledge/factsheets/pestle-analysis-factsheet/

Indeed Editorial Team. (2025, March 4). What is a TOWS analysis? (Definition and how to conduct it). *Indeed*. https://uk.indeed.com/career-advice/career-development/what-is-tows-analysis

Jurevicius, O. (2025, June 16). SOAR analysis demystified: Your go-to guide. *Strategic Management Insight*. https://strategicmanagementinsight.com/tools/soar-analysis/

Martins, J. (2025, February 2). What are SMART goals? Examples and templates. *Asana*. https://asana.com/resources/smart-goals

von Moltke, N. (n.d.). [Free] SOAR analysis template and SOAR matrix guide. *Academy to Innovate HR*. https://www.aihr.com/blog/soar-analysis-template/

10 Case Studies

Marie Segares

Case 10.1 Crafty Chica: Thriving, Not Just Surviving

Maker Profile

Kathy Cano-Murillo is a third generation Mexican-American living in Phoenix, Arizona, who has always been a "hyper-creative" and "multi-passionate" person. In her early 20s, she made earrings from watercolor paper and brought them to a boutique where they quickly sold (Figure 10.1.1).

> The feeling of receiving a check for something that I had so much fun creating – I just anchored that moment for the rest of my life. I was like, 'This is what I want to get paid for: doing what I love.'

In the 1990s, Kathy and her husband, who is also an artist, funded their lives through their creative work which they sold **wholesale** to boutiques, galleries, museum stores, and large **retailers** around the United States. Eventually, they found **manufacturing** and **production** to be too overwhelming to manage with two small children at home. They stopped doing wholesale

Figure 10.1.1 Kathy Cano-Murillo, founder of Crafty Chica.

Source: Courtesy of Kathy Cano-Murillo/Crafty Chica.

DOI: 10.4324/9781003588771-10

orders and Kathy went to work at a newspaper, quickly moving from the features department to writing a weekly craft column that was eventually syndicated in 130 publications. While at the newspaper, Kathy was introduced to the craft **industry**. Through attending industry events, she met other creative professionals, manufacturers, and publishers, "and suddenly my love of this hobby turned into a professional career." She learned to be a designer,

> and that was so valuable because I knew when I signed on for a design project, it's all about meeting people where they're at, filling a need in the industry, making the client's work shine … whereas as an artist, I could just create whatever I want.

Introduction to Crafty Chica

In 2001, while still writing her weekly craft column, Kathy realized, "there was no representation in the [craft] industry" and "decided to do something for my Latino community." She launched Crafty Chica as a craft blog, where she would add "a Latin spin to celebrate culture" to current trends.

Mindset Shifts

After meeting a manufacturer at a trade show, in 2007 Kathy was invited to design a **product line**. Kathy knew she wouldn't be able to balance her work at the newspaper and her family life as a married mother of two with designing a large product line for national retail **distribution**. Kathy explains,

> I thought, 'this is my chance to try something new.' I put together a wishlist for the company that was double my newspaper salary, that included where I would only use their **products** on my blog, and I would be their national spokesperson because I would be showing their products to new audiences in my Latino community. Basically, it was a long-term brand partnership – which didn't really exist back then.

When the company agreed, Kathy was able to quit her job at the newspaper to work on this brand partnership while maintaining her health insurance and retirement plan and getting additional time to focus on Crafty Chica.

In 2015, Kathy felt ready to focus on Crafty Chica full-time. She contracted with a business manager so that she could focus on creative work while her manager would develop business opportunities for a 20% **commission**. Kathy knew from previous experience that she didn't want to rely on vending her art because it was difficult to scale, nor did she want to manufacture her own products because it would involve hiring (and managing) many people. Kathy was inspired by large lifestyle brands, such as Martha Stewart, Jennifer Lopez and Oprah Winfrey, and knew that in addition to "their main thing," each also had books and other product lines they built community around. She applied this same "blueprint" to Crafty Chica, developing experiences like the Crafty Chica Cruise, writing books, teaching workshops and designing products to **license** to manufacturers. Kathy notes,

> I really had to look at the big picture of how to make this work because I didn't want to just survive. I wanted to thrive. I wanted to have a nice cushy life doing what I love to do and change that stigma of the starving artist.

As part of the transition to being a full-time **creative entrepreneur**, Kathy was inspired by a speaker she met at a conference to think differently about money. The speaker encouraged her to reframe her thinking from "losing" money when leaving a job to *gaining time*

> to use to make as much money as you want. When you work for a company, you're limited to what they think you're worth, and you get that same paycheck every month. When you are an entrepreneur, you can find ways to make more money than your paycheck. That blew my mind. My husband and I had lived a life of squeezing a dollar out of a dime because that's how we were conditioned from our parents and society, that artists are always scraping to get by. This flipped my mindset from squeezing a dollar out of a dime

Figure 10.1.2 A bookstore endcap featuring Crafty Chica products.

Source: Courtesy of Kathy Cano-Murillo/Crafty Chica.

> to turning one dollar into a hundred dollars. After that, everything changed. It just made me be daring and add extra zeros to my quotes [to brand partners].

Diversifying Crafty Chica

Crafty Chica is no longer "just" a craft blog. Kathy recently submitted a new book proposal, she has been designing pottery for paint-on-pottery studios, she teaches local workshops and online and destination retreats, and she continues to work with brand partners on sponsored content. Additionally, Kathy is the author of 12 non-fiction and fiction books and has designed licensed fabric, stationery, greeting cards, blank ceramics, and craft supplies such as die sets and stencils (Figure 10.1.2). She also sells art prints and mugs, jewelry, stickers, and craft kits through the Crafty Chica store. While the Crafty Chica blog originally included personal stories, Kathy has updated her site to focus on craft projects, recipes, and tutorials. The **advertising** revenue she earns from the Crafty Chica blog and YouTube channel is still an important **revenue stream**. In fact, Kathy relies on this **passive income** to pay her mortgage each month.

Planning for Success

As she plans for what is next for Crafty Chica each year, Kathy asks herself,

> what are the life experiences I want to have while I'm here on this earth? It's a little non-traditional from the business aspect of things, but I want to get my work out to the masses in all different avenues. Every year, I pick three things that I'm going to focus on for the year.

Every quarter, Kathy checks in to see if any adjustments are needed to her annual plan. In the summer (end of the second quarter), she focuses heavily on the third and fourth quarter because the last half of the year is her "money-making season." From past experience, she knows that new designs or products have to be finished by the end of the second quarter before her busy end-of-the-year season.

Kathy finds that if she doesn't plan and schedule her work, "I will just wander. I get lost in the weeds and I'm not really that productive." She makes a monthly to-do list, and on Sunday nights, she makes a weekly to-do list which she updates each night before bed. During busy times of year, such as when she travels frequently for workshops and events, she will make an hourly schedule for herself for each day. Kathy says, "there's something about **timeboxing** [the to-do list]. It's so wild. I get everything done." This is possible through Kathy's years of experience as she is able to accurately predict how much time different activities will take.

Partnerships and Supports

Even after more than 20 years in the craft industry, Kathy is always learning and looking for collaborations. She works with several Arizona-based organizations in her local community including Ella, a nonprofit organization that works with Latina entrepreneurs; Amor Collective, an **incubator** for Latinas; and the J. Orin Edson Entrepreneurship + Innovation Institute at Arizona State University. Kathy teaches and mentors other entrepreneurs as a way to give back to the community, but she also learns from other speakers and entrepreneurs. As she notes, "There's always time to try something new. You can always pivot or change or evolve to try something new."

Crafty Chica's Tips for Emerging Creative Entrepreneurs

- Create a bingo card where you write down everything you want to achieve with your business during the year and cross achievements off as they happen. Kathy says, "they don't all have to be super serious. It could be having a national celebrity buy one of my earrings. It could be whatever fun things that you want to put on there."
- Document your feelings as you're creating and doing work in your business, but not necessarily to share on social media. Write things down, use a journal app or voice memos, or snap a picture, and use these notes to reflect on your feelings later. Kathy also jots down when she doesn't enjoy activities because "I have to remind myself this is why I stopped doing this."
- Use a Pinterest board to curate the vibe or color story for a new collection or series to help everything stay in sync.
- Read business books or listen to business podcasts so that you're constantly learning new ways to grow your business.
- It's OK not to want to be an artist full-time for a living. If you'd rather have a steady paycheck from a job, spend your free time working on your art, and not focus on growing your business, do that instead.

Case Concepts, Reflections, and Resources

Concepts

- Business planning (Chapter 9)
- Entrepreneurial mindset (Chapter 1)
- Money script (Chapter 1)
- Operations management (Chapter 8)

Reflection Questions

1 Kathy works with a business manager who identifies business opportunities in exchange for 20% commission. What are the benefits and challenges of contracting with a business manager? Is this an option you would consider for your business? Why or why not?
2 Which elements of the **entrepreneurial mindset** described in Chapter 1 does Kathy's journey highlight? What has she learned during her career that could be helpful to you and your business?
3 Kathy describes shifting her views about money from that of a "starving artist." Chapter 1 highlights several **money scripts**. Is there one you observed Kathy using at any point during her entrepreneurial journey? Is there anything about how Kathy views money that could be helpful to you or your business?
4 Kathy uses a time management approach called timeboxing when she is managing multiple deadlines to schedule a start and end time for specific tasks. (See Further Reading and Viewing below for more information about timeboxing.) During less busy seasons, she uses to-do lists to guide her daily activities. Could either of these time management approaches work for you and your business?
5 Kathy works closely with many local organizations that support entrepreneurs to find opportunities, share knowledge, and learn. If you don't already have a local network, search for arts councils, business improvement organizations, business networking organizations, **economic development organizations**, or **entrepreneur support organizations** near you.

Which organizations offer helpful resources? Which host **networking** events? Are there any you would consider joining or becoming more involved with?

Additional Resources

Kathy maintains several websites.

- Crafty Chica (craftychica.com) is her site for consumers.
- Crafty Chica Store (craftychicastore.com) is her retail shop, which also includes licensing information for prospective business customers.
- Kathy Cano-Murillo (www.kathycanomurillo.com) highlights her brand partnerships and **business-to-business** services.

Further Reading and Viewing

Licensing

Elyse Breanne Design. (2024, July 12). Art licensing 101: How I used licensing to grow my million-dollar art business! [Video]. YouTube. https://youtu.be/HFVe4AdiO3w

Lentz, M. (n.d.). Licensing 101: A guide for artists and creatives. *Molly Marie Pea*. https://www.mollymariepea.com/blog/licensing-101-a-guide-for-artists-and-creatives

Networking

Johnson, J. (2023, July 19). Networking with other entrepreneurs: Why it matters and how to do it right. *CO–U.S. Chamber of Commerce*. https://www.uschamber.com/co/grow/thrive/tips-for-networking-with-other-entrepreneurs

Dobush, G. (2016, December 23). Networking tips for introverts. *Craft Industry Alliance*. https://craftindustryalliance.org/networking-tips-introverts/

Timeboxing

Martins, J. (2025, January 28). Timeboxing 101: The goal-oriented time management technique. *Asana*. https://asana.com/resources/what-is-timeboxing

Zao-Sanders, M. (2018, December 12). How timeboxing works and why it will make you more productive. *Harvard Business Review*. https://hbr.org/2018/12/how-timeboxing-works-and-why-it-will-make-you-more-productive

Case 10.2 The Punny Quilter: From Hobby Blogger to Product Inventor

Note: The author has disguised names and other identifying information to protect confidentiality at the entrepreneur's request.

Maker Profile

After graduating from college, Nina Shaw worked for an **advertising** agency before transitioning to sales positions in other **industries**. After moving to a new state, Nina took a job at a quilt shop doing **marketing** and special events. "I had been a quilter since I was 12, so that was a really natural fit," she said.

When her second child was born in the early 2010s, Nina made the difficult decision to exit the workforce. "Quilt shops don't pay a lot of money because the margins are so slim. The cost of daycare for two children basically negated any salary that I would be bringing in." Nina had never planned to be a stay-at-home mother, but had already started The Punny Quilter blog, and she found that blogging was a good fit with her new lifestyle staying at home with two young children.

> Blogging was really flexible because if I don't post this week, it's okay. And if I post [twice] because I have extra time, then it's okay. I didn't have a specific blog schedule. I kept it very freeform in any assignments that I took on. I made sure that they fit within my life. We weren't trying to make an income from [the blog]. It was just some extra money here and there.

Nina took on freelance writing roles for large craft publishers and started a separate general crafts blog, shifting her focus there for several years while her children were young. Though she still maintained The Punny Quilter,

> I found that the sewing and quilting blogging world was harder to break into. I just felt a lot more gatekeeping. There was a craft blogging conference [in the western United States where] you got to physically meet with craft brands and there wasn't a similar opportunity in the sewing and quilting world to get that face time with brands.

At the same time, Nina had an eye towards the future. She knew that "having young children is temporary. My goal was: I'm starting this now so that I can have time to build a really strong, sturdy platform to grow off of."

Evolution of the Punny Quilter

Nina had always planned to continue her education, and when her children were scheduled to have the same drop off and pick up times in elementary school, she thought it would be the perfect opportunity. She enrolled in a graduate program at a nearby university for a Master of Business Administration (MBA) degree with a focus on entrepreneurship. Nina was selling her quilt patterns as digital downloads through a large third-party website that closed its pattern **marketplace**. Rather than give up on selling digital downloads, Nina set a goal to add **e-commerce** to The Punny Quilter website within 12 months. Because of her experience in the quilt shop, Nina also knew the importance of printed paper patterns. She says, "paper patterns are still the **distribution** method of choice if you want to work with **distributors** and shops." Her long-term plan was "to take my five most popular PDF patterns and turn them into printed patterns." After launching The Punny Quilter online shop to sell pattern PDFs, Nina began to grow her pattern **inventory** and track their sales.

Becoming a Notions Inventor

While still in graduate school, Nina continued both blogs, began growing her YouTube channel, and was doing freelance writing and sponsored posts for publishers and brands in the crafts and sewing industries in addition to selling PDF patterns. Her transition to an inventor started as a class project in her graduate degree program. "One of the classes we had was an **ideation** class, and I came up with the idea for this notion." Notions are the tools and accessories – excluding a sewing machine and fabric – used in sewing and quilting. Some examples include needles and threads, marking tools, rulers, and cutting tools (Figure 10.2.1).

Nina continues,

> I didn't have the **manufacturing** background to be able to figure out how to get [the notion] made myself. But I had a friend who I'd met at one of those [craft blogger] conferences who at that point worked for [a large distributor of craft, sewing, and quilting products] that also manufactures a lot of their own notions.

After reaching out to her contact, Nina ended up licensing her notion to that company who handled both manufacturing and distribution to **retailers**.

While Nina was happy with the **licensing agreement** she signed with the company, "looking back, I would make some changes to the contract that I signed. You can only make the best decision you can with the information you have at that time." Her licensing agreement is for "very small" **royalties** on each notion sale. "Any increase in royalty percentage would increase the

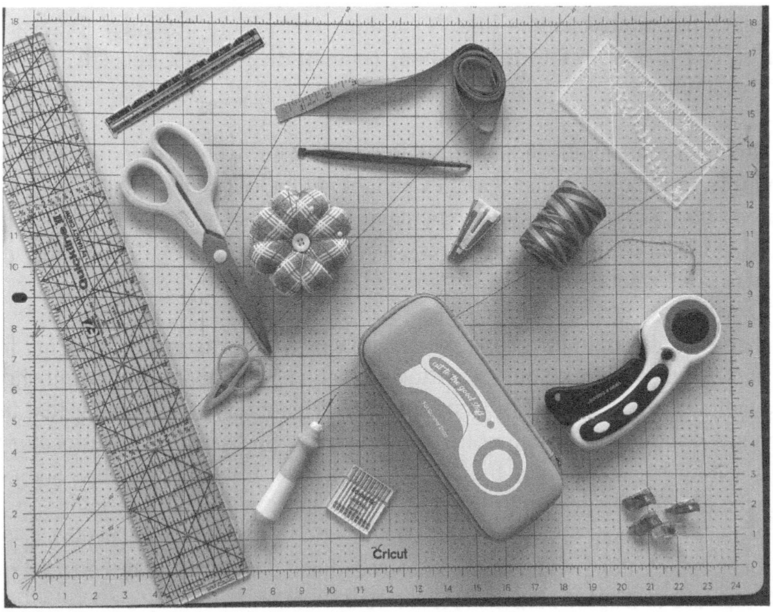

Figure 10.2.1 Quilting and sewing notions, including measuring and cutting tools, pins and clips, thread, needles, a container, and other tools.

Source: Marie Segares

price of the product and then the product wouldn't be sellable," Nina explains, "so that's fine. But [the company has] the license to continue to manufacture and sell the product exclusively until they don't want to anymore." With her experience now, Nina would have negotiated an option for getting the rights back "if sales fall below a certain number." The company does little to market her notion, and Nina ends up doing a lot of **promotion** for it while earning relatively little in exchange. Nina also notes,

> I might have put a time limit on [the agreement so that] after five years the contract gets renegotiated. If the industry changes in a big way, maybe I could renegotiate that royalty percentage. My name is on the product, but my name wasn't as known in the industry then as it is now. So, five years later, maybe having my name on a product is more valuable.

Nina reflects,

> Those are things that I would have changed, but I don't regret signing that contract. That's how you learn. You make leaps and sometimes they work out great and sometimes they don't. This one worked out fine. It wasn't a failure by any stretch.

She comments that with licensing and a "royalty situation, you don't have to send anything out. I didn't have to manufacture, I didn't have to do **fulfillment**. They did all that work." From this first experience as a notions inventor, Nina learned, "I like coming up with an idea and selling someone else the idea and then getting checks in the mail every month."

Launching from Her "Strong, Sturdy Platform"

Nina's slow work of building a platform for The Punny Quilter began to pay off when she was ready to launch her printed pattern line. "One thing that pattern designers forget when you're looking at selling [patterns] into [quilt] shops [is that] distributors, honestly, don't care what they sell," Nina reflects.

> Distributors only care about demand from the shops. They want to carry what the shops want. The shops have some aesthetics that they're looking for, but shops want to sell what customers want to buy. So, in order to drive demand from shops and from distributors, really you just need to create demand in **consumers**. Then, the rest of that will take care of itself. So, I wanted to create that demand.

To launch her printed pattern line, Nina set up a giveaway on Instagram, asking her followers to share the name of their favorite quilt shop to enter. Nina generated a list of quilt shops that her most engaged fans loved. Nina then went onto the website for the distributor that licensed her first notion and would be distributing her print patterns. She used the store locator to identify quilt shops selling her notion near the 25 largest cities in the United States. She added those retailers to the ones named by her followers to create a list of 200 quilt shops.

When Nina placed her first print order of her most popular quilt patterns, she ordered 200 additional copies along with branded letterhead and envelopes, and the small plastic bags that quilt shops use to display patterns (Figure 10.2.2). Nina explains,

> I sent the shops a letter saying, 'One of my followers on Instagram says that you're their favorite quilt shop. And, since they follow me and they're a fan of yours, I thought that would be a good

Figure 10.2.2 Paper quilt patterns are typically printed on letter paper, folded in half, and packaged in clear plastic bags. Quilt shops display patterns on hooks on peg boards or in shelves on rotating literature stands.

Source: Marie Segares

> connection.' Or, 'because you already sell [my notion]....' I sent them the letter along with actual physical copies of the pattern. Having worked in a quilt shop, I know that [shops] worry about the actual quality. They could look through it and see if it was a well written pattern. In [the letter], I said, 'If this [pattern] isn't a good fit for you and you don't want to order them, feel free to give these to an employee or use them in a giveaway,' Because the worst thing for me would be for [the patterns] to end up in the trash, or even for them to sit on that shop owner's desk. I want them to go into circulation somehow because that'll be a secondary chance.

Before sending these letters and samples to the quilt shops, Nina "looked at how much it was going to cost and I said, 'I want to make this money back in three months.'" Although Nina encouraged the shops to buy her patterns through her distributor – thereby decreasing her earnings on each unit – she was able to make back the money from her marketing activities within one month. An added benefit was that her reputation with the distributor was enhanced "because, 'Wow, she's a brand new designer and she's moving product.'"

Nina soon came up with an idea for her next notion, a specialized acrylic ruler, and she went back to her distributor to see if they would be interested in licensing her latest invention. Nina's contact was now less popular within the company, and her pitch to the committee about the new product was rejected. When Nina's contact left the distributor soon after, her replacement saw the proposal and asked Nina if she could "pitch it to the committee again." Nina agreed, thinking, "I've got nothing to lose, [but] the committee said, 'We already said no to this.'" Nonetheless, her new contact advised Nina not to abandon the product, saying "This is a cool idea. I really think that you should move forward with it and figure out how to make it yourself."

Journey to Manufacturing

Inspired by that feedback, Nina sought out other people she had met at events who had designed acrylic rulers. "I didn't know them well," Nina said, but she asked each one, "Could you give me 10 minutes of your time and let me know what I should know and where do you get it manufactured?" She spoke to about six different people, including some who were referred by others she spoke with. Reflecting back on those exploratory conversations, Nina notes,

> If you hadn't called them, you wouldn't have the information. So, you've got nothing to lose. There's a lot of really, really nice, generous people. There were people who would offer to help me in different ways. It's like, 'If you have any more questions, give me a call,' and 'I'm happy to put in a good word for you.'

From these conversations, Nina narrowed her options down to a list of "three different potential manufacturers. Two of them got back to me with quotes. One was significantly cheaper than the other. And, so that's what I went with."

The first step was for this manufacturer to create **prototypes** for Nina. Prototypes are samples that can be further iterated on to develop the final product. Nina remembers that "it was like $300 for prototyping, and that was a lot of money for me." Once she was satisfied with the product, Nina had to decide how many rulers to include in her initial order. Nina considered the balance between the total cost and the **economies of scale**. For the total costs, she weighed "how much money I was willing to invest," since, at the time, her business was entirely **self-funded**. Nina asked herself, "Is it worth the extra risk to buy a thousand because I'm going to save, let's say 47 cents per unit, but it's going to cost me $3,000 more total?" Nina decided to place her first order for 500 rulers. At the time, Nina was running a business from the small home she shared with her husband and two children. Nina remembers,

> I had no concept of how much space 500 rulers was going to take. So, I ordered them. They came in. It was the biggest check that I'd ever written up until that point. And, they sold out in less than two weeks.

Since these first successful product launches, Nina has continued to introduce two to three new notions products each year, develop more patterns, and grow her platform.

From Hobby to Business

Looking back, Nina describes The Punny Quilter as

> more a hobby at the beginning and now it's an actual business. And, the difference between hobby and business is the expectation of bringing in money. To me, if you lose money at a hobby, you don't care. If you make a little bit [of money] at a hobby, it's like, 'Oh, that was nice. I've got fun money.' If a business loses money, there's a problem. You have an expectation and goals of how much money the business needs to bring in.

As she continues to develop The Punny Quilter, Nina has stepped away from her craft blog and is considering selling it. She has experimented with different ways to **finance** manufacturing, including **business loans** and **pre-orders**. Nina moved The Punny Quilter to its own office space which allows her to keep more inventory on site, more easily manage fulfillment, and establish a more functional set up for filming videos and photographing products. "But," she notes, "now the business needs to make enough to pay the rent on space. As your business grows, the risk of what you have to consider gets bigger as well." Thinking back, Nina comments that

> as creatives, if you can – especially early on – not count on the business, that makes it easier for you to take risks. Now I've taken enough risks, I feel comfortable taking the risks. They feel less risky because really risk is that area between what you know and what you don't know. The more experience you have, the more you're able to close that gap of what you don't know.

Case Concepts, Reflections, and Resources

Concepts

- Breakeven analysis (Chapter 6)
- Economies of scale (Chapter 3)
- Effectuation (Chapter 1)
- Manufacturing (Chapter 8)
- Prototyping (Chapter 4)
- Target markets (Chapter 4)
- Unit economics (Chapter 7)

Reflection Questions

1 Nina initially turned to manufacturing when she had difficulty licensing a product with her preferred distributor. If you had a product concept, would licensing or manufacturing work better for your business? Why? (You can find more information about licensing and manufacturing in Chapter 8 and the Further Readings and Viewings for Case 10.1 and Case 10.3.)
2 Nina shared the lessons she learned from signing her first licensing agreement. Have you signed any agreements for your creative venture? How do you decide if an agreement or contract is beneficial for you?
3 Nina's plan for launching her paper patterns in quilt shops was very successful. Are there elements of her product launch marketing plan that you could adapt for your own venture? How?
4 Nina weighed the balance between total costs and economies of scale when making her first product order with the manufacturer. Research something you would order in bulk. You can look at wholesale options for supplies you use regularly, or visit a site like Alibaba.com to explore manufacturing options. How would you determine which volume makes the most sense for your business at this point in time? When would you know when your business is ready to order at the next higher volume?
5 Nina conducts a **breakeven analysis** (described in Chapter 6) before each major expenditure for her business and sets a target timeline for earning back the investment. For example, she expected to earn back the costs associated with her print pattern launch in three months. Do you conduct breakeven analyses for your business? If yes, what information have you learned that helps you with planning? If not, conduct a breakeven analysis for a major expense for your business. Estimate how long it will take to earn the funds back.

Additional Resources

Nina's case is confidential at her request. She discussed several business events during her interview that may be helpful for your creative business. You can find these and other helpful organizations listed in Appendix B.

Further Reading

Agreements and Contracts

Shores, A. (2025, July 19). Contracts for creatives: What you actually need and where to get them. *Our Arts Magazine*. https://ourartsmagazine.com/blog/contracts-for-creatives-what-you-actually-need-and-where-to-get-them/

Stahle, K. (n.d.). How to write a contract for your creative business. *The Artist's J.D.* https://theartistsjd.com/drafting-contracts-for-creatives/

Prototyping

Interaction Design Foundation. (n.d.) Prototypes. *Interaction Design Foundation*. https://www.interaction-design.org/literature/topics/prototypes

Shopify. (2025, July 8). How to get a prototype made and protect your design. *Shopify*. https://www.shopify.com/blog/7076768-tim-ferriss-on-manufacturing-and-prototyping-a-product

Trade Shows

Key, S. (2015, February 10). 13 tips for getting the most out of trade shows. *Inc*. https://www.inc.com/stephen-key/how-to-get-the-most-out-of-attending-a-trade-show.html

Nichols, J. (n.d.) Trade show success: Insider tips for attendees without a booth. *Julie Nichols Marketing*. https://www.julienicholsmarketing.com/blog/trade-show-attendee

Case 10.3 Cognitive Surplus: From Apartment-Based to 36,000 ft^2 Warehouse, Distribution Center, and Retail Store

Maker Profile

Although Geoff Zephyrus earned a Bachelor of Fine Arts degree at the Massachusetts College of Art and Design, he initially planned to study business because he dreamed of launching his own company. After graduating, Geoff worked at startups, attended entrepreneurship meetups, and continued dreaming of one day starting his own business, while his then girlfriend, Kristen, worked in film and television post-production. Eventually, Kristen "just got so sick and tired of hearing [Geoff] talk" about starting a business that she gave him an ultimatum: he would have to start a business based on his next idea. Geoff remembers, "I had this idea of doing screen printed wrapping paper or making wrapping paper out of figure illustrations. I'd seen how to screen print, but I'd never actually taken a class." Kristen told him, "You have to buy materials right now. You have to make steps, you have to commit yourself." While considering the type of designs to focus on, Kristen mentioned to Geoff that it was difficult to buy science gifts for her mother, a teacher, and her father, a doctor. Geoff recalls Kristen telling him "'it'd be cool if we did science stuff. And, if you do it science themed, I'll somewhat help you.'" Geoff decided "that's as good an idea as any. Constraint is helpful."

Figure 10.3.1 Geoff and Kristen Zephyrus, founders of Cognitive Surplus.

Source: Courtesy of Geoff and Kristen Zephyrus/Cognitive Surplus

Geoff had studied **startups** for years, and he knew that as many as one in five in the United States fail in the first year. Knowing this was liberating; as Geoff notes,

> we heard that even if you fail, your second startup is more likely to be successful. There's really no reason not to fail. Get that first failure out of the way as quickly as possible. That's the attitude we approached [starting the business] with: 'we'll just do this, but obviously it's going to fail. We have no idea what we're doing and it's not going to work, so we'll just keep doing it until it's clearly died, and then we'll move on to some other idea.' But we just kind of kept doing it, and it didn't really fail.

The Early Days at Cognitive Surplus

With the idea they could fail faster if they just started a business, Geoff and Kristen launched Cognitive Surplus in 2013 from their small New York City apartment. Geoff worked full-time in the business from home, designing and screen-printing all of their **products**, while Kristen continued working externally to fund their startup. Their plan was to eventually **outsource production** with Geoff continuing to focus on design (Figure 10.3.2).

Geoff explains,

> We knew at the beginning that we weren't going to be the best at making things because it's not my background. The vision was to try and create a Target-sized store of science products where it's this whole lifestyle store where you could get everything from curtains to glassware, t-shirts and notebooks – all science themed, a whole brand specifically for scientists and science enthusiasts.

(Target, one of the largest retailers in the United States – with stores in every state and the District of Columbia – operates hypermarkets combining supermarket and department store features.)

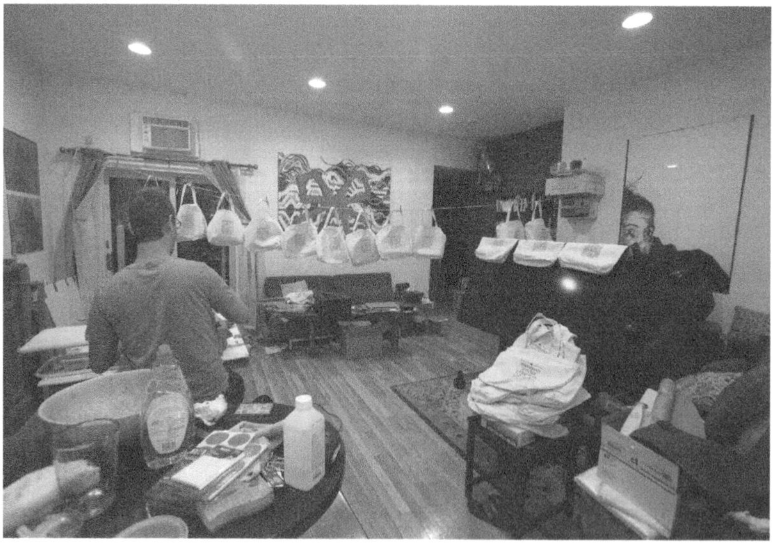

Figure 10.3.2 Geoff screenprinting bags in their New York City apartment, circa 2013.

Source: Courtesy of Geoff and Kristen Zephyrus/Cognitive Surplus

Cognitive Surplus launched a website and vended at in-person markets from the start. While initially their "policy was just say 'yes' to everything," eventually the couple realized that they should focus their vending efforts on venues that were a better fit for their products, such as **wholesale markets** like NY NOW (nynow.com), established craft events like Renegade Craft (www.renegadecraft.com), and **trade shows** for the health care and science community. After a year and half, Geoff and Kristen found that the business was outgrowing their apartment and they moved to a larger place in New Jersey, continuing to produce everything in-house and launching an Etsy shop.

Expanding and Experimenting with Outsourcing

Since each **product line** included variations across many scientific disciplines (such as astronomy, biology, medicine, physics, or psychology), Cognitive Surplus was limited to working with **manufacturers** that offered low minimums in its early years. Initially, Cognitive Surplus worked with a company in the United States to produce glassware with Geoff screenprinting the boxes "because we couldn't afford large enough runs of packaging." After buying notebook blanks with binding they didn't like and with Geoff's screenprinted covers not being "high **quality** enough" for their own standards, Cognitive Surplus decided it was time to expand into overseas manufacturing. Through Alibaba – a **publicly traded** multinational company with an online **business-to-business** platform to connect manufacturers, **suppliers**, **exporters**, **importers**, **buyers**, and wholesalers – they identified a Chinese manufacturer to produce notebooks. While Geoff and Kristen were satisfied with the quality of their first order, there was a learning curve. "We didn't understand the difference between pages and sheets. Our first notebook order went in and we got half the number of pages that we wanted," Geoff explains. While Geoff describes himself as "a perfectionist," Kristen is much more focused on action, so they agreed to sell the notebooks as is. "And, [the notebooks] sold, and then we were able to fix it for the next order," Geoff notes.

Geoff was fulfilling orders every morning to ship out, and gradually was making fewer products by hand and ordering more from manufacturers. As their **product mix** expanded, Cognitive Surplus began to pick up wholesale **customers** and outgrew their space in New Jersey. By 2015, they had to decide whether to move to a larger home office or to try another option.

A friend recommended a **third-party logistics (3PL)** company in Chicago, Illinois. 3PL companies handle **fulfillment** services for other businesses including **warehousing**, picking orders (retrieving items from the warehouse and preparing for shipment) and shipping. Kristen and Geoff decided to hire this 3PL company to do their product fulfillment and sent all of their **inventory** to Chicago while moving their home to Portland, Oregon. Although initially planning to find a job in Portland, Kristen realized, "I had always been paying the bills, and we looked down and suddenly the company was able to pay the bills." Kristen began working for Cognitive Surplus full-time.

Expansion Challenges and Opportunities

As Cognitive Surplus expanded, they outgrew some of their partners. Within seven months of moving to Portland, Kristen and Geoff learned the 3PL company had hundreds of their orders outstanding and would not be able to ship in time for Christmas. The 3PL company prioritized a larger customer with even more outstanding orders. As approximately 50% of their **revenue** was made from orders placed in the last two months of the year, Geoff and Kristen decided to fly to Chicago, pick and pack their own orders, and fire the 3PL company. After this experience,

Figure 10.3.3 The first Cognitive Surplus warehouse in Medford, Oregon.

Source: Courtesy of Geoff and Kristen Zephyrus/Cognitive Surplus

Cognitive Surplus was ready for a different fulfillment solution. A friend suggested they hire her husband to do fulfillment, and Cognitive Surplus had all inventory shipped to a rented warehouse in Medford, Oregon, five hours south of their home (Figure 10.3.3).

Kristen and Geoff spent a month training their first employee. Geoff describes the transition from 3PL to managing their own fulfillment as a critical one for Cognitive Surplus.

> [It] allows us to have a lot more control over how we fulfill our products, how we store our stuff, just making sure that we can have a good customer service experience. Because if something's wrong with an order, it's our company. We can make sure the problem's dealt with immediately.

Similarly, Cognitive Surplus expanded faster than some of their manufacturers' capabilities. This would sometimes result in receiving poor-quality products or unexpected changes in payment terms. Nevertheless, as Cognitive Surplus grew, Kristen notes that

> we were able to meet the minimums of better companies and the better companies had better quality and better practices. We've really been able to find far stronger manufacturing partners who we really, really like. But that process took some time.

In addition to Alibaba, Cognitive Surplus has found manufacturing partners through trade shows and recommendations from other businesses.

Within two years, Cognitive Surplus had outgrown their Medford warehouse, was storing some products in a separate location, and the ten-hour round-trip was getting challenging. In 2018, Cognitive Surplus moved to a larger warehouse in Portland, Oregon, but soon, even that space was bursting at the seams. In 2020, Cognitive Surplus used a **Small Business Administration** loan to purchase a 36,000 square foot warehouse in Redmond, Oregon. The United

Figure 10.3.4 Shelving being installed at the Redmond, Oregon warehouse of Cognitive Surplus.

Source: Courtesy of Geoff and Kristen Zephyrus/Cognitive Surplus

Figure 10.3.5 The Cognitive Surplus retail shop in Redmond, Oregon.

Source: Courtesy of Geoff and Kristen Zephyrus/Cognitive Surplus

States Small Business Administration (www.sba.gov) is a federal agency that supports small businesses and entrepreneurs through a variety of services, including lending programs and Small Business Development Centers in each state (Figure 10.3.4).

In 2021, Cognitive Surplus established an international warehouse partner in the Netherlands to make shipping within Europe and the rest of the world easier and more affordable. In 2024, they opened a retail shop in downtown Redmond (Figure 10.3.5).

Cognitive Surplus currently has 20 employees, with Geoff serving as the chief designer and Kristen as the chief executive officer. Cognitive Surplus is an inclusive workplace and has been recognized for providing employment opportunities for people with disabilities.

Analyzing Success at Cognitive Surplus

Geoff and Kristen highlight several factors that have contributed to their long-term success, including **self-funding**, **focus strategy** and **branding**, **pricing**, and role clarity.

Self-funding. Other than the low-interest loan for their warehouse, the business operates without **debt**. Kristen states,

> My philosophy of business is that I do not like debt. The entire business has been cash-based from the very beginning. I financed it to start with, by supporting [Geoff] and supporting [our] rent. We always fold the profits back in. If we can't produce something and then sell it profitably to start, we don't do it. We've been able to grow really quickly, which was awesome. But then also, we didn't ever have the drag of debt behind us.

Focus strategy and branding. Cognitive Surplus focuses on an underserved, niche market by making "scientifically accurate" products that "really celebrate science and math and engineering." Kristen notes their customers have been "very forgiving [because] no one had ever seen some of this stuff on a notebook or on a bag before." This has allowed Cognitive Surplus to make incremental improvements in quality for their loyal audience while avoiding competing in a general market.

As Kristen shares, by "making that commitment from the very beginning to making the highest quality product that we could with the resources that we had, and making things as sustainably as we could," Cognitive Surplus has built their reputation with retailers and distributors, as well as with consumers.

Pricing. Over the years, Kristen has found that a markup based on the **landed cost** works best for Cognitive Surplus. Landed cost is the expenditure that the product has incurred from its origination until it arrives at the company, including manufacturing costs, shipping or transportation costs, and insurance and customs fees. Using a markup of eight times the landed costs to establish the retail price has allowed Cognitive Surplus to "run profitably" and be able to pay for costs throughout the supply chain including their distribution and warehousing partners and retail markups.

Role clarity. While in the earlier stages of the business, everyone was expected to "put on eight different hats," Kristen is proud to report that now

> we've been able to solidify everyone into the roles that they did best. Everyone has a single title. We have very defined roles, and that's been a completely wonderful experience. Finally, getting to give people actual titles where they're able to do one thing that they're excellent at, rather than trying to cross-train everyone and hope everyone's really awesome at lots of different things, which is not as typical.

This also allows Geoff more time for designing while Kristen can focus on "the numbers" and being the "problem solver" as CEO.

Tips from Cognitive Surplus for Emerging Creative Entrepreneurs

- "Just shut up and do it," advises Geoff. In other words, get your business started. If you struggle with perfectionism, Geoff recommends that you "do the best job you can on a timer, get [the product] out, and then do a revision." You can make incremental improvements and changes as you go along.

- "Always do the math. Make sure your choices are profitable," Kristen says. She reminds entrepreneurs to consider all of their costs, including less visible **fixed costs** and **variable costs** like web hosting and electricity.

Case Concepts, Reflections, and Resources

Concepts

- Branding (Chapter 5)
- Effectuation (Chapter 1)
- Focus strategy and growth strategy (Chapter 3)
- Funding through self-funding and business loans (Chapter 7)
- Operations management (Chapter 8)
- Pricing (Chapter 6)

Reflection Questions

1. When Geoff and Kristen founded Cognitive Surplus, they assumed it might fail but instead it has expanded into an international company with 20 employees. What did Geoff and Kristen learn during their business journey that could be helpful to you and your business?
2. Geoff and Kristen described their trial-and-error process of learning about manufacturing and finding manufacturing partners in the United States and abroad. They have found partners through Alibaba, referrals from their network, and through trade shows. If you were to manufacture a product, how would you research the options available to you?
3. Geoff and Kristen's first experience with a third-party logistics company didn't go well, but many entrepreneurs have successful collaborations with 3PL partners. Would 3PL work for your venture? Why or why not?
4. Kristen feels that self-funding contributed to the success of Cognitive Surplus. Which of the approaches to financing outlined in Chapter 7 (self-funding, friends and family, grants, crowdfunding, investor funding, and debt) make sense for your venture now? Which might you consider using in the future?
5. Based on their experience, the team at Cognitive Surplus now uses a formula of 8 x [Landed Cost] to determine the retail price for their products. This allows them to earn profit on items they wholesale as well as on items they sell **direct-to-consumer**. What is your approach to pricing for your venture? Are there alternative approaches to pricing you might consider using in the future?

Additional Resources

The Cognitive Surplus website (cognitive-surplus.com) is their primary home online. Cognitive Surplus also operates an Etsy shop (www.etsy.com/shop/CognitiveSurplus).

Further Reading and Viewing

Funding with Bootstrapping and Business Loans

Anthony, L. (2024, April 22). Bootstrapping: Definition and pros and cons. *Nerd Wallet.* https://www.nerdwallet.com/article/small-business/bootstrapping

Webber, M.R. (2024, August 19). How do business loans work. *Investopedia.* https://www.investopedia.com/how-do-business-loans-work-7550170

Manufacturing Partnerships

First Citizens Bank. (2021, April 15). How to have a successful business partnership with your manufacturer. *First Citizens Bank.* https://www.firstcitizens.com/commercial/insights/finance/business-partnership-with-your-manufacturer

Graham, V. (2016, April 12). Small batch manufacturing: Dream big, think small. *Craft Industry Alliance.* https://craftindustryalliance.org/small-batch-manufacturing-dream-big-stay-small/

Wholesale Markets and Trade Shows

Tory Burch Foundation. (2023, August 23). Trade show tips for small businesses [Video]. YouTube. https://youtu.be/EyyFxGofWyY

Vertical Ledge. (n.d.). Mastering wholesale trade shows: A comprehensive guide. *Vertical Ledge.* https://verticalledge.com/blogs/news/mastering-wholesale-trade-shows-a-comprehensive-guide

Case 10.4 Exalting in Beauty: From Necessity Entrepreneur to the Entrepreneurial Pivot

Maker Profile

After high school, Aaliyah Taylor went to college in Tennessee for graphic design, but transferred to a school in Atlanta, Georgia to study fashion design after a year "because that's where my heart was." Unfortunately, that school soon closed and Aaliyah decided to "take a step back from art school." While working in retail, she was looking for ways to "keep my creativity going," and she turned to Perler beads: small, colorful beads that can be fused with heat from an iron (Figure 10.4.1).

Introduced to Perler beads as a child, Aaliyah had several sets purchased while in art school in her apartment, and she became curious about whether she could use them to make jewelry. Her experiments "led me to realize that I love making things and if I can make this into a business, I would not mind it."

Introduction to Exalting in Beauty

In 2013, Aaliyah began Exalting in Beauty as a **side hustle**, selling her unique handmade Perler bead jewelry creations at hair salons and barbershops in Atlanta (Figure 10.4.2).

Initially,

> everything was $10 no matter how extravagant the design was. I was selling the pieces because of the current financial situation that me and my mom were in. I was **pricing** them at a point that I know people won't turn away from it [to make money quickly].

Figure 10.4.1 Perler beads, tweezers, and pegboards.

Source: Marie Segares

Figure 10.4.2 The Exalting in Beauty logo.

Source: Courtesy of Aaliyah Taylor/Exalting in Beauty

Figure 10.4.3 Several Exalting in Beauty jewelry designs made with Perler beads.

Source: Courtesy of Aaliyah Taylor/Exalting in Beauty

Aaliyah didn't have business cards and she didn't focus on developing recurring customers – though she did gather a few. She opened a small online shop using the free Storenvy platform.

Aaliyah moved back to Birmingham, Alabama in 2015, continuing to work in retail, and transitioned her creative practice to painting on wood … but, she kept being drawn back to the Perler beads. Aaliyah had "a big box of thousands and thousands of beads. I hate being wasteful. I was just like, 'I can't just let you sit here and collect dust.'" Aaliyah continued to create Perler bead jewelry, setting up an Etsy shop and starting to sell on Instagram (Figure 10.4.3).

The creative scene in Birmingham was growing, and in 2017, Aaliyah was invited to vend at the Woodlawn Street Market (now the Woodlawn Marketplace). Aaliyah recalls, "It wasn't until then I realized how serious this business can be, because I kept looking at it still as a hobby, or as a quick fix for those financial dire situations."

Connecting with Supports for Entrepreneurs

From 2017 to 2019, Aaliyah started learning more about running a business. She worked with REV Birmingham, a **non-profit**, local **economic development organization**. When Nest, a non-profit organization that provides education and resources for artisans around the world, launched its Makers United program in Birmingham, Aaliyah and her mother, who is also an artist, were active participants. Aaliyah began to be "mindful of how to take the pictures, making sure that people are seeing the craftsmanship" for her Etsy listings. Aaliyah also made limited edition pieces, created business cards, and started building a stronger social media presence.

Building Community Leads to Expansion

By 2020, Aaliyah was working full time as a children's librarian. As the COVID pandemic emerged, it was unclear whether she would be able to keep her job. Aaliyah reflects,

> even though it was such a dark time for our nation and our world, I had to take a moment and sit down and say, 'Okay, you have this gift. You've done pretty well so far on Etsy, why not take it serious?'

Aaliyah continued to focus on Exalting in Beauty, taking webinars offered by Etsy, REV Birmingham, and Create Birmingham. While attending a book reading by her favorite author, Aaliyah felt moved to give her some jewelry. When the author posted pictures wearing the earrings on social media the next day, Aaliyah's Etsy shop quickly sold out. "Even in a dark moment, I was realizing, the time you put on your social media, this actually has worked," Aaliyah remembers.

As a Black creator, Aaliyah started getting approached by companies online as they launched or strengthened their diversity, equity, and inclusion (DEI) efforts in response to the growing Black Lives Matter movement in the United States. In October 2020, Aaliyah was one of 20 Black women creators selected by JOANN for its first annual Minority Creative Grant program. (JOANN was a specialty arts and crafts retail chain founded in 1943 with over 800 stores in the United States. After filing for bankruptcy twice within 12 months, the company **liquidated**, with all of its stores closing by May 2025.) With her prize of $5,000 in JOANN gift cards, Aaliyah focused on getting equipment that she might need in the future, such as an electronic cutting machine, an upgraded sewing machine and sewing table, and a serger. Soon after,

> Perler reached out to me on Instagram to just say, 'Congratulations.' They wanted to send me a big box of Perler beads, and I was like, 'Yes! I waited years for you guys, I feel like y'all were never going to notice me.'

Soon after, Perler's parent company reached out to Aaliyah via email, inviting her to collaborate on a jewelry kit. Perler identified three designs from Aaliyah's jewelry collection to license in exchange for **royalties** from kit sales. The kit launched in 2022 with a two-year **licensing agreement** and was sold through Perler's website and craft and general retailers (Figure 10.4.4).

Besides Aaliyah's initial investment of her Perler bead inventory in 2013, Exalting in Beauty financed much of its growth through **grants**. In addition to the JOANN Minority Creative Grant program, Aaliyah has been a recipient of funds from Nest's Makers Future Fund, the Tory Burch Foundation Fund, and the Fearless Fund. Her website was built for free as part of a prize package she won through Magic City Fashion Week. Aaliyah has also used grant funds to purchase supplies, equipment, and technology.

Figure 10.4.4 Perler licensed several of Aaliyah's designs for use in a fused bead jewelry kit with 2,467 pieces including beads, pegboards, studs with clasps, fish hook and kidney hook wires, jump rings, tweezers, an adhesive sheet, a pattern sheet with instructions, and ironing paper.

Source: Courtesy of Aaliyah Taylor/Exalting in Beauty and Perler

Aaliyah shares,

> I always tell people at the highest height of my business, I was in the lowest point of my life. I'm open to share that story. Me and my mom were practically homeless. We were living in a hotel room.

Through funds from her licensing agreement, online and market sales, and grant funds, Aaliyah was able to secure an apartment, get a car, and set up an emergency fund and savings for her business.

The Future of Exalting in Beauty

Exalting in Beauty is a part-time venture for Aaliyah, who is back to working full-time as a children's librarian. While Aaliyah intentionally takes a break from social media and Exalting in Beauty every January and February to "reset my business so that I can do my **taxes** and get prepared for the upcoming season," in 2023, Aaliyah paused the business completely. She says,

> I didn't create anything, only did things for me like crochet. I did everything [creatively] that did not require me to sell, just because I was burnt out from 2022. A lot of great things happened, but it was overwhelming. That was where my business got a bit too successful, but I wasn't in the mindset to handle that success.

Currently, Aaliyah is considering "**scal[ing]** my business into creating slow fashion designs for mid-size or plus-size women." She is active in different online and local artisan and fashion collectives and continues learning from programs for entrepreneurs, such as CO.STARTERS. As she thinks about her future clothing line, Aaliyah notes, "I have to be honest with myself about pricing. I'm coming from in 2013, selling jewelry that should have been priced \$50 to \$70 for \$10. And, so I struggle with pricing what it's worth." Aaliyah is currently selling commissioned custom clothing designs, creating **prototype** garments while calculating the **process time** and materials **costs** required, sharing her slow fashion makes on social media, and

Figure 10.4.5 A slow fashion design by Aaliyah at a fashion show.

Source: Courtesy of Aaliyah Taylor/Exalting in Beauty

continuing the conversations with her network about how to **position** and price her fashion pieces (Figure 10.4.5).

As Aaliyah reflects on the retracting of DEI programs for entrepreneurs in the United States, she notes

> There's so many stats of how difficult it is for Black-owned businesses specifically to receive any type of **capital**, any type of **investment**. Already you have this inherent feeling that 'I have to prove myself.' Now the pressure and burden of that is going to be 10 times more felt. We're going to have to be burdened to make sure we are seen. We are deserving of inclusion.

At the same time, she is not surprised to see the support for DEI diminishing. "Unfortunately, in a capitalist, consumer-based society, a lot of us are so **trend** focused." After the initial interest in supporting minority-owned businesses, "it gets quieter."

While previously, Aaliyah relied on community referrals for grant funding, she is now "intentional of applying for grants where I'm not relying on relationships." She is doing this to stretch herself as part of her **entrepreneurial pivot** of Exalting in Beauty, because DEI programs in the United States are shrinking in the current political climate, and "because the [funders] that I did rely on, they're giving other people a chance. I don't want to be out there just repeating the same thing and not allowing someone else to do it." Aaliyah has found that tailoring her pitch to different grant proposals has tightened her ability to "articulate who I am, who my brand is, and also where my business is going."

Aaliyah is trying to challenge herself in other ways, too. She notes, "sometimes as a business owner, I get a little too comfortable with the familiarity. I deal with not liking change and not pivoting when I should pivot." In the past, she has relied on gentle prodding from her network to push her business forward by vending at larger or more reputable markets or by applying for grants. Now that she has begun to save money from her grants and business earnings, "I feel like I'm ready to grow and scale my business. I would now have enough money to take those risks and not be in such a loss."

Case Concepts, Reflections, and Resources

Concepts

- Entrepreneurial pivot (Chapter 1)
- Funding through self-funding and grants (Chapter 7)
- Necessity entrepreneurship (Chapter 1)
- Networking (Chapter 9)
- Pricing (Chapter 6)

Reflection Questions

1 Aaliyah has developed relationships with local and international **entrepreneur support organizations** to receive free training, coaching, opportunity matching, and grant funding. Which entrepreneurship support organizations are you connected with? Research and identify at least two local, regional, national, or worldwide organizations that you haven't yet connected with that offer services, **networking** opportunities, or events that would be valuable for your business.

2 Aaliyah has begun an entrepreneurial pivot from jewelry into fashion, even though that required moving outside of her comfort zone and managing change. What is your approach to change for your business? Are there changes or pivots that you are proud of? Are there changes or pivots that you have avoided? What did Aaliyah learn about pivoting from her journey that might be useful for your business?
3 Aaliyah shared her struggles with pricing her work. Which **pricing objectives** outlined in Chapter 6 did you observe Aaliyah using during her journey? Is there anything from Aaliyah's learnings about pricing that could be helpful to your business?
4 Aaliyah takes an intentional break from social media each year to reset creatively and to focus on administrative matters such as filing taxes. Are there parts of your business you put on hold or scale back temporarily to refresh? If so, how has it worked for your business? If not, is this something you could plan for?
5 Aaliyah has been awarded grant funding from various sources to support the expansion of Exalting in Beauty. These grants have included cash, services, and products or gift cards. Aaliyah noted that applying for grants has helped her to describe her business concisely. How might you use grant funding for your business today or in the future? Find a grant application (current or expired) that is relevant to your business and review it. Draft one or more sections to explore how you might articulate your needs and your **venture**. What did you learn from this process that could be helpful for your business?

Additional Resources

Exalting in Beauty can be found on its website (exaltinginbeauty.com).

Aaliyah has received grant funding from national and international organizations including the Nest's Makers Future Fund, the Tory Burch Foundation, and the Fearless Fund. More information about these organizations can be found in Appendix B.

Further Reading and Viewing

Emergency Savings for Business

Bortner, G. (2025, September 2). Building financial stability in uncertain times. *Craft Industry Alliance*. https://craftindustryalliance.org/building-financial-stability-in-uncertain-times/

Tara Wagner Coaching. (2021, November 2). How to build a small business savings account/emergency fund [Video]. YouTube. https://youtu.be/PBUWkalPpuU

Entrepreneurial Pivot

TEDx Talks. (2013, October 2). The power of entrepreneurial pivoting: Steve Rogers at TEDxUNPlaza [Video]. YouTube. https://youtu.be/s3xcJptA9_g

Wayra Telefónica. (n.d.). In the face of change: An entrepreneur's guide to startup pivots. *Wayra Telefónica*. https://www.wayra.de/blog/pivot-startup

Funding with Grants

OpenGrants. (2025, January 24). How to apply for a grant for small business: A step-by-step guide. *OpenGrants*. https://opengrants.io/how-to-apply-for-a-grant-for-small-business-a-step-by-step-guide/

U.S. Chamber of Commerce. (2025, August 28). 100+ grants, loans, and programs to benefit your small business. *CO–U.S. Chamber of Commerce*. https://www.uschamber.com/co/run/business-financing/small-business-grants-and-programs

Case 10.5 Elizabeth Caven: A Tech Startup in the Sewing Industry

Maker Profile

Elizabeth Caven is "an entrepreneur by background. I was one of those kids that had profitable lemonade stands." After graduating from college, she worked for a **startup** which was soon acquired by a **publicly traded** company. She didn't enjoy working for the slower paced larger company and realized that startups and entrepreneurial environments were a better fit for her. At 24, Elizabeth started her first business. It **scaled** quickly to 14 employees with multimillion dollars in **revenue** and was later **acquired** (Figure 10.5.1).

When Elizabeth started a family, she wanted to sew for her daughter, just as her mother had made clothes for her. Borrowing a family member's sewing machine, Elizabeth bought a paper sewing pattern from a craft supply store, but

> it was another language that I clearly had not been taught how to speak. I started going down the rabbit holes of all the YouTube videos, trying to find bloggers that were explaining terms

Figure 10.5.1 Elizabeth Caven, founder of UpCraft Club and KITE.

Source: Courtesy of Elizabeth Caven

> and teaching basics on how to sew. The first [project] I tried was a failure, but it was the start of a passion.

Elizabeth was soon blogging about her "Fraken-patterning" experiences of using pieces from multiple patterns to sew unique projects for her kids. At this time, in the early 2010s, paper patterns were still the norm but "indie pattern designers were starting to pop up."

An Introduction to Paper Sewing Patterns

Paper patterns for home sewists are typically sold in packets including the pattern and an instructional pamphlet. Patterns are printed on large-format tissue paper that is folded multiple times to fit into the packet (Figure 10.5.2).

Many patterns include several pages of tissue paper, each with multiple pieces the sewist would use in the final project printed onto the same page. For projects available in multiple sizes – such as clothing and accessories – several sizes are displayed as nested outlines of the same pattern piece. The sewist selects the appropriate size for their intended finished project to follow, cuts out pattern pieces and uses those to trace an outline onto fabric, and then cuts the fabric before assembling it into the sewing project (Figure 10.5.3).

When independent designers began creating patterns for digital download, most were PDF files sized for printing at home on letter paper. These patterns require the home sewist to print and assemble the pattern before use. For larger projects, such as pants, one pattern piece might extend over multiple pages of letter paper, requiring the home sewist to cut parts from multiple pages and tape together to assemble into a single pattern piece. Digital patterns have proliferated in the last decade and are now sold by both indie designers and large companies. Many now have the option to print on letter paper and assemble, or to print on A0 paper – a large-format paper used for architectural blueprints, posters, and maps – that prints on plotters. Some fabric and sewing supply stores have introduced A0 pattern printing as an available service for sewists.

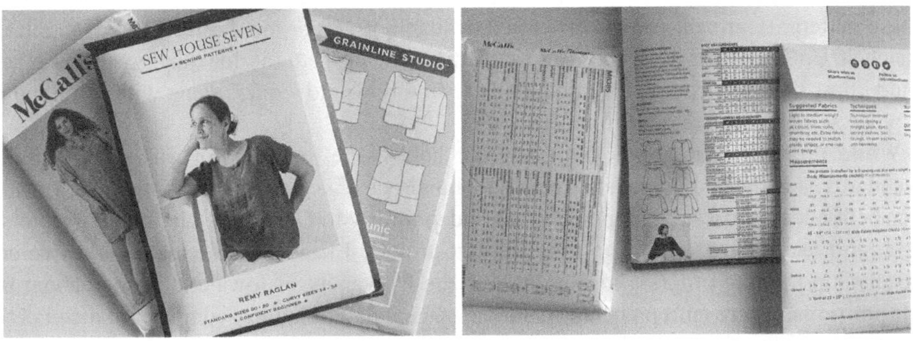

Figure 10.5.2 Paper sewing patterns from three different brands in packets. The front of the packet shows the finished garment or project while the back lists available sizes and required supplies. Sewing and craft supply stores usually display catalogs with numbered pictures of each pattern, while the packets are stored in numbered drawers.

Source: Marie Segares

Figure 10.5.3 Cut out paper sewing pattern pieces are positioned on fabric using pins or pattern weights. The fabric is then cut in the shape of the pieces before assembling by sewing.

Source: Tima Miroshnichenko via Pexels

The Early Days: UpCraft Club

After getting positive feedback from her followers, Elizabeth dipped her toe into pattern design, but discovered there were several challenges. At the time, online **marketplaces** didn't offer instant digital downloads – for example, Etsy sellers had to email the customer the PDF after purchase. There was also a continuum of independent pattern **quality**, as more home sewists like Elizabeth tried their hands at designing patterns. These designers often lacked a background in drafting or in grading, the process of adding additional sizes (larger or smaller) after making a base pattern. (Garment patterns are often available in ten or more sizes.) In 2014, Elizabeth launched UpCraft Club with the idea to "certify sewing patterns for quality so that a sewist could know that they could get a product that actually would work," along with an online marketplace selling certified quality patterns.

While Elizabeth started UpCraft Club as a hobby, she found that it was growing quickly. Eventually, it expanded to include patterns by hundreds of designers from around the world and Elizabeth added subscription options and a video library to UpCraft Club. In an effort to scale faster and learn about options to fund the fast growth, Elizabeth participated in a free entrepreneurship training program locally through the University of Iowa and learned about **pitch competitions**, where entrepreneurs "come on stage, talk about their company in a competition format," and win prizes. Elizabeth entered multiple pitch competitions, winning "seven or eight different competitions and over $100,000" in **seed funding** (Figure 10.5.4).

Solving for Pain Points in the Retail Space

Using some of her winnings, Elizabeth attended a sewing convention and connected with a large sewing product **distributor**. Speaking with a distributor opened her eyes to the impact digital

Figure 10.5.4 Elizabeth pitching UpCraft Club at an event in Peru.

Source: Courtesy of Elizabeth Caven

patterns would have in a brick-and-mortar **retail** setting. "If you're a sewing supply distributor with a digital product, how do you get the physical representation of that in store?" she explains. This conversation was the genesis of Elizabeth's next business concept. She used more competition funds to write and obtain a **patent** for a retail product using near-field communication, a technology that allows short-range communication between two devices that are in physical proximity. Elizabeth developed cards for display in a brick-and-mortar setting with images of the finished projects and a supply list for making the pattern. Sewists could scan a QR code, visit a URL, or tap their phone to purchase and instantly download the pattern. Each store had a unique URL to earn **royalties** for sales generated through their shop. Elizabeth remembers, "Nobody else was doing anything like this to get distribution in physical stores for digital patterns." UpCraft Club had hundreds of patterns at the time, and "it was really thrilling to offer a way that pattern makers could distribute their designs and make a living because they were getting a **revenue-share** of all the patterns" that were sold offline.

Scaling Up as a Tech Company

By 2015, Elizabeth was "learning more about **venture capital** and the idea that you could take an investment" in your company in exchange for **shares** of **equity**. She was able to connect with 500 Startups (now 500 Global), a startup **accelerator** program and early-state venture capital fund. The challenge for Elizabeth was that "when people would hear that you're building [a business] in sewing, they thought about it as being old fashioned – and a small **market**." She wanted to enter the sewing industry from a tech perspective because the sewing "market is large enough to support a really big company. I set out to build a billion-dollar company in the space."

Elizabeth realized that her pattern card idea shared some of the challenges facing printed patterns, but also that "it was really hard to sell [to retail customers at a trade show] because people spend their money, but they leave with nothing [but] an email." Elizabeth decided to go "back to basics" and imagine, "if I was going to create sewing patterns today – invent them – how would they function?" She knew that working with the paper pattern "is nobody's favorite part of what they're doing when they want to sew. The fun part is bringing the garment to life, not putting together a puzzle of pieces of paper and then cutting it out." She envisioned a **process** where

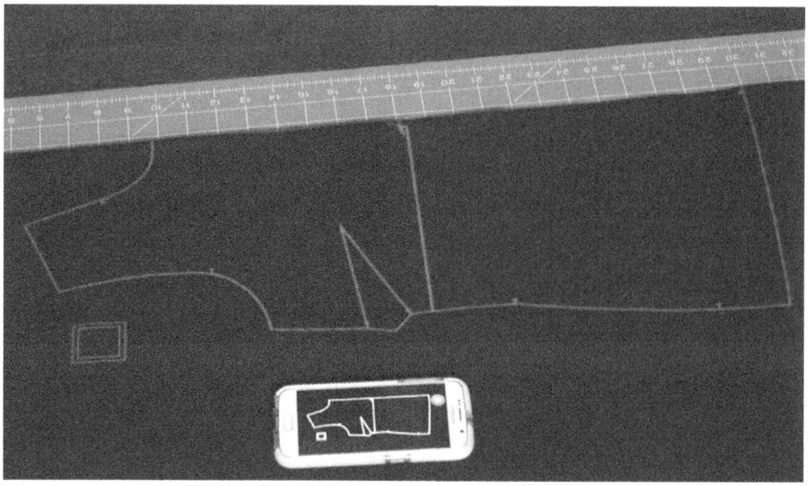

Figure 10.5.5 A KITE prototype in use.

Source: Courtesy of Elizabeth Caven

"I would never have to touch a piece of paper" using a mobile phone to project the pattern's cutting lines onto fabric while the phone could provide instructions for sewing. Using a very small projector with a mini tripod, Elizabeth named this new business idea KITE "because it would 'fly' above your fabric. It would project the image of the pattern, and you'd just cut it out." Elizabeth explored options for calibrating the projector for accurate sizing, finding the right brightness to project onto both light and dark fabrics, and how to deal with patterns in multiple sizes. After getting venture capital investment in early 2016, Elizabeth moved to San Francisco with an employee for six months while her husband stayed with their four young children in Iowa (Figure 10.5.5).

Elizabeth wrote and obtained patents for paperless sewing patterns using projectors or augmented reality. When she showed KITE to sewists, "they immediately got it, I didn't have to sell them on it. It made sense. They wanted it." But, when she introduced KITE to the large pattern companies, hoping to partner so their pattern libraries would be available through her projector, Elizabeth learned that

> there was no appetite for [this product] because the status quo was really hard to break. You have an incumbent like the sewing pattern companies that had been doing this for a hundred years, that had all of their **operating costs** tied up in the physical printing, the physical folding, the distribution of these actual physical patterns, and what I was presenting to them would make that business irrelevant. If they embraced this new idea, it would cannibalize their own business.

While UpCraft Club was already selling digital patterns in 83 countries, Elizabeth was still learning about the sewing **industry** and distribution through retail **channels**. Elizabeth found that

> the leadership of most of the companies in the sewing industry were made up of non-sewers. At company after company, I would show them this amazing thing that if you showed any sewer, they would say, 'Yes! That should exist.' Then you show it to these non-sewers, and it was really difficult for them to understand.

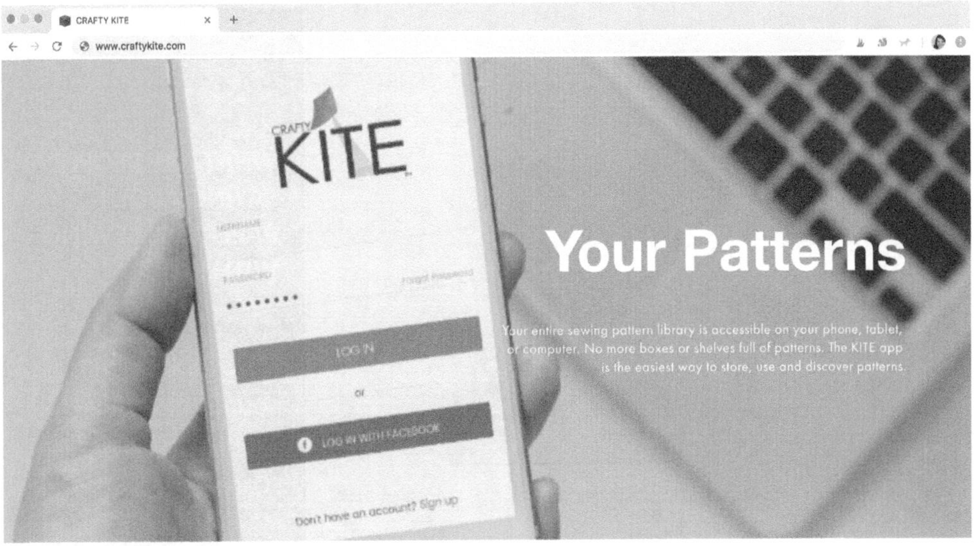

Figure 10.5.6 The KITE homepage.

Source: Courtesy of Elizabeth Caven

Similarly, Elizabeth found that venture capital firms didn't understand the sewing industry or the home sewing market, and therefore, weren't initially interested in investing.

Nonetheless, Elizabeth explains that

> nobody can argue with the actual data. When you have growing revenue, you have growing customers, you have evidence that they really want the thing you're creating, the opinion of an **investor** doesn't matter. The market was pulling this product into existence. I knew it was a matter of 'when and how,' not a matter of 'if.'

She already had "purchase orders to the tune of millions and millions of dollars. I was working on funding and getting the **supply chain** all set up" (Figure 10.5.6).

An Unexpected Exit: From KITE to Ditto Patterns

By 2019, Elizabeth's company was fully virtual and she was living in Minnesota. She had been recognized by the United States **Small Business Administration** and had been invited to the White House to speak about women's entrepreneurship. "I was building my business at this point. I was still raising money. I was still developing the product. It wasn't a household name yet. [The business] still was centering around me" (Figure 10.5.7).

When Elizabeth was unexpectedly diagnosed with cancer, she wanted to make sure her company could "land somewhere that could sustain it in the future." She thought, "Maybe selling now is the thing to do because then it can outlive me if the worst case scenario happens." Elizabeth had been in talks with a large craft and sewing supply retailer that wanted 100% ownership so the product could be sold exclusively through their stores. She made the decision to sell the business and exit the company in 2019 to focus on her health. (Elizabeth has now been cancer-free for six years.)

Four years after the sale, Ditto Patterns launched as a partnership between the retailer and Singer, a large sewing machine manufacturer. The product looked different from Elizabeth's

Figure 10.5.7 A promotional one-pager for KITE.

Source: Courtesy of Elizabeth Caven

initial concept, and launched as a closed system where only patterns from specific manufacturers could be accessed. Ditto Patterns eventually added an option to upload patterns from other sources. When the retailer filed for bankruptcy in 2024 and 2025, with all 800 of its stores being **liquidated** by May 2025, it was unclear what the future of Ditto Patterns would be. However, in June 2025, SVP Worldwide, Singer's parent company, announced that Ditto Patterns

> joined the SVP Worldwide family of brands… Ditto Patterns has reimagined how sewists of all skill levels interact with patterns. By replacing traditional paper templates with a digital, body-inclusive, and fully customizable projection system, Ditto Patterns removes common frustrations and empowers users to cut fabric with speed, precision, and confidence.… This change in ownership brings renewed momentum to Ditto Patterns' mission of making sewing more seamless, efficient, and inclusive than ever before.

Reflecting on her experience now, Elizabeth says

> **Exit [events]** are important to think about. When you start a business on day one, you need to know that your role in the business will end somehow. It might end because your involvement with it will end, it might end because you die and you're no longer running [it], it might [end] because it goes bankrupt, it might end because you don't want to do it anymore, and you just shut it down. It might end because it goes public, and you aren't the sole owner anymore because the public gets to help own it, too. You need to have some ideas of what you will or won't be open to. I was open to everything.

At the same time, she notes,

> You can't prepare yourself for after you exit. It's a really complicated set of feelings. On one hand, you want it to completely fail without you to show how valuable you were. And on the other hand, it's your name still tied to that forever. And so you don't want it to fail. You want it to be incredibly successful because you always get to say you started that thing.

Case Concepts, Reflections, and Resources

Concepts

- Exit events through acquisition (Chapter 7)
- Funding with self-funding, seed-funding, equity investment, and venture capital (Chapter 7)
- Opportunity recognition (Chapters 1, 2, and 4)
- Pain points and value proposition (Chapter 2)
- Serial entrepreneurship (Chapter 1)

Reflection Questions

1 Elizabeth's sewing business evolved over time from sewing pattern design to a pattern marketplace to a video-supported membership platform to developing a tangible product, the sewing pattern projector. What did Elizabeth learn during her sewing business journey that might be useful for your business?

2 Elizabeth was able to fund many of her startup costs through pitch competitions. Find a pitch competition application (current or expired) that is relevant to your business and review it. Develop a pitch for your business that meets the time guidelines for this competition. What did you learn from this process that could be helpful to your business?
3 Elizabeth talked about the importance of considering the types of **exit strategies** you would accept at the start of your business. Which type(s) of exit (closing/ending the business, selling the business or its assets, becoming publicly traded, transitioning ownership to a successor such as a child or other family member) would be possible options for your business? Is there any exit option you would not consider? Why or why not?
4 Elizabeth protected her inventions using patents. Patents, along with **copyright**, **trademarks**, and **trade secrets**, are important ways of securing **intellectual property**. Which, if any, intellectual property protections do you use for your creative **venture** now? Which might you use in the future? Often, misinformation about intellectual property protection is shared in online communities. Seek out the government agencies responsible for intellectual property law in your country. How long does each type of protection last? How does one secure it?
5 Elizabeth iterated on her concept for a sewing pattern projector, developed **prototypes**, and talked to prospective customers to gather data as described in Chapter 4. Do you already have an intentional system for **market testing**, data collection and reflection, and product iteration? If not, are there elements of Elizabeth's process that you could adapt for your business?

Additional Resources

While the UpCraft Club and KITE websites are no longer active, Elizabeth maintains her own website (www.elizabethcaven.com) as an investor. Ditto Patterns (www.dittopatterns.com) can also be found online.

Further Reading and Listening

Evolution of Sewing Patterns

Frey, H. & Wilson, T. (Hosts). (2025, July 14). Paper sewing patterns, part 1 [Audio podcast episode]. In *Stuff You Missed in History Class.* iHeart Radio. https://www.iheart.com/podcast/105-stuff-you-missed-in-histor-21124503/episode/paper-sewing-patterns-part-1-285761676/

Frey, H. & Wilson, T. (Hosts). (2025, July 16). Paper sewing patterns, part 2 [Audio podcast episode]. In *Stuff You Missed in History Class.* iHeart Radio. https://www.iheart.com/podcast/105-stuff-you-missed-in-histor-21124503/episode/paper-sewing-patterns-part-2-286230085/

Glassenberg, A. (2023, February 21). JOANN and Singer launch Ditto, the first projector made just for sewing. *Craft Industry Alliance.* https://craftindustryalliance.org/joann-and-singer-launch-ditto-the-first-projector-made-just-for-sewing/

McDowell Hopper, L. (2020, June 2). Shining a new light on sewing: The growing trend of sewing with projectors. *Craft Industry Alliance.* https://craftindustryalliance.org/shining-a-new-light-on-sewing-the-growing-trend-of-sewing-with-projectors/

Product Development and Iteration

Jakicic, C. (2025, May 27). Happy accidents: When a product unexpectedly becomes a favorite among crafters. *Craft Industry Alliance.* https://craftindustryalliance.org/happy-accidents-when-a-product-unexpectedly-becomes-a-favorite-among-crafters/

Nusselder, A. (n.d.) Iterating. *Design Thinking for Higher Education.* https://designthinking.nusselder.org/iteration/

Case 10.6 Fake Cakery: Explosive Growth After "Going Viral"

Maker Profile

Julie Nguyen is a recent graduate of the Massachusetts College of Art and Design (MassArt). Julie recalls, "Food had always been something that I was interested in. As a kid growing up, I loved to bake." She attended a career-focused high school with the intent of preparing for a career in culinary arts. Though Julie enhanced her skills, by the end of high school she knew that the culinary **industry** wasn't the right fit for her. Instead, she decided to focus on film studies in college with the hopes of entering a career in food media (Figure 10.6.1).

In the summer between high school graduation and starting college, Julie continued working at a bakery while using her free time to experiment with sculpture, polymer clay, resin, and acrylic paints. Julie was responsible for making the display cakes for her job, "and, around the same time, there was a **trend** that was starting to emerge on Instagram and it was this idea of fake cakes." These fake cakes appearing on social media could be used for decoration, as photo props, or might be fully functional, such as a jewelry box disguised as a cake.

As the trend shifted from making fake cakes using edible ingredients towards ones where "everything was inedible" with spackling and acrylic paint used to decorate, Julie decided to order supplies and try it out. "That first batch was so fun. It was almost like an addiction. I just

Figure 10.6.1 Julie Nguyen, founder of Fake Cakery.

Source: Courtesy of Julie Nguyen/Fake Cakery

Figure 10.6.2 Julie decorating a fake cake.

Source: Courtesy of Julie Nguyen/Fake Cakery

started creating more." Without the need to bake a cake and let it cool, Julie could focus entirely on decorating her fake cakes. Julie's mother "didn't love the fact that I was accumulating so many" fake cakes, so Julie listed them on Depop, an **e-commerce** app, in the home decor section. The fake cakes sold quickly, and Julie decided to create a separate Instagram account for her fake cakes. She had previous experience with YouTube and Instagram, and asked her existing followers to check out her new account (Figure 10.6.2).

Introduction to Fake Cakery

After starting her Fake Cakery account, Julie spent the first four months making custom orders and experimenting, creating magnets and trying different designs. As Julie began school at MassArt, she set aside the Instagram account for a few months, concentrating on the transition into college. But soon, financial pressures led Julie to refocus on Fake Cakery. She decided to "start doing collections," beginning by asking herself, "What's going on in the world of cakes right now? What's trending?" Her business "started picking up" and she was contacted by a quirky boutique in San Francisco, who asked her to create fake cakes for their storefront display. There was also an opportunity for further collaboration including **licensing** and teaching workshops. Julie remembers,

> That was the first time I was really having this experience of working professionally with another **brand**. It ended up doing very well for both of us. Because of that experience, it gave me a little bit of confidence to push a bit further with my ideas.

Explosive Growth and Unexpected Outcomes

While considering her next collection, Julie observed that cannabis grinders have a similar shape to cakes. Julie bought some grinders at a local dispensary, painted them pink, and decorated them as fake cakes. By this time, she already had a website. The fake cake grinders sold out "almost immediately" after listing, which surprised Julie. Then she began getting messages from people asking, "'Hey, are you going to make more? Because I would love to get one. I couldn't buy one.'" Julie began accepting **pre-orders** for grinders and then a nearby cannabis dispensary messaged Julie to express interest in carrying her grinders. Julie agreed, explaining that "it was kind of a new experience for me to realize I need to meet demands now."

Julie's first year at MassArt was coming to an end, and she was preparing for a summer craft fair. She thought that launching a fake cake grinder collection at the craft fair would be ideal. She ordered grinders through Alibaba – a **business-to-business** platform that links **manufacturers** with **buyers** – and began testing new designs. Julie contacted a friend who was interested in modeling and they did a photo shoot in a park, "kind of like a picnic, but with fake cakes." Julie uploaded one photo to Instagram that day, and it got a lot of attention. She followed up by putting together "a video demonstrating how the grinders work, and I posted that, and overnight it essentially had a million views." Julie followed up by posting more videos about the grinders and directing people who were interested in ordering to the craft fair. On the day of the craft fair, she made her first sale "five minutes before doors opened because some people had actually snuck in early, and by the end of that day, we'd fully sold out. We had nothing left."

Julie had promised her followers that she would post remaining grinders for sale on her website after the craft fair, but instead, she had to tell them, "'We don't actually have anything.'" She estimated how many grinders she could realistically make, and decided to list 100 for pre-order on her website. "The website crashed and they sold out in about two minutes," Julie remembers. In order to meet **demand**, Julie quit her job at the bakery and found an affordable studio space to rent in Rhode Island. Her plan was "to make all these pre-orders and additional [**inventory**] because people are expecting more things," but she recalls that she soon realized,

> This is a lot more serious than I intended for it to be. And, it pretty much took over my whole life. I spent every day that summer trying to meet demand, and I still never really met it for that year. It kept on carrying over.

While Julie was thrilled to get "special requests from big companies and celebrities" and learned a lot about working with collaborators, as she prepared to return to MassArt for her sophomore year, she found that

> the air was kind of weird to me. I was just joining this major and I was meeting all the film students for the first time. When we were doing introductions, some people already knew who I was. I was like, 'that's kind of weird.' I've never had that experience before.

Figure 10.6.3 Fake Cakery products, including keychains, cannabis grinders, and jewelry boxes.

Source: Courtesy of Julie Nguyen/Fake Cakery

Ultimately, Julie found that she couldn't balance school and completing her pre-orders in the studio, so she decided to take a semester off. Julie hoped that her time away would allow her to catch up with demand, but she found that it "just kept on getting busier and busier" (Figure 10.6.3).

When it was time to return to MassArt for the next semester, Julie realized that she was no longer interested in a career in food media and instead wanted to take more classes focused on business. She decided, "I'll just figure out how to warp the film [major] to be in relation to my business." Additionally, she was beginning to find the drive to Rhode Island exhausting and her studio had experienced some flooding. Julie decided to move into a larger apartment and operate the business from home rather than rent a separate studio space.

As Julie returned to school for her sophomore year classes and began working from home, she found that "because I took such a long break from the business at that point, the audience that was so patiently waiting for new stuff [and] wasn't getting anything new, I kind of lost them a little bit slowly." Julie needed to revive the business to financially support her new apartment and return to school. She connected with a hand model she had worked with before and shot videos for a new collection. The videos resonated with her audience, and Julie recalls that "I was rebuilding that momentum up again. But, I think that first experience with losing that audience made me realize, 'Okay, the virality doesn't last forever.'"

Next Steps for Fake Cakery

As she graduated from MassArt, Julie notes that

> we're at a point where the demand has definitely been met. My business is running at a pace that is much more ideal. It still leaves a lot of room where I'm allowed to experiment and try new things. There will generally be some audience that is receptive to it, and I'm not really looking for the 'next viral thing' anymore. I think I'm kind of done with it.

Julie no longer uses pre-orders "because I think that first experience really traumatized me from the demand" (Figure 10.6.4). As an art student, Julie initially was just

> making whatever I wanted, whenever I wanted and kind of putting it out to the world. It was a very drastic shift when it was going from 'I make what I want, whenever I want' to customers going, 'I want this and I want it by this date.' It was a big thing for me to go from this artistic freedom of making things how I like to the repetitiveness of going, '50 people want this specific design and I have to make that 50 times.' It killed that spark a little bit because it wasn't what I was used to.

While she was a teenager, meeting the pre-order demand for Fake Cakery from her studio space in Rhode Island, Julie would work long days, often without taking breaks, to make the long drive worthwhile. Now, from her home studio, "the process has shifted." Julie sets aside one day weekly for administrative work like bookkeeping and "any work that just needs to be done on a screen." She aims to be in the studio for at least three hours a day, but not longer than ten hours. She takes regular breaks and has her partner and an assistant who work on **fulfillment** and customer service issues. She has returned to listing collections, small batches, or one-of-a-kind items, rather than using pre-orders. Julie **self-funds** by allocating some of her profits for supplies for future materials, rather than expecting to fund materials with pre-order sales. While Julie is open to considering partnerships and collaborations with others, she has

Figure 10.6.4 Fake Cakery marketing materials.

Source: Courtesy of Julie Nguyen/Fake Cakery

found that most would require manufacturing agreements and she is still focused on making her products by hand.

Case Concepts, Reflections, and Resources

Concepts

- Branding (Chapter 5)
- Funding through self-funding and pre-orders (Chapter 7)
- Marketing (Chapters 2 and 4)
- Operations management (Chapter 8)
- Pricing (Chapter 6)
- Strategy (Chapter 3)

Reflection Questions

1 Julie found pre-orders draining but many creative entrepreneurs prefer using pre-orders for financing and to accurately predict demand. Would pre-orders be a good fit for your business?

Why or why not? What can you learn from Julie's journey that might impact if or how you use pre-orders?

2 Julie successfully created a brand identity and leveraged social media virality for Fake Cakery. Review Julie's website and Instagram profile linked in Additional Resources below. How would you describe her brand voice and style? What can you learn from Julie's approach to branding that would be beneficial to your business?
3 As Julie's business has evolved, she began dedicating a specific day for non-creative and administrative work and has also set limits for her studio time. What aspects of Julie's approach to organizing her schedule might be relevant to your business?
4 Julie became selective about partnerships over time because she wants to continue to create handmade fake cakes. Have you collaborated with other organizations on special collections, new products, or marketing? If yes, how do you decide if a partnership is a good fit for your business? If not, what type of partnerships would you be open to? What can you learn from Julie's collaborations that could impact your business?
5 Which of the effectuation principles outlined in Chapter 1 did you observe Julie practicing? Which effectuation principles have you practiced? Which principles could you incorporate further into your creative business practice?

Additional Resources

Fake Cakery can be found on its website (fakecakery.com) and also maintains an active presence on Instagram (www.instagram.com/fakecakery).

Further Reading and Viewing

Branding

Canva Team. (2025, August). Building brand guidelines: How-tos, templates, and tips. *Canva*. https://www.canva.com/docs/brand-guidelines/

Matthew Encina. (2025, May 29). Building a brand - Redesigning a business start to finish [Video]. YouTube. https://youtu.be/ZvxpaklnMXI

Sventeckis, A. (2025, August 19). Craft your best brand voice: Expert tips, examples, and templates. *HubSpot*. https://blog.hubspot.com/marketing/brand-voice

Pre-Orders

Arvind. (2025, January 7). The ultimate guide to pre-orders: How they work, benefits, and the best practices. *OneCart*. https://www.getonecart.com/the-ultimate-guide-to-pre-orders-how-they-work-benefits-and-best-practices/

Dopson, E. (2025, June 7). Preorder: Meaning and how to boost sales in 2025. *Shopify*. https://www.shopify.com/blog/shopify-pre-orders#

Link, K. (2016, January 19). Crowdfunding your next project? 7 good questions to answer before you launch. *Craft Industry Alliance*. https://craftindustryalliance.org/crowdfunding-your-next-project-7-good-questions-to-answer-before-you-launch/

Case 10.7 Allpa: Transforming Artisans into Entrepreneurs in Peru

Introduction to Allpa Perú

Allpa Perú (Allpa) was founded in 1986 by sociologists Maria del Carmen de la Fuente and Nelly Canepa. Maria and Nelly had been working with a **non-governmental organization** for several years to support low-income producers throughout Peru. Maria recalls that while "we wanted to help everybody," their work could have more **impact** by focusing on artisans. As Maria explains,

> crafts-making is an economic activity which creates jobs in a very easy and affordable way – meaning you don't need to have a lot of money to invest in a factory or in a piece of land to grow. You only need some money, some tools, and skills.

Most of the artisans Maria and Nelly had already worked with practiced traditional crafts, and "received these skills from their ancestors" (Figure 10.7.1).

Allpa was established as a **for-profit** company and began with a **business loan** from a German financial institution. These funds were used to "start the company, to do traveling, to visit customers, and to start projects with different groups of artisans," and were repaid within two years. Initially, Allpa worked with artisans in 200 workshops throughout Peru making a broad array of **products** using many artisan crafts and techniques. Eventually, Maria and Nelly decided that "we needed to focus, reduce the scope of the designs and the crafts and the projects that we were developing." Today, Allpa has a staff of 25 people and primarily works with artisans who create textiles, metals, pottery, and wall art in 80 workshops. Maria notes that "all of our production goes to abroad. We **export** everything." Allpa's motto is "to transform artisans into entrepreneurs." Maria explains that "even if they keep the traditions [at] the core of the product they produce," the artisans who work with Allpa "need to learn to become entrepreneurs." This is especially true in the 2020s, as

Figure 10.7.1 The Allpa Perú team holding Allpa logo mugs.

Source: Courtesy of Allpa Perú

Figure 10.7.2 Maria speaking with an artisan in one of the workshops Allpa Perú works with.
Source: Courtesy of Allpa Perú

the international markets that Allpa artisans export products to have "changed enormously" (Figure 10.7.2).

Contemporary Challenges in the International Marketplace

When Allpa launched, Asian producers didn't have a presence at the international **trade shows** and **retail** shows Allpa attended. "China didn't exist as a **competitor**," Maria says, but now Peruvian artisans compete with producers from countries throughout Asia including China, the Philippines, and Cambodia. Additionally, Maria explains, "the **market** has become very demanding." In the early days of Allpa, consumers appreciated the "authenticity of the products," which were easier to sell "as they came out of the hands of the artisans without important changes." However, to remain competitive in today's market, Allpa works with artisans to develop products that are more functional than purely decorative, and that meet other consumer preferences (Figure 10.7.3).

As consumers have become more environmentally and socially conscious, Allpa has obtained and maintained **third-party certifications** that customers value while also ensuring that the artisans remain in compliance with certification requirements. In addition to environmental certifications indicating that products are non-toxic, there are also certifications clarifying that Allpa artisans don't use child labor or allow discrimination, and that they pay appropriate wages. Maria notes that

> these days, we compete with Asian producers. It is difficult because Asian producers, they have much lower wages than in Peru. Latin America is much more expensive than Asian countries. For example, many American companies produce in Bangladesh, in Vietnam, and they pay much lower wages than what we pay here in Peru.

Today, 80% of Allpa's exports go to the United States. Because of Peru's proximity, it is easy for American buyers to visit Allpa's facilities. Maria also notes that "there's a longer tradition

Figure 10.7.3 Allpa's products include (from left to right): traditional ceramics from Chulucanas, textiles and pottery, jewelry, and accessories.

Source: Courtesy of Allpa Perú

in selling crafts to the United States. This tradition started in the [1940s]. Then also, [the United States is] a very large market" with a population of over 340 million people who are "very high consumers. Americans love to buy, love shopping."

Allpa develops all of its collections, either in-house or "according to our customer requirements [and] technical specifications." Maria highlights that "designing and developing new products is core in our business. And, our artisans have learned how to follow the instructions, how to respect the size, the color, the material, et cetera."

The pressures of the international marketplace are a main factor for "why it is very important that our artisans, other than use their skills to make beautiful products, these products need to comply with a lot of requirements. So we need [our artisans] to become entrepreneurs."

Facilitating The Transition from Artisan to Entrepreneur

Allpa's initial step is to "check if this artisan wants to be an entrepreneur, because not everybody wants to." Maria explains that many Peruvian artisans are happy producing one-of-a-kind products without formalizing into a business where they will need to, for example, pay wages and maintain payroll records for tax purposes. One-of-a-kind products are too expensive to produce and too difficult to **merchandise** to fit into Allpa's export model. If the artisan is interested in collaborating, Allpa will "start developing products with them in a small scale to see if they understand what we need," and to observe whether the artisan is willing to make the adjustments needed "because the market wants those changes" (Figure 10.7.4.1–10.7.4.2–10.7.4.3). If this is successful, Allpa provides technical assistance through partnerships with local universities and professionals, supporting the artisan entrepreneur in adapting techniques and materials and building infrastructure. "Most of the times, the workshops are very small family workshops, and if we need them to grow and they don't have the means to do it on their own, we give them loans," Maria says. Allpa also sends personnel to the workshop sites to ensure compliance with the certifications.

Additionally, Allpa has obtained loans and other funding to develop or adapt tools for the artisans in the workshops, such as specialized washing machines for textiles or systems to control the use of alpaca yarns in weaving to reduce waste. This is necessary because many commercial machines are too large for use in small workshops, or existing software requires higher literacy levels than their artisans have. The specialized tools that Allpa has worked with experts to develop or modify operate at a scale between handmade and large industrial.

FICHA TECNICA				allpa
ESPECIFICACIONES DE ARTICULO				
ARTICULO:	MANTA	DISEÑO		TAFETAN , ESPIGA
CODIGO ALLPA:	TTPE02027	PESO DE ARTICULO FINAL		0.530 KG. PESO APROX.
MEDIDA FINAL (ANCHO X LARGO)	120 X 84	FLECOS	SI	BORDE / no
ACABADO	SI / X / NO	MEDIDAS (CM)	12	MEDIDAS (CM) / ...

DATOS DE PRODUCCION		LONGITUD TOTAL A URDIR POR PIEZA	
TECNICA	TAFETAN ESPIGA	LARGO DE BORDE	...
NUMERO DE MARCOS Y PEDALES	MARCO 6 /PEDAL 8	LARGO DE FLECOS EN TELAR (CM)	26
DATOS DE URDIMBRE (2 HEBRAS ALPACA 1 HEBRA ALPALOOP = 3 HILOS XLISO)		LARGO DE TEJIDO EN TELAR (CM)	90 (para que quede en 84CM)
PEINE	4	MERMA	3
ANCHO DE TEJIDO EN PEINE (cm)	131 cm para que quede en 120 cm)	TOTAL LARGO DE TEJIDO (CM	119
HILOS POR (cm)	4 HILOS X 3 HEBRAS = 12 HILOS	RESTA EN TELAR	120 cm
HILOS DE FONDO SIN GRUPOS NI ORILLOS	131X12 =1572		
HILOS DE ORILLO	NO HAY ORILLO VA DIRECTO SIN TORCER	DATOS DE LA TRAMA	(2 HEBRAS ALPALOOP)(3 HEBRAS ALPACA ESPIGA)
TOTAL HILOS DE URDIDO	1572	HILOS POR CM	(ALPACA 22 HILOS APROX) (ALPALOOP 11 HILOS)

COMPOSICION	TITULO	COLOR	HILOS	DISTRIBUCION
100/ ALPACA	2/16	211	1048	URDIDO
ALPALOOP 89% ALPACA	1/5	ZD28	524	URDIDO
			1572	

COMPOSICION	TITULO	COLOR	HILOS	DISTRIBUCION
100% ALPACA	2/16	SFN10	422	TRAMA
ALPALOOP 89% ALPACA 11% POYAMIDE	1/5	HUESO BO	160	TRAMA
ALPALOOP 89% ALPACA 11% POYAMIDE	2/16	ZF91	472	TRAMA
100% ALPACA	2/16	282	198	TRAMA
			1252	

Figure 10.7.4.1, 10.7.4.2, 10.7.4.3 An Allpa ficha tecnica (technical sheet) for a woven shawl. This document provides production details to the artisan workshop, including the fiber content and color of threads or yarns used, the patterning, and the finished product dimensions.

Source: Courtesy of Allpa Perú

	DISTRIBUCION DE LA TRAMA TTPE02027							
	COMPOSICION	TITULO	COLOR	HEBRA	DESCRIPCION DEL TEJIDO	TELA	TELAR	TOTAL HILOS
1	100% ALPACA	2/16	SFN10	2	TAFETAN NORMAL 2 HEBRA	2.50	2.7	37
2	ALPALOOP	1/5	BO	2	PISADA 1,7,3,8 boucle salteado) (2 HEBRAS 22 PASADAS)	3.50	3.8	44
3	100% ALPACA	2/16	SFN10	3	ESPIGA HORIZONTAL (3 HEBRAS 29 PASADAS)	4.00	4.3	87
4	ALPALOOP	1/5	BO	2	PISADA 1,7,3,8 boucle salteado (2 HEBRAS 6PASADAS)	1.00	1.1	12
5	100% ALPACA	2/16	282	3	ESPIGA HORIZONTAL (3 HEBRAS 29 PASADAS)	4.00	4.3	87
6	ALPALOOP	1/5	BO	2	PISADA 1,7,3,8 boucle salteado (2 HEBRAS 6 PASADAS)	1.00	1.1	12
7	100% ALPACA	2/16	SFN10	3	ESPIGA HORIZONTAL (3 HEBRAS) 29 PASADAS	4.00	4.3	87
8	ALPALOOP	1/5	BO	2	PISADA 1,7,3,8 boucle salteado (2 HEBRAS 6 PASADAS)	1.00	1.1	12
9	100% ALPACA	2/16	282	2	TAFETAN NORMAL 6 PASADS 2 HEBRA	1.00	1.1	12
10	ALPALOOP	1/5	ZF91	2	PISADA 1,7,3,8 boucle salteado (2 HEBRAS	20.00	21.4	236
					MEDIO DE LA MANTA REPITE AL ESPEJO			
11	ALPALOOP	1/5	ZF91	2	PISADA 1,7,3,8 boucle salteado (2 HEBRAS)	20.00	21.4	236
12	100% ALPACA	2/16	282	2	TAFETAN NORMAL 6 PASADS 2 HEBRA	1.00	1.1	12
13	ALPALOOP	1/5	BO	2	PISADA 1,7,3,8 boucle salteado (2 HEBRAS 6 PASADAS)	1.00	1.1	12
14	100% ALPACA	2/16	SFN10	3	ESPIGA HORIZONTAL (3 HEBRAS) 29 PASADAS	4.00	4.3	87
15	ALPALOOP	1/5	BO	2	PISADA 1,7,3,8 boucle salteado (2 HEBRAS 6 PASADAS)	1.00	1.1	12
16	100% ALPACA	2/16	282	3	ESPIGA HORIZONTAL (3 HEBRAS 29 PASADAS)	4.00	4.3	87
17	ALPALOOP	1/5	BO	2	PISADA 1,7,3,8 boucle salteado (2 HEBRAS 6 PASADAS)	1.00	1.1	12
18	100% ALPACA	2/16	SFN10	3	ESPIGA HORIZONTAL (3 HEBRAS 29 PASADAS)	4.00	4.3	87
19	ALPALOOP	1/5	BO	2	PISADA 1,7,3,8 boucle salteado (2 HEBRAS 22 PASADAS)	3.50	3.8	44
20	100% ALPACA	2/16	SFN10	2	TAFETAN NORMAL 2 HEBRA	2.50	2.7	37
						84.00	90.0	1252

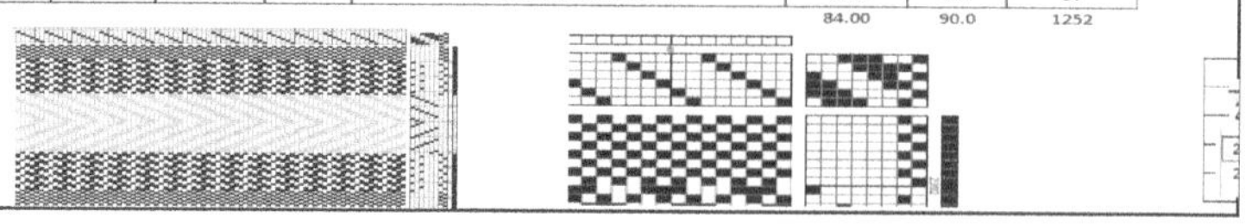

Figure 10.7.4.1, 10.7.4.2, 10.7.4.3 (Continued)

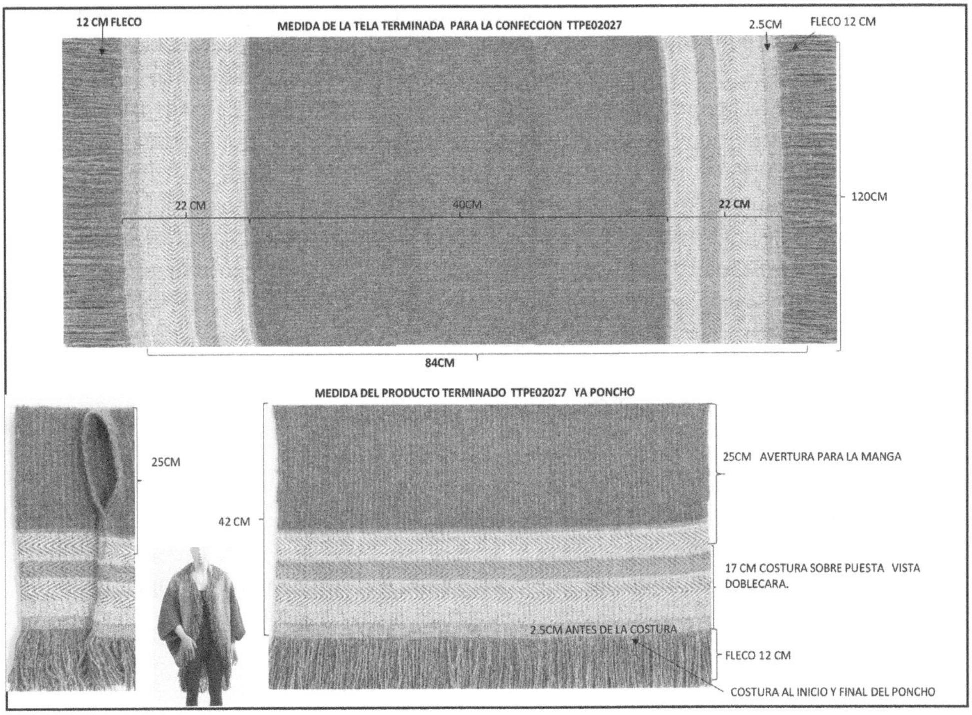

Figure 10.7.4.1, 10.7.4.2, 10.7.4.3 (Continued)

While most artisans begin their journey with Allpa as home-based ventures, Maria explains that Allpa has

> pushed them to grow. We are not happy when we see an artisan remaining at home forever. That is not a sign of success. We want them to grow, to make sure they bring jobs to the communities, [and] they improve the quality of their living conditions.

These changes include sending their children to school.

The Future of Allpa

While Allpa has built a successful model over four decades, they face several challenges as they look to the future. Maria and Nelly began planning for **succession** five years ago, thinking "we need to create a new generation of people who can continue Allpa" when they retire. As younger workers have developed a preference to stay with employers for shorter intervals, it has been difficult to hire and train employees who are committed to working at Allpa for a decade or longer. Additionally, Maria notes that "not everybody likes to work with artisans." While Allpa's headquarters is in Lima – Peru's capital and a cosmopolitan city with a population over 10 million – many of the artisans live elsewhere in Peru, speak indigenous languages rather than Spanish, have low literacy, or "have a different culture." In addition to seeking employees who want to continue Allpa, Maria and Nelly want "to find people who appreciate" the diversity of the artisans that collaborate with Allpa "and want to work with" those artisans.

E-commerce is an area that Allpa is just beginning to explore. They are "scared about losing money" by selling **direct-to-consumer** using **marketplaces** like Etsy or Amazon. Their current systems are built on exporting in volume to **distributors** or retailers, rather than directly to consumers. They have yet to develop an infrastructure for marketing to consumers who aren't able to touch their products and observe the quality, or for **fulfillment** of small, international orders in a cost-effective way.

Additionally, the United States government is becoming more resistant to importing and is exploring imposing high **tariffs** which may impact Peruvian **imports**. Increasing unemployment and inflation in the United States may also limit the disposable income of consumers in Allpa's largest market at the same time as the effective price of Allpa's exported products may increase due to tariffs.

Case Concepts, Reflections, and Resources

Concepts

- Business model (Chapter 2)
- Entrepreneurial mindset (Chapter 1)
- Operations management including process mapping and sustainability (Chapter 8)
- Strategy (Chapter 3)

Reflection Questions

1. Maria describes Allpa's motto as "to transform artisans into entrepreneurs." What aspects of Allpa's work supporting artisans as they transform into entrepreneurs are relevant for your own creative business?
2. Allpa uses *fichas tecnica* (technical sheets), documents including information like finished product dimensions, materials used, and patterning so that multiple artisans in a workshop can produce nearly identical items at a specific cost. How could a technical sheet (or **process mapping**) be used for a sole creator business rather than for a multi-creator business? Are there aspects of a technical sheet that could be useful in your creative business?
3. Allpa obtains and manages third-party certification and compliance on behalf of the artisans it works with, including environmental certifications, and social responsibility and **fair trade** certifications. Are there any third-party certifications that would be useful for your business (or your suppliers) to have? If so, which one(s) would be most valued by your customers?
4. Allpa has recently begun **business-to-consumer (B2C)** e-commerce using Etsy's marketplace after years of selling **wholesale** through **business-to-business (B2B)** relationships and marketplaces. Does your creative business sell both to consumers and to businesses? If so, what aspects of your B2C activities could inform your B2B activities and vice versa? If not, what challenges and opportunities might you experience by adding either B2C or B2B activities to your business?
5. As Allpa plans for succession, Maria noted they are looking for someone who wants to work at Allpa for multiple years and who also enjoys working with the artisan workshops outside of Lima. As you consider bringing in independent **contractors** or employees to work with your creative business (including experts like accountants or lawyers), what are the characteristics you are looking for?

Additional Resources

Allpa Perú can be found online on their website (allpaperu.com), Instagram (www.instagram.com/allpaperu.pe), and their recently launched Etsy shop (www.etsy.com/shop/CasaAllpape). Allpa is certified with Nest's Ethical Handcraft seal, which you can learn more about in Appendix B.

Further Reading and Viewing

Selling Internationally

Crafts Council. (2022). Maker support resources: Sell and showcase your work overseas. *Crafts Council.* https://www.craftscouncil.org.uk/sector-support/craft-business-resources/sell-and-showcase-your-work-overseas

Ewi Macrame. (2025). The challenges of selling handmade abroad. *Ewi Macrame.* https://www.ewimacrame.com/blog/challenges-of-selling-handmade-abroad

Work in Culture. (n.d.) How to sell your work internationally: Export readiness. *Work in Culture.* https://workinculture.ca/resource/how-to-sell-your-work-internationally/

Third-Party Certifications

B Lab. (2023, October 6). About B Corp Certification. *B Lab.* https://www.bcorporation.net/en-us/certification/

Fair Trade Federation. (n.d.) Eligibility requirements. *Fair Trade Federation.* https://www.fairtradefederation.org/screening-process/

Nest. (n.d.). Ethical handicraft. *Nest.* https://www.buildanest.org/ethical-handcraft

Case 10.8 That Zaire: Planning with Three Pillars and Exploring Income Streams

Maker Profile and Introduction to That Zaire

Zaire Miles-Moultrie is a recent graduate of the University of North Carolina at Greensboro. Drawing was always a hobby for Zaire, and he began selling small drawings on commission at the end of high school. Zaire entered college with a focus on business and pre-law. His plans changed when he took a course in arts entrepreneurship that opened his eyes to possibilities he hadn't considered, and he was introduced to printmaking, which "just took my life over." Zaire ultimately earned a Bachelor of Fine Arts with concentrations in printmaking and drawing. Zaire describes his work as "rooted deeply in my upbringing in the Southern United States," and he explores blackness, identity, and culture through drawing, collaging, and printmaking (Figure 10.8.1).

As a student, Zaire developed a five-year plan for his arts business. His first five-year plan ended last December, and he is currently on his second five-year plan. "The previous five-year plan was actually really beneficial, and I hit just about all the marks that I wanted," Zaire says, though "there are some [**goals**] that had to push to this five-year plan. It's much more feasible." Remembering his early days developing the plan, Zaire says, "it was very tumultuous. It was a lot of trying to navigate what I want, what's feasible, what's not feasible."

In addition to selling commissioned work, Zaire has experimented with a variety of **revenue streams**, including vending, partnering with mission-driven organizations, using print-on-demand services and **marketplaces**, and selling his work through open studio events and galleries.

Examining Multiple Revenue Streams

That Zaire had a larger focus on vending initially, but Zaire soon found that

> even though [vending] can be beneficial, it was too much of an expense to get to and from, along with time that I couldn't really waste. I would have to take a day to make sure that I have all my **inventory**. I would have to take a few hours to make sure that I have my table situated. I had to make sure that I made advertisements, I had to make sure that my prices was correct, I had to do research on where I was going to be, and also the audience where I was going to be selling at.

Figure 10.8.1 A selection of Zaire's work from his That Black Feeling solo exhibit at the Greensboro Project Space.

Source: Courtesy of Zaire Miles-Moultrie/That Zaire.

Zaire found that even within his local area, the audience for different venues could vary greatly. For example, while at one event "the majority of individuals that bought my work were older white women that had money" and who would buy larger, more expensive pieces, at another event "it was a lot more younger folk that wasn't able to reach my price points. And, that's my fault because I wasn't able to do research on them in time."

Currently, Zaire is an emerging artist-in-residence at a **non-profit** visual arts center in Raleigh, North Carolina that hosts events and open studio hours. During his residency, Zaire shifted his focus to selling work directly through his studio. Through open studio hours,

> people can come in and out, I get to talk to them. I'm not trying to capture their attention within an outside court where there's 20, 30, 40, 50 other artists. With them coming to my studio, it gives me the time to actually talk to them, [show] my work, and for them to get involved.

Zaire prefers selling through his studio to vending as his prep is minimized, the audience is interested in art, and he can bring potential customers into his space to "see my world." Another benefit of the studio environment is **networking**. Zaire has found that

> other artists, especially those that's been in the **industry** for a lot longer, they are more than happy to give you information about how to operate, how to price, where to go, who to talk to, and many other things.

Zaire has learned about grant and fellowship opportunities and has explored possibilities for creative collaborations through networking with other artists as well.

Zaire also collaborates with several mission-driven organizations to get his art into the community. The North Carolina Museum of Art carries Zaire's work in the gallery store and he has also taught workshops for teenagers through their education program (Figure 10.8.2).

Figure 10.8.2 The North Carolina Museum of Art partners with local artists and artisans like Zaire to sell their work in the museum store and exhibition store.

Source: Curtis Adams via Pexels

Zaire worked with ArtGivers, an organization that aims to make the "healing power of original art available to more people in more places" by purchasing art to install in organizations including low-cost clinics, shelters, and substance abuse rehabilitation programs. Zaire has partnered with elementary schools to teach "the power of print" to children. Zaire has discovered that teaching is a "very beneficial source" of **revenue**, but also that through teaching "I get to be creative." These collaborations allow Zaire to earn money through providing services, selling his work, or earning a **commission** or **revenue sharing** with the organization.

In That Zaire's early days, Zaire used INPRNT, an online marketplace that makes "gallery quality art prints" in their studio and also handles shipping and customer service. However, Zaire found that the revenue share with INPRNT wasn't beneficial; he cautions young artists against using similar services like Redbubble which provide the artist with a small commission for each sale. He recently was able to acquire a large format printer for free and has plans to eventually print and ship his own prints.

Zaire has also worked to get his art into galleries, but has found that when he applies to gallery shows, even when his work is accepted, it may not be the right fit. Zaire notes that "being invited and being scouted" by the gallery is "more appealing" as each gallery has "very specific requirements and aesthetics."

While Zaire continues to do commissioned work, he explains that "I'm much more selective about what I do."

Planning for Success

Zaire explains that

> when I'm making plans [for my business], there's a few factors that I take in mind. Personal goals, economic goals, and then artistic goals. So, those were the three big pillars. Initially, when I did my first five-year plan, it was like artistic: How do I become an artist? How do I be an artist? Personal goal was graduate college, have a foundation for my business. And, then, economic goal was – which I moved to my new five-year plan – make $500 a month from my art-related ventures.

In his current five-year plan, Zaire's goals have become more nuanced. His economic goals include allocating funds to maintain his equipment and purchase supplies. His personal goals include participating in gallery shows and researching concepts. His artistic goals include the number of pieces he creates, where they are shown, and fellowships and residency opportunities. Zaire also keeps his costs low by working full-time at a university where he can access printmaking resources and supplies more affordably.

That Zaire's Advice for Emerging Creative Entrepreneurs

Zaire shares advice for emerging artists that he learned from a professor: "Do not worry about making money immediately, because if you are money driven, your audience will know. They will." He also reminds **creative entrepreneurs** to

> have a reason for why you're making your art and why you're pursuing this as a passion. An **artist statement** is important, even though it changes over time. It is important to have and it is important to know why you're doing it. Another thing: most artists that are making art or practicing [art] have a day job. I have a day job. Always have a backup plan,

have an artist statement, and don't quit your day job unless you're making God knows how much money to support yourself, your business, and your expenses.

Case Concepts, Reflections, and Resources

Concepts

- Business model (Chapter 2)
- Business planning (Chapter 9)
- Portfolio of revenue streams (Chapter 2)
- Pricing (Chapter 6)

Reflection Questions

1 Zaire has explored a variety of revenue streams including art shows and craft fairs, consignment sales, print-on-demand, and teaching, and has found collaborations with non-profit organizations helpful both creatively and financially. Have you explored collaborations with local arts organizations, charities, and educational groups for your business? If so, what have the challenges and benefits been? If not, are there partnerships you'd like to explore?
2 Zaire found that vending at art shows and craft fairs was not a good fit for his business, but many creative entrepreneurs find vending lucrative. Would vending at art shows or craft fairs events be a good fit for your business? Why or why not? What can you learn from Zaire's journey that might impact if or how you use vending at art shows or craft fairs as part of your **business model**?
3 Zaire enjoys open studio events and has found these helpful for building relationships with customers. Have you organized or participated in open studio events for your business? If yes, how have they impacted your business? If not, would you consider open studio events for the future?
4 Zaire creates five-year plans for his (currently part-time) business including goals and **objectives** that are personal, financial, and artistic. Would long-term planning be helpful or challenging for your business? Why? Would using these three pillars be a helpful structure or too limiting or difficult for your business? Why?
5 Zaire emphasizes the importance of an artist statement. Do you have an artist statement? Why or why not? If so, is it publicly viewable? Why or why not?

Additional Resources

Zaire can be found online at the That Zaire website (thatzaire.wixsite.com/website), as well as on Instagram (www.instagram.com/that_zaire).

Further Reading

Artist Statement

ArtConnect. (n.d.) Writing an artist statement: Dos and don'ts. *ArtConnect*. https://www.magazine.artconnect.com/resources/writing-an-artist-statement-dos-and-donts

Hotchkiss, S. (2018, October 18). How to write an artist statement. *The Creative Independent*. https://thecreativeindependent.com/guides/how-to-write-an-artist-statement/

Mitchell, C. (n.d.) How to write an artist statement: A step-by-step guide. *C4E*. https://www.callforentries.com/pages/how-to-write-an-artist-statement-a-step-by-step-guide.html

Open Studios

ARTDEX. (n.d.) The artist's guide for creating the best open studio art event and art walk. *ARTDEX.* https://www.artdex.com/the-artists-guide-for-creating-the-best-open-studio-art-event-and-art-walk/

Berman, Harriete Estel. (2010). Professional guidelines: Open studios: Artist checklist. *Harriete Estel Berman.* https://harrieteestelberman.com/open-studios-artist-checklist

Cole, C. (2023, November 23). Preparing for an open studio: Tips from professional artists. *Artwork Archive.* https://www.artworkarchive.com/blog/preparing-for-an-open-studio-tips-from-professional-artists

Case 10.9 Curate Essentials: Getting Off the Treadmill and Owning the Vision

Maker Profile

Leslie Pearson is a multimedia artist, educator, community arts advocate, and **serial entrepreneur** living and working in Fayetteville, North Carolina. With her husband, she opened Vizcaya Villa, a wedding and event space, in 2015. To provide "an all-inclusive package for our brides, we found a restaurant and catering space we could work through" and ended up opening a restaurant in 2016. The second business grew rapidly as the Fayetteville Pie Company. Leslie remembers, "it was just very well received, became very popular, and it was just a lot of hard work. It wasn't really my passion, but I learned so much about working with staff [and] understanding the practicalities of ordering **wholesale**" (Figure 10.9.1). Leslie also learned that as an entrepreneur, people

> will flood you with all the things that they think you should be doing because they want to be doing those things, and they don't have the courage or the money or the strength. And, so I learned to fight through some of those things to say, 'What is my vision?'

Introduction to Curate Essentials

While Leslie "learned a ton" at Fayetteville Pie Company, she "realized that I don't really want to work in the restaurant [**industry**], and my heart was pulling me back toward focusing more on my art practice, and doing my own sort of personal health journey." Her initial vision for Curate Essentials was to create a studio space for herself in a "a really beautiful historic home" built in 1914 that Leslie owned and had begun renovating in 2018. Because the building is "centrally located in the community," Leslie imagined that it would be a space where she could make art, "have some classes, have some showings, exhibitions, stuff like that"

Figure 10.9.1 Leslie Pearson, founder of Curate Essentials, with her products.

Source: Courtesy of Leslie Pearson/Curate Essentials

Figure 10.9.2 The entrance to Curate Essentials with a view of the herbal garden.
Source: Courtesy of Leslie Pearson/Curate Essentials

(Figure 10.9.2). When the COVID pandemic began in 2020, Leslie turned her focus towards gardening. She remembers,

> Everything slowed down. It slowed down at my other business, and I was able to just focus on renovating the space, and I was kind of gardening at the same time. I was playing around with different herbs and making things for myself, making soaps and lotions, and things like that. And, I realized there was starting to become a **market** for that. My niece got pregnant and I started focusing on an all natural mommy and baby product line that drew some attention. And, before I knew it, I [realized] this is starting to become more than just a gallery space where I'm going to be selling whatever the things are that I like to make and sell, that there was a real need for holistic wellness options in the community.

Leslie opened Curate Essentials in 2022 with a soft launch, selling herbs, tea blends, and soaps.

> I did a soft opening because I just wanted to see what the vibe was like, who are coming in, will people know what an herbal apothecary is? We have a small cafe included, too. I knew people would know what a coffee shop was. It also allows people to taste our functional tea blends, so they can actually get a treatment when they walk in the door.

The location is "tranquil and peaceful," with a wraparound porch and herbal teaching gardens out front.

Leslie began to slowly expand her products "based off the things that people would come in and ask for." Because Fayetteville is a military town with a transient population, Leslie assumed that her audience would be military spouses in their 30s from around the United States who were used to having local options for holistic shopping. Soon, she realized that, "I'm 50. It was people my age and older who were coming in saying, 'do you have anything for stress and anxiety, have anything for menopause or perimenopause?'"

Since opening, Curate Essentials has "really become a community space more than I expected." The space hosts meetup groups for moms and is open to children. Leslie notes, "it's a great, healthy environment for the kids to be in. They're learning about the earth, and about botany and plants." Curate Essentials has expanded its **product mix** to include herbal remedies such as tinctures and essential oils, local honey, soy wax candles and melts, bath and body products including sugar scrubs and beard balm, art supplies like eco-printing kits, affirmation and gratitude cards, and branded merchandise.

Changing Priorities

Three years into the business, Leslie describes herself as being "in a very different place than I was when I began." She compares her previous approach to business as being on

> the treadmill cycle. If I stopped, my business stopped. If I didn't show up, my business didn't work, nobody got paid if I weren't producing, and it was like 12-hour days, 15-hour days, you never stop. There was just so much to do. I was developing the product, the recipes, the labels, the packaging, the website, all the content, all the things that a small business owner has to do.

Leslie notes that she no longer wants "to just keep grinding. How much do you want to keep saying yes to? How much do you want to keep working for that extra money so you can hit that next level? Those priorities have changed for me."

These days, Leslie takes Wednesdays off and leaves Curate Essentials at 5 pm. She makes time with her family a priority and also "take[s] breaks and go[es] out into the garden." While she is currently satisfied with this approach, Leslie initially struggled to find the right balance after **delegating** tasks and roles at Curate Essentials. She explains,

> when I started hiring more people to take some of the responsibility off of me, I thought, 'what the hell am I supposed to do with myself?' I was actually a little bit lost. I [didn't] even know what is my role in this business anymore.

Figure 10.9.3 Curate Essentials soaps curing.

Source: Courtesy of Leslie Pearson/Curate Essentials

Leslie realized that she had achieved her **goals** for **product development**. Her sister is working as the manager, overseeing product **quality** control and doing "administrative tasks that I feel no longer serve the highest and best use of my time." Leslie has shifted her attention to the evolving "decor, customer relations, [and] building the relationships with the people" (Figure 10.9.3). Curate Essentials is preparing to expand its classroom options, and Leslie has

> been connecting with people that I think might be willing to teach a class. I realize I don't have to be the one bringing all that air, that other people can do it, and bring it, and they can own it. And, that's even way more meaningful to me than if I were out there just like, 'no, I'm the teacher and it's my ego and I've got to be the one.'

Embracing the Vision

As with her previous companies, Leslie has found that she receives a lot of unsolicited business advice. She says,

> I get a lot of people who come up to me and say, 'You could be doing this,' or 'You should be doing this to expand the business.' And, I've kind of come to the idea that I like the **cottage industry**. I like the very much one-on-one relationship I have with my customers, because while I don't prescribe things, my business is really about holistic, mostly preventative medicine. Treating things upfront and teaching them about their own health. I like that because I can really hone in on the specific thing that my customer needs. It doesn't have to be so generic.

As she looks towards the future, Leslie remembers that when she first started sharing her vision for Curate Essentials, people were skeptical. But, now that it has "actually worked," Leslie hopes to one day buy several neighboring buildings to expand Curate Essentials to have a larger presence as a community space. She has already begun saving so that "if the opportunity comes up, my bank account is ready."

Case Concepts, Reflections, and Resources

Concepts

- Branding (Chapter 5)
- Entrepreneurial mindset (Chapter 1)
- Funding through self-financing (Chapter 7)
- Operations management (Chapter 8)
- Serial entrepreneurship (Chapter 1)
- Unique value proposition (Chapter 3)

Reflection Questions

1 Leslie talks about the unsolicited advice entrepreneurs get about their businesses. Think about unexpected feedback you've received about your business. How do you decide which input is relevant and which should be ignored? If you are seeking input, who are the trusted advisors you turn to and why?
2 Leslie's initial assumption about who her customers would be has evolved based on her experiences owning and operating Curate Essentials for three years. Consider the different

approaches to identifying your customers explored in Chapter 2. Which, if any, of these apply to Leslie's business? Which might apply to your own creative business?

3 How would you describe the **unique value proposition** of Curate Essentials? What can you learn from Leslie's journey that can help you better articulate the unique value proposition of your creative business?
4 Leslie describes changing her approach to her business from a "treadmill cycle" to wanting to stop "grinding" and devote more time to family life and being outdoors. Are you comfortable with the amount of time you spend on creative expression, your business, and other aspects of your life? If so, how would you describe your philosophy or approach to balance? If not, is there anything you can learn from Leslie's venture to apply to your own situation?
5 Leslie is a **serial entrepreneur** who has owned and operated multiple ventures during her career. Which elements of the entrepreneurial mindset described in Chapter 1 does Leslie's journey highlight? What has she learned during her journey that could be helpful to you and your business?

Additional Resources

Leslie can be found online at the Curate Essentials website (curateessentials.com) and their Facebook (www.facebook.com/curateessentials) and Instagram (www.instagram.com/curateessentials) accounts, as well as on her artist website (www.lesliekpearson.com).

Further Reading and Viewing

Market Segmentation

Carpenter, A. (n.d.). Market segmentation: Definition, types, benefits, & best practices. *Qualtrics*. https://www.qualtrics.com/experience-management/brand/what-is-market-segmentation/

Hoenig, H. (2025, September 8). Understanding market segmentation: A comprehensive guide. *Investopedia*. https://www.investopedia.com/terms/m/marketsegmentation.asp

Salesforce. (n.d.) Psychographics for marketing: A complete guide. *Salesforce*. https://www.salesforce.com/marketing/psychographics/

Self-Care

ArtistsThrive. (n.d.). Self-care resources. *ArtistsThrive*. https://www.artiststhrive.org/selfcare

McCormick, K. (2024, April 22) 7 ways successful entrepreneurs manage stress. *University of Michigan Center for Entrepreneurship*. https://cfe.umich.edu/7-ways-successful-entrepreneurs-manage-stress/

Tsaousides, T. (2015, October 14). How entrepreneurs can protect their most valuable asset: 5 strategies to guard your mental health from the challenges of entrepreneurship. *Psychology Today*. https://www.psychologytoday.com/us/blog/smashing-the-brainblocks/201510/how-entrepreneurs-can-protect-their-most-valuable-asset

Case 10.10 Larson Wood Designs: The Journey to Full Time Entrepreneurship

Maker Profile

David Larson started his career as a licensed journeyman plumber. In 2020, David was diagnosed with spondylolisthesis, a painful condition of the spine. It became difficult for David to walk or do other activities. He was "trying to avoid surgery, and life got to be really nightmarish for me because of that." While David explored alternative treatments, he

> started doing a lot of woodworking because they shut the world down [due to the COVID pandemic]. I like to build things. I like to do things with my hands. I started framing and building houses when I was 15. So, I have a basic understanding of tools and wood.

David was making gifts for friends and family, but soon he discovered that "I found a love. The first thing I built was a workbench for myself. I felt differently when I was out there at my workbench. I felt great. I just felt really good." With gardening becoming more popular during and after COVID shutdowns, David generated interest in planter boxes he made and began to sell them. By 2021, David's woodworking "started doing well from a monetary standpoint." In 2022, he made "a significant amount of money," doubling his earnings from the year before. By 2023, David realized his woodworking was no longer a hobby. David explains, "When you have this much money coming in, you got to tell somebody at the government."

Introduction to Larson Wood Designs

At the beginning of 2023, David and his wife moved to Lexington, Kentucky. Using Facebook Marketplace ads, he "generated almost $50,000 in sales" in just two months. Facebook Marketplace is an **e-commerce** platform where Facebook users can buy and sell **products**. David's wife encouraged him to start a business and David formed Larson Wood Designs as a **limited liability company**. In addition to planter boxes, David's products include patterned cutting boards and blanket ladders for quilts. David initially relied on Facebook Marketplace ads to market his creations, but found these ads had declining effectiveness starting in 2024.

Transitioning from Employee to Entrepreneur

Thinking about his previous career, David reflects, "I was into the plumbing and pipe fitting stuff because I chased money. I didn't have any passion. I can't say I really looked forward to going to work. It was really hard work in a lot of pain." While David has financial **goals** for Larson Wood Designs, he has experienced a lot of satisfaction from seeing his handmade products helping people, such as when his planter design was the perfect height for a gardener in a wheelchair. David has also found "priceless" gratification from developing custom products for organizations – such as elevated garden beds for a nursing home – and from selling his products to domestic violence shelters and elementary school teachers for classroom use. "I love what I'm doing," David shares.

At the same time, David has discovered that entrepreneurship is

> such a lot harder than you might think. I feel like we get trained from a young age to live these lives that are not going to be fulfilling. Go work at this place where you walk in, and essentially check your soul in at the door. You just go in there and all you have to worry about to provide for yourself is just doing what some other guy tells you to do. And, that is not at all what my life is now. I am scavenging for time to work. I need 40 hours in a day. I really do.

In addition to the demands of juggling his woodworking production with **marketing**, **networking**, **fulfillment**, and administrative tasks, David expressed concerns about the financial uncertainty that emerging **creative entrepreneurs** face. David has also observed that working from home takes a toll on his mental health. "Never leaving home is not good for you at all," he says,

> so part of my job is making sure I'm taking particular certain administrative tasks and going to a coffee shop or a park. Because you'll find it's real easy to have this long to-do list, and you just stay [home] all day.

Next Steps for Larson Wood Designs

David has met several mentors who have provided useful guidance. He notes that he "taught myself a lot by the time I got to the Nest Uplift Makers group, but gosh, what I would've given to had access to the literature in the learning programs they've given me two years ago." In addition to his work with Nest, David has "gotten involved in a lot of good, positive things" since moving to Kentucky. He recently received a Citation of Achievement from the Kentucky House of Representatives, which acknowledged him as "an extraordinarily gifted woodworker who seeks to create heirloom-quality pieces that honor the beauty of natural materials and are inspired by the landscape, heritage, and culture of Kentucky and Appalachia" (Figure 10.10.1).

The citation included an invitation to vend at Kentucky Crafted, a market for the best visual and craft artists in the state. He has also been invited to vend at the Woodland Art Fair, the largest art fair in his area. Being invited to these prestigious events just two years after formalizing his business has signaled to David that the aesthetics and quality of his work are being recognized.

As he considers the next steps for Larson Wood Designs, David explains,

> I'm just so close to the beginning of the business. I've had a big focus on building my reputation, networking, trying to establish myself in the community. That's been one of my big goals, learning where all these markets are. It's hard for me to apply for them when I don't even know about them.

He believes that "as far as a hobby and my creative side, it's all a success. But the part where this is what I'm doing for a living, I have to make money." As long as David continues to meet his financial **objectives**, he considers his business a success.

Case Concepts, Reflections, and Resources

Concepts

- Channels (Chapters 5 and 8)
- Entrepreneurial mindset (Chapter 1)
- Social media marketing (Chapter 5)
- Operations management (Chapter 8)

Reflection Questions

1 David formed Larson Wood Designs as a limited liability company. Research the **business structures** available in your area. (If you live in Australia, Canada, the United Kingdom, or the United States, you can find helpful links in the Further Reading section below.) Is your business formalized? If so, does your current business structure still meet your needs or is

The House of Representatives

Commonwealth of Kentucky

Citation of Achievement

The House of Representatives of the Commonwealth of Kentucky hereby recognizes and honors

Larson Wood Designs

upon being selected by the Kentucky Arts Council for inclusion in the Kentucky Crafted program. This worthwhile initiative is an adjudicated arts marketing assistance program that provides visual and craft artists with arts business training, networking, sales, exhibits, and promotional opportunities. The business is owned by David Larson, an extraordinarily gifted woodworker who seeks to create heirloom-quality pieces that honor the beauty of natural materials and are inspired by the landscape, heritage, and culture of Kentucky and Appalachia. He is now also eligible to exhibit at the popular Kentucky Crafted Market, an annual showcase of the best visual and craft arts and artists in the Commonwealth. Inasmuch as David Larson has distinguished himself as a vital member of Kentucky's rich arts community and has brought immense honor and pride to his family, his community, and to this Commonwealth as a whole by his skill and achievement, the members of this distinguished body are delighted to join Representative Vanessa Grossl in offering him sincere congratulations upon having earned this well-deserved distinction and in extending to him best wishes for the utmost success and good fortune in the future.

Done in Frankfort, Kentucky, this thirteenth day of May, in the year two thousand twenty-five.

Speaker, House of Representatives

Member, House of Representatives

Figure 10.10.1 The Citation of Achievement the Kentucky House of Representatives awarded to Larson Wood Designs.

Source: Courtesy of David Larson/Larson Wood Designs.

there another available structure you should consider? If it isn't formalized, what type of business structure would you consider for the future? Why?

2 David talks about some of the challenges of creative entrepreneurship including balancing production with administrative tasks, working from home, financial uncertainty, and isolation. What resources and supports do you have for coping with these challenges? What resources and supports do you need to build or find?
3 David has been successful in building a reputation locally but he wants to learn more about prestigious markets in his region. What **channels** for marketing or **distribution** would you like to learn more about for your creative ventures? What sources of information could you use to get more information?
4 David explains that working from home constantly is bad for his mental health. Do you work from one location or multiple locations? Does this setup work for you, or do you need to have more or fewer locations for your own mental health? If you need more or different locations, investigate local options for coworking and studio space, as well as options for informal working such as coffee shops and libraries. Were you able to find something that might work better for you and your business?

Additional Resources

David can be found online at the Larson Wood Designs website (larsonwooddesigns.com) and on Facebook (www.facebook.com/larsonwooddesigns) and Instagram (www.instagram.com/larson_wood_designs). David recently launched an Etsy shop (www.etsy.com/shop/LarsonWoodDesigns).

Further Reading

Business Legal Structures

BDC. (2025, March 14). How to choose the right legal form for your business. *BDC*. https://www.bdc.ca/en/articles-tools/start-buy-business/start-business/advantages-different-business-structures

Desprez, A. (2024, December 17). Business structure in UK: A complete guide for choosing the right one. *Yousign*. https://yousign.com/blog/business-structure-uk

Johnson, J. (2024, August 11). How to choose a legal entity for your startup. *CO–U.S. Chamber of Commerce*. https://www.uschamber.com/co/start/startup/choosing-legal-entity-for-small-business

Solo, A. (2025, May 20). Comparing different business structures in Australia. *Sprintlaw*. https://sprintlaw.com.au/articles/comparing-different-business-structures-in-australia/

Coworking

Adam, J. (2023, December 15). Should you use a coworking space? *U.S. News & World Report*. https://careers.usnews.com/advice/articles/should-you-use-a-coworking-space

Roos, D. (n.d.). The pros and cons of coworking spaces. *How Stuff Works*. https://money.howstuffworks.com/deal-with-difficult-coworkers.htm

Appendix A

Glossary

3PL See third-party logistics.

5 Ps The fundamental elements of marketing strategy: Product, Price, Place, Promotion, and People. Also known as the marketing mix.

accelerator A program that provides startups with mentorship, resources, and often funding in exchange for equity, typically lasting three to six months.

acceptable loss The maximum amount of money, time, or resources an entrepreneur is willing to risk or lose when pursuing a new business or opportunity.

account ledger A detailed record of all financial transactions for a specific account, showing debits, credits, and running balances over time.

accounting The systematic recording, measuring, and communication of financial information about a business to various stakeholders.

accounting methods The specific rules and procedures used to record and report financial transactions, such as cash accounting or accrual accounting.

accounts payable Short-term debts a company owes to suppliers or vendors for goods and services received but not yet paid for. This appears as a liability on the balance sheet.

accounts receivable Money owed to a company by customers for goods or services delivered but not yet paid for. This appears as an asset on the balance sheet.

accrual accounting An accounting method where revenues and expenses are recorded when earned or incurred, regardless of when cash is actually received or paid.

achievable One of the SMART criteria for creating objectives that are realistic and attainable given available resources and constraints.

acquisition The purchase of one company by another, where the acquiring company takes control of the target company's assets and operations.

adaptation One of eight traits and behaviors in the entrepreneurial mindset. The ability to adjust strategies, products, or approaches based on changing market conditions, customer feedback, or unexpected challenges.

advertising Paid promotional communication designed to inform, persuade, or remind target audiences about a product, service, or brand through various media channels.

affordable loss principle An effectuation principle where entrepreneurs limit risk by only investing what they can afford to lose, rather than calculating expected returns.

AI See artificial intelligence.

amortization The process of gradually paying off a debt over time through regular payments, or spreading the cost of an intangible asset over its useful life.

anchoring A cognitive bias where people rely too heavily on the first piece of information they receive (the "anchor") when making decisions.

angel investor An individual who provides capital for a business startup, usually in exchange for convertible debt or ownership equity.

Ansoff matrix A framework for identifying growth opportunities based on new and existing products and services through four growth strategies: market penetration, market development, product development, and diversification. Also known as the product/market expansion grid.

anticipated revenue Projected income that a business expects to generate from sales of products or services over a specific period. Used in channel analysis.

artificial intelligence Technology that enables computers and software to perform tasks that typically require human intelligence, such as understanding language, recognizing patterns, making decisions, and automating processes.

artist statement A written description that explains an artist's work, creative process, inspiration, and artistic vision or philosophy.

assets Resources owned by a business that have economic value and can contribute to competitive advantage. Shown on the balance sheet.

assets + competitive advantage Resources and capabilities that give a micro-enterprise a superior position over competitors and are difficult to replicate. An element of the micro-enterprise for creatives canvas.

automation The use of technology and systems to perform tasks with minimal human intervention with the aim of increasing efficiency and/or reducing costs.

avatar A detailed representation of a target customer or user, including demographic, behavioral, geographic, and psychographic needs and motivations used to guide marketing and product decisions.

B2B See business-to-business.

B2C See business-to-consumer.

backward planning A project or time management approach that starts with the desired end result and works backward to determine necessary steps and timelines.

balance sheet A financial statement showing a company's assets, liabilities, and shareholders' equity at a specific point in time.

bargaining power of buyers See buyer power.

bargaining power of suppliers See supplier power.

barriers to entry Obstacles that make it difficult for new companies to enter a market, such as high capital requirements, regulations, brand loyalty, or economies of scale.

baseline measurement The initial data point or standard against which future performance or progress is compared and measured.

BCG matrix See growth-share matrix.

behavioral segmentation Grouping customers based on their purchasing behavior, usage frequency and intensity, usage situations, and desired benefits, including perceived value, pain points, and required features.

belonging framework An approach focused on creating inclusive environments and communities where customers feel valued and connected to the brand.

benefit corporation A for-profit corporation that is legally required to consider the impact of its decisions on society and the environment in addition to shareholders. This business structure must meet higher standards of accountability and transparency while pursuing both profit and positive social and/or environmental impact.

benefits The positive outcomes or value customers receive from using a product or service.

bespoke Custom-made or tailored specifically to individual customer requirements, often commanding premium pricing due to personalization.

best-cost provider strategy The strategy of offering customers the best value for their money by combining elements of low cost and differentiation.

bird-in-hand principle An effectuation principle where entrepreneurs start with available resources (skills, knowledge, network) rather than waiting for ideal conditions or resources.

blocked task A work action that cannot proceed due to dependencies on other incomplete tasks or external factors.

blue ocean An uncontested market space where competition is irrelevant and demand is created rather than fought over.

blue ocean strategy Creating new market spaces by making competition irrelevant through value innovation.

bootstrapping Building and growing a business using personal funds and resources and revenue generated by the business.

Boston Consulting Group matrix See growth-share matrix.

bottleneck A point in a process where the flow of work is restricted, limiting overall system capacity and efficiency.

bottom line See net income.

brand guidelines A set of rules and standards that define how a brand should be visually and verbally presented across all communications and touchpoints.

branding The process of creating a distinctive identity, image, and reputation for a product, service, or company in consumers' minds through consistent messaging and visual elements.

breakeven analysis A calculation to determine the point at which total revenue equals total costs, resulting in neither profit nor loss.

broad differentiation strategy See differentiation strategy.

business loan Debt financing obtained from banks or financial institutions that must be repaid with interest. Can be used to fund business operations or expansion and often requires collateral and/or a business plan.

business model The framework describing how a company creates, delivers, and captures value, including how it generates revenue and its cost structure.

business model canvas A visual tool with nine building blocks (key partners, key activities, key resources, value propositions, customer relationships, channels, customer segments, cost structure, and revenue streams) for developing, analyzing, and communicating a business model.

business partnership A business structure available in the United Kingdom where two or more people share ownership and responsibility for running a business, with partners sharing profits, losses, and unlimited personal liability for business debts unless structured as a limited partnership.

business plan A comprehensive document outlining a company's objectives, strategies, market analysis, financial projections, and operational plans.

business structure The legal and organizational framework of a company. Examples include partnership, corporation, and cooperative. In the United States, additional options include sole proprietorship, benefit corporation, and limited liability company (LLC). In the United Kingdom, additional options include sole trader, limited company, and social enterprise.

business-to-business (B2B) Commerce transactions between companies rather than between a company and individual consumers.

business-to-consumer (B2C) Commerce transactions directly between a company and end-use consumers.

buyer power The influence customers have to influence prices, quality, or sales or service terms. Strong when buyers are large, concentrated, or have many alternatives. Examined through the five forces analysis.

buyers Individuals or businesses that purchase goods or services for their own use or for resale.

C corporation A business structure in the United States for corporations wherein it is taxed as a separate entity, resulting in double taxation where profits are taxed at the corporate level and again when distributed as dividends to shareholders.

canvas See modeling canvas.

capacity The maximum amount of work, production, or output that a system, process, or organization can handle within a given timeframe.

capacity building The process of developing and strengthening skills, abilities, processes, and resources within an entrepreneur or an organization.

CAPEX See capital expenditure.

capital Financial resources, assets, or funds used to start, operate, or grow a business.

capital expenditure (CAPEX) Money spent on acquiring, upgrading, or maintaining fixed assets like property, technology, or equipment that will benefit the business long-term.

cash Liquid financial assets including currency, bank deposits, and other readily convertible monetary instruments. Shown on the balance sheet.

cash accounting An accounting method where transactions are recorded only when cash is actually received or paid out.

cash cows High-market-share products in low-growth markets that generate substantial cash with minimal investment as shown on a growth-share matrix.

cash flow The movement of money in and out of a business over a specific period, crucial for understanding liquidity and operational health.

cash flow from financing activities Cash movements related to borrowing, repaying debt, issuing stock, paying dividends, and other financing transactions as shown on the statement of cash flows.

cash flow from investing activities Cash movements related to buying and selling long-term assets, investments, and capital expenditures as shown on the statement of cash flows.

cash flow from operating activities Cash movements generated from the core business operations, including sales receipts and operating expense payments, as shown on the statement of cash flows.

cash flow statement See statement of cash flows.

causal logic A traditional business planning approach that starts with a goal and identifies the means to achieve it.

chamber of commerce A business association that promotes commercial interests and provides networking opportunities for local businesses.

channel analysis The evaluation of different distribution methods and pathways used to deliver products or services to customers.

channel costs The expenses associated with using specific distribution channels, including fees, commissions, and operational costs. Evaluated as part of a channel analysis.

channel reach The number of potential customers that can be accessed through a particular distribution channel. Evaluated as part of a channel analysis.

channel risks Potential threats and vulnerabilities associated with using specific distribution channels or sales pathways. Evaluated as part of a channel analysis.

channels The pathways or networks through which products or services move from the producer to the end consumer. These can include direct channels (selling directly to customers through websites, retail stores, or sales teams) or indirect channels (using intermediaries like wholesalers, distributors, retailers, or online marketplaces). One of the nine building blocks of the business model canvas.

client communications The various ways businesses interact with and relay information to their customers. An element of the micro-enterprise for creatives canvas.

cognitive bias Systematic patterns of deviation from rationality in judgment and decision-making. Mental shortcuts or tendencies allow people to process information quickly but in ways that can lead to flawed conclusions through errors in thinking, perception, and memory.

COGS See cost of goods sold.

collaboration Working together with others, including partners, customers, or stakeholders, to create mutual value. When paired with communication, it is one of eight aspects of the entrepreneurial mindset.

collaborators Parties working together on projects or initiatives, often with shared goals and complementary skills. Part of the partners, collaborators, stakeholders block of the micro-enterprise for creatives canvas.

comfort with risk An entrepreneur's willingness to accept uncertainty and potential losses in the pursuit of opportunities. One of eight aspects of the entrepreneurial mindset.

commission A payment structure where individuals earn money based on a percentage of sales or transactions they generate, or a percentage of sales or transactions paid to an agent or another business.

communication The exchange of information, ideas, and feedback between entrepreneurs and stakeholders. When paired with collaboration, it is one of eight aspects of the entrepreneurial mindset.

compensation The total package of monetary and non-monetary rewards provided to employees in exchange for their work and services. Micro-enterprise owners/entrepreneurs can choose how they are compensated, including with wages or salary, withdrawing funds as needed (if they are sole owners), profit distributions, and/or by commission.

competitive advantage Strengths or circumstances that allow companies to outperform competitors and deliver superior value to customers, thereby establishing a superior business position.

competitor Other businesses offering similar products or services to the same target market.

consignment An arrangement where goods are placed with a retailer who only pays the supplier after the goods are sold, with unsold items typically returnable.

consumer An individual or entity that purchases and uses goods or services for consumption rather than resale.

content creator An individual or entity that produces digital content such as videos, articles, and social media posts to engage audiences and to monetize.

contractor An independent service provider who performs work for a company without being hired as an employee.

contributed income Revenue from donations, grants, or gifts, typically used by non-profits, non-governmental organizations, and social enterprises.

contribution margin The difference between revenue and variable costs, representing the amount available to cover fixed costs and generate profit.

convergent thinking A problem-solving approach focused on finding a single, best solution by narrowing down possibilities.

cooperative A business structure where the organization is owned and democratically controlled by its members (customers, employees, or suppliers) who share in the profits and/or decision-making based on their participation rather than investment.

copyright Legal protection granted to creators of original works, giving them exclusive rights to use, reproduce, and distribute their creations.

corporation A business structure available in the United States and Canada that creates a legal entity that exists separately from its owners (shareholders), providing limited liability protection while being subject to corporate taxation and formal governance requirements.

cost leadership strategy A strategy based on achieving the lowest costs of production and distribution while maintaining acceptable quality.

cost of goods See cost of goods sold.

cost of goods sold (COGS) The direct costs associated with producing goods sold by a company, including materials, labor, and manufacturing overhead. Shown on the income statement.

cost structure The arrangement and proportion of fixed and variable costs in a business model. One of nine blocks in the business model canvas.

cost-benefit analysis Systematic evaluation comparing the costs of an action against its expected benefits.

cost-plus pricing A pricing strategy where the selling price is determined by adding a markup percentage to the total cost of producing the product or service.

costs The expenses incurred in running a business, including fixed costs such as rent or salaries and variable costs such as materials commissions.

cottage industry A small-scale manufacturing company, typically using handmade or artisanal crafts and privately owned by an individual or family.

crazy quilt principle An effectuation principle that emphasizes building partnerships and alliances with diverse stakeholders who commit resources to the venture.

creative entrepreneur An individual who builds a business around their artistic talents, creative skills, or cultural products.

creative entrepreneurship Entrepreneurship in creative industries like arts, crafts, media, design, or entertainment.

creative spacemaking Developing environments or opportunities that foster creativity and innovation.

creativity The ability to generate novel and useful ideas, solutions, or approaches. When paired with innovation, it is one of eight aspects of the entrepreneurial mindset.

critical thinking Objective analysis and evaluation of information to form reasoned judgments and decisions. When paired with problem-solving, it is one of eight aspects of the entrepreneurial mindset.

crowdfunding Raising capital by collecting small amounts of money from a large number of people, typically via online platforms.

crowdfunding campaign An effort to raise funds through crowdfunding for a specific product, service, or business including marketing to raise awareness of both the business, product, or service and the fundraising activities.

current assets Short-term assets that can be converted to cash within one year, including cash, inventory, and accounts receivable. Shown on the balance sheet.

current liabilities Short-term debts and obligations that must be paid within one year. Shown on the balance sheet.

current ratio A liquidity ratio calculated by dividing current assets by current liabilities to measure short-term financial health.

customer decision-making process The stages consumers go through when making purchase decisions including problem recognition, information search, evaluation of alternatives, purchase decision, and post-purchase behavior.

customer gains See gains.

customer pains See pain points.

customer profile A detailed description of ideal customers, including demographics, behaviors, needs, and preferences. Shown on the value proposition canvas. Also known as an avatar or buyer persona.

customer relationships The types of relationships a company establishes with specific customer segments including personal assistance, self-service, automated services, and/or communities. One of nine building blocks of the business model canvas.

cyclical advantage A temporary competitive advantage that arises from market fluctuations or short-term trends.

D2C See direct-to-consumer.

debt Money owed by a company to creditors, including loans, bonds, and other financial obligations.

debt financing Raising capital by borrowing money, which must be repaid with interest. Also known as debt funding.

debt to assets A financial ratio that measures the percentage of a company's assets financed through debt rather than equity.

delegation The process of assigning tasks and responsibilities to others while maintaining accountability for results.

demand The quantity of a product or service that consumers are willing and able to buy at various prices.

demographic segmentation Dividing markets based on statistical characteristics like age, gender, income, education, ethnicity, occupation, and family status.

depreciation The systematic and gradual decrease in the value of a tangible asset over time due to wear and tear or obsolescence. Shown on the income statement.

design thinking A human-centered approach to innovation and problem-solving that emphasizes empathy, ideation, prototyping, and testing to create solutions.

differentiation A competitive strategy that involves making products or services distinct from competitors through unique features, benefits, or branding.

differentiation strategy A strategy based on offering unique products or services that customers perceive as providing superior value and are willing to pay premium prices for.

digital entrepreneurship Entrepreneurship that leverages digital technologies to create and grow businesses.

digital marketing Marketing products or services using digital channels like websites, social media, email, and search engines.

direct costs Costs directly attributable to the production of a specific product or service.

direct-to-consumer Selling products directly to customers without intermediaries. Also known as D2C or DTC.

distribution channels See channels.

distributors Intermediaries who purchase products from manufacturers and sell them to retailers or end customers, often providing storage and logistics services.

divergent thinking A creative thinking process that generates multiple ideas, solutions, or possibilities for a given problem.

diversification Entering new markets with new products. One of four growth strategies explored through the Ansoff matrix.

dogs Low-growth, low-market-share products or businesses, as shown on a growth-share matrix

DTC See direct-to-consumer.

durable assets Long-lasting physical assets such as equipment, machinery, and buildings that provide value over multiple years.

e-commerce Buying and selling goods and services online.

earned income Revenue generated from selling products or services, rather than from donations or investments.

Earnings Before Interest, Taxes, Depreciation, and Amortization A measure of company profitability that excludes certain non-operating expenses to assess core business performance as shown on the income statement. Also known as EBITDA.

EBITDA See Earnings Before Interest, Taxes, Depreciation, and Amortization.

economic analysis The systematic exploration of economic factors and conditions that may impact business decisions and market opportunities. Part of a PESTLE analysis.

economic development organization An entity that promotes economic growth and business development within a specific region or community.

economies of scale Cost advantages achieved when production or purchasing increases, leading to lower per-unit costs.

effectiveness The degree to which objectives are achieved and desired results are accomplished.

effectuation An entrepreneurial decision-making approach that starts with available means and focuses on controlling outcomes rather than predicting them.

efficiency The ratio of useful output to total input, measuring how well resources are utilized to achieve desired results with minimal waste.

end user The final consumer or person who will ultimately use a product or service.

end-user empathy The ability to understand and share the feelings, needs, and experiences of the final consumer or user of a product or service.

enterprise A business organization, especially one that involves considerable risk, initiative, or complexity.

entrepreneur support organization An entity that provides resources, guidance, and assistance to help entrepreneurs start and grow their businesses.

entrepreneurial mindset A set of behaviors, characteristics, skills, and ways of thinking focused on creating value, including eight elements: future orientation, creativity & innovation, comfort with risk, communication & collaboration, flexibility & adaptation, critical thinking & problem-solving, initiative & self-reliance, and opportunity recognition.

entrepreneurial motivations The driving forces that inspire individuals to start and run businesses and organizations like independence, financial gain, or social impact.

entrepreneurial pivot A radical strategic shift where a business changes its products, services, market focus, or business model dramatically based on market feedback and learning.

environmental analysis The systematic exploration of factors in the physical environment that may impact business decisions and market opportunities. Part of a PESTLE analysis.

environmental sustainability Business practices that meet current needs while preserving resources and minimizing environmental impact for future generations.

equity (equity funding) Ownership interest in a business, represented by shares of stock.

equity dilution The reduction in ownership percentage when new shares are issued.

evaluation of alternatives The third stage in the customer decision-making process, where consumers compare different options based on their criteria and preferences.

exemplars Entrepreneurs who are doing what you want to do in your business with an established level of success.

exit event An event that allows investors to liquidate their investment such as an acquisition or IPO.

exit strategy A plan for how entrepreneurs or investors will eventually leave or sell their stake in a business.

export The sale and shipment of goods or services from one country to buyers in another country.

exporters Businesses that sell and ship goods to customers in other countries.

external environment All factors outside of a business that can affect its success. A PESTLE analysis is one framework for exploring these factors.

features Specific attributes, characteristics, or functionalities of a product or service that distinguish it from competitors.

financial assets Non-physical assets that derive value from contractual claims such as stocks, bonds, and bank deposits.

financial statements Formal records of the financial activities and position of a business, including the income statement, balance sheet, and statement of cash flows.

financing The process of obtaining funds or capital to support business operations, growth, or investment activities.

firm infrastructure The support systems and organizational structure that enable a company to function effectively. Examined as part of the support activities in a value chain analysis.

five forces analysis A framework analyzing competitive intensity within an industry through five forces: buyer power, rivalry among existing competitors, supplier power, threat of new entrants, and threat of substitutes.

fixed costs Costs that remain constant regardless of the level of production or sales such as rent or insurance.

flexibility The ability to change direction quickly in response to new information or circumstances. When paired with adaptation, it is one of eight aspects of the entrepreneurial mindset.

flowchart A visual diagram used in process mapping that represents a process or workflow using symbols and arrows to show the sequence of steps.

focus strategy A strategy based on concentrating on a narrow market segment or niche.

focused differentiation strategy A strategy based on offering unique products or services to a narrow market segment.

focused low-cost strategy A strategy based on being the low-cost provider within a niche market.

for-profit An organization operated with the primary goal of generating profit for owners or shareholders.

founder The person who establishes and initially develops a business or organization.

four-action framework Tool for blue ocean strategy asking what to eliminate, reduce, raise, and create in your value proposition.

fragmented market A market with many small competitors and no dominant players.

friends and family funding Initial capital raised from personal relationships rather than formal investors or financial institutions.

fulfillment The process of receiving, processing, and delivering customer orders, including inventory management and shipping.

funding Financial resources that organizations use to start, operate, or expand.

funding source The origin of capital used to finance business operations, including self-funding, debt, investments, and grants.

future orientation A focus on long-term goals and planning for future opportunities and challenges. One of eight aspects of the entrepreneurial mindset.

GAAP See Generally Accepted Accounting Principles.

gains The outcomes and benefits customers want to achieve or would be surprised to receive. Shown on the value proposition canvas.

general partnership A Canadian business structure where two or more individuals or entities carry on business together with the intention of making a profit, sharing management responsibilities and unlimited personal liability for partnership debts and obligations.

Generally Accepted Accounting Principles (GAAP) Standardized accounting rules and procedures used in the United States to ensure consistency and transparency in financial reporting.

generative engine optimization (GEO) Optimizing content and websites to improve visibility and ranking in AI-powered search engines and generative AI tools that provide direct answers rather than traditional search result links.

generic competitive strategies Fundamental strategies for achieving competitive advantage across an industry.

GEO See generative engine optimization.

geographic segmentation Dividing markets based on physical location, density, and climate or seasonality, such as country or region; urban, suburban, or rural; or cold or humid subtropical.

Goal A desired outcome or target that an individual or organization aims to achieve within a specific timeframe.

goods Tangible products that can be manufactured, stored, and sold to customers.

grant Non-repayable funds provided by a government agency, foundation, or other organization for a specific purpose.

grantmaker An organization or individual that provides grants or funding to support specific projects, causes, or organizations.

gross margin The difference between revenue and cost of goods sold, expressed as a percentage of revenue and shown on the income statement.

growth strategy A plan for expanding a business's operations, revenue, and/or market share.

growth-share matrix A portfolio management tool that classifies business units based on market share and market growth rate into four quadrants: stars (high growth, high market share), cash cows (low growth, high market share), question marks (high growth, low market share), and dogs (low growth, low market share). Also known as the BCG matrix or Boston Consulting Group matrix.

hidden costs Unexpected or undisclosed expenses that are not immediately apparent in the initial price of or budget for a product or service.

highly concentrated market A market dominated by few large players with significant market share.

HR (HRM) See human resources management.

human resources management The approach to managing people within an organization, including recruitment, training, and employee relations. Evaluated as part of the support activities in a value chain analysis. Also known as HR management or HRM.

ideal client The perfect customer who derives maximum value from your offering and represents the most profitable segment. An element of the micro-enterprise for creatives canvas.

ideation The process of generating, developing, and communicating new ideas. An element of design thinking.

impact The effect or influence a business has on customers, communities, or society. An element of the micro-enterprise for creatives canvas.

import The purchase and receipt of goods or services from sellers in other countries for use domestically.

importers Businesses that bring goods into a country from foreign suppliers for domestic sale or use.

inbound logistics The processes involved in receiving, storing, and distributing inputs and raw materials for production. Evaluated as part of the primary activities in a value chain analysis.

income statement A financial statement showing revenues, expenses, and net income over a specific period. Also known as a profit and loss (P&L) statement.

incubator A program or facility that provides early-stage startups with office space, mentorship, resources, and support services over an extended period (typically one to two years) to help them develop their business ideas into viable companies, usually without taking equity or with minimal equity requirements.

Indiegogo A crowdfunding platform that allows entrepreneurs and creators to raise money for projects, products, or causes through small contributions from many backers, offering both all-or-nothing and flexible funding options.

indirect costs Costs that are not directly attributable to a specific product or service but support the overall operation of the business, such as utilities.

industry See sector.

industry life cycle See market stage.

information search The second stage in the customer decision-making process where consumers actively seek information about products or services to meet their identified needs.

initial public offering (IPO) The first sale of a company's stock to the public, transitioning from private ownership to being publicly traded and owned.

innovation The implementation of new ideas, methods, products, or services that create value.

intellectual property Intangible assets created by human intellect, including patents, trademarks, copyrights, and trade secrets.

interest The cost of borrowing money, typically expressed as a percentage of the principal amount and shown on the income statement.

internal process refinement The ongoing improvement and optimization of internal business processes to increase efficiency and quality.

initiative The ability to take action and begin projects without being prompted by others. When paired with self-reliance, it is one of eight aspects of the entrepreneurial mindset.

introvert Personality type characterized by inward focus, preference for solitude, and energy drawn from internal reflection.

inventory Raw materials, work-in-progress, and finished goods held for sale. Shown on the balance sheet.

inventory turnover A ratio that measures how frequently a company sells and replaces its inventory over a specific period.

investments Assets purchased with the expectation of generating income or appreciating in value over time. Shown on the balance sheet.

investor An individual or entity that provides capital to businesses in exchange for financial returns or equity ownership.

IPO See initial public offering.

key activities The most important actions a company must perform to operate successfully and deliver its value proposition. One of nine building blocks in the business model canvas.

key partners The network of suppliers, allies, and partner organizations that help the business model function effectively. One of nine building blocks in the business model canvas.

key performance indicators (KPIs) Specific, measurable metrics used to evaluate how effectively a business is achieving its objectives, and to provide quantifiable data to track progress, make informed decisions, and identify areas for improvement.

key resources The most important assets required to make a business model work, including physical, intellectual, human, or financial resources. One of nine building blocks in the business model canvas.

Kickstarter A rewards-based crowdfunding platform where creators seek funding for creative projects by offering backers various rewards or early access to products, using an all-or-nothing funding model where projects must reach their goal to receive any money.

KPIs See key performance indicators.

Landed cost The total cost of importing goods, including purchase price, shipping, insurance, customs duties, taxes, and other fees until the product reaches its destination.

lean canvas A simplified, one-page business model template adapted from the business model canvas and emphasizing problem-solution fit and key metrics.

legal analysis The systematic exploration of legal factors, regulations, and requirements that may impact business operations and decisions. Part of a PESTLE analysis.

lemonade principle An effectuation principle describing making the best of unexpected situations by turning setbacks into opportunities.

liabilities A financial obligation or debt owed by a business to others, shown on the balance sheet.

licensing The practice of granting permission to use intellectual property or assets in exchange for fees or royalties.

licensing agreement A legal contract that outlines the terms and conditions for using another party's intellectual property or assets.

limited company A UK business structure where the company's finances are separate from shareholders' personal finances, providing limited liability protection to owners.

limited liability company (LLC) A business structure available in the United States that combines the liability protection of a corporation with the tax benefits and operational flexibility of a partnership, where owners (called members) are not personally liable for business debts.

liquid assets Assets that can be quickly and easily converted to cash without significant loss of value.

liquidate The process of converting assets into cash, often when closing a business or selling off inventory or investments.

liquidators Companies that purchase excess, returned, or discontinued inventory at discounted prices and resell it to recover value.

low-cost provider strategy See cost leadership.

maker Artists, artisans, designers, and others whose primary form of expression is through the making of goods and/or services.

makerspace A collaborative workspace equipped with tools, equipment, and technology such as 3D printers, laser cutters, and metalworking tools where entrepreneurs, inventors, and creators can prototype, build, and test their product ideas while sharing resources and knowledge with other makers.

manufacturers Companies that produce finished goods from raw materials or components.

manufacturing The process of converting raw materials into finished products through various production methods and techniques.

MAP See minimum advertised price.

margin See profit margin.

market The potential customers of a product or service, or the place where buyers and sellers come together to exchange goods and services. The latter is also known as a marketplace.

market concentration The degree to which a market is dominated by a small number of firms.

market demand See demand.

market development Selling existing products in new markets. One of four growth strategies explored through the Ansoff matrix.

market growth The rate at which a market is expanding, typically measured annually.

market penetration Increasing sales of existing products in existing markets. One of four growth strategies explored through the Ansoff matrix.

market research The systematic collection and analysis of information about target markets, customers, and competitors.

market segmentation The process of dividing a broad market into smaller, distinct groups of consumers who share similar characteristics, needs, behaviors, or preferences to identify subsets of customers that can be targeted with tailored marketing strategies and products. Includes behavioral, demographic, geographic, and psychographic segmentation.

market share A company's portion of total market sales or volume.

market size The total revenue or unit volume potential of a market.

market stage (industry life cycle) The stages of growth and decline that industries experience over time, progressing from introduction to growth, maturity, and decline.

market testing Evaluating customer response to a product or service before full-scale launch.

marketing The activities and processes involved in creating, communicating, delivering, and exchanging offerings that have value for customers and stakeholders.

marketing & sales Business activities focused on promoting products or services and converting prospects into paying customers. Evaluated as part of the primary activities in a value chain analysis.

marketing mix See 5 Ps.

marketing plan A comprehensive document outlining marketing strategies, tactics, and objectives for achieving business goals.

marketing strategy A plan for how a business will reach its target market and achieve its marketing objectives, ideally aligned with the business strategy.

marketplace The environment where buyers and sellers interact to exchange goods, services, or information.

measurable One of the SMART criteria for setting objectives and referring to objectives that can be tracked and assessed.

merchandizing The practice of promoting and selling products through strategic presentation, pricing, and placement.

metric Quantifiable measures used to track and assess business performance and progress toward goals. Visualized in the lean canvas.

micro-enterprise for creatives canvas A specialized canvas tailored for creative professionals to map their business model, considering unique aspects of creative work.

micro-enterprises Very small businesses, typically with fewer than 20 employees and limited startup capital.

mindset The attitudes, beliefs, and mental approaches that shape how people think.

minimum advertised price (MAP) The lowest price that retailers are allowed to advertise a manufacturer's products to maintain price consistency and brand value.

minimum viable products (MVP) A simple version of a product that can be released to test core assumptions with early customers.

modeling canvas Visual framework used to map, analyze, and communicate aspects of a business and its business model.

money avoidance A money script where individuals avoid thinking about or dealing with financial matters.

money script inventory An assessment tool that identifies underlying beliefs and attitudes about money.

money scripts Unconscious beliefs about money developed in childhood that influence financial behaviors.

money status A money script linking self-worth and social status to wealth and material possessions.

money vigilance A money script characterized by being secretive or anxious about money matters.

money worship A money script that equates money with happiness and believes money solves problems.

mood board A visual collage that communicates the aesthetic, style, or concept for a creative project or product.

multi-sided business model A business model that serves multiple customer groups simultaneously, often facilitating interactions between them.

MVP See minimum viable product.

nascent entrepreneurship The early stage of entrepreneurship when individuals are actively trying to start a business.

necessity entrepreneurship Starting a business based on financial necessity due to precarious employment, underemployment, or unemployment.

need recognition See problem/need recognition.

net income The total profit of a company after all expenses, taxes, and costs have been deducted from revenue. Shown on the income statement.

net profit margin A profitability ratio calculated by dividing net income by total revenue, expressed as a percentage.

networking The process of building and maintaining professional relationships to exchange information and create business opportunities.

niche strategy See focus strategy.

non-current assets Long-term assets that are not expected to be converted to cash within one year, such as property and equipment. Shown on the balance sheet.

non-current liabilities Long-term debts and obligations that are not due within the next year. Shown on the balance sheet.

non-governmental organization A private organization that operates independently of government and typically serves public or social purposes.

non-profit An organization operated for purposes other than generating profit, typically focused on social, educational, or charitable missions.

noncustomers People who currently don't use your industry's products but could become customers through value innovation. An important aspect of blue ocean strategy.

objective A target or outcome that supports the achievement of a broader goal.

offerings The products or services that a company provides to its customers or market.

operating costs The ongoing expenses required to run a business's day-to-day operations. Shown on the income statement.

operating cycle The time it takes for a business to purchase inventory, sell it, and collect cash from customers.

operational activities Specific tasks and processes involved in the core functioning of a business, such as production, inventory management, and service delivery. Visualized on the micro-enterprise for creatives canvas.

operations The core business activities involved in producing and delivering products or services to customers. Can be evaluated as part of the primary activities in a value chain analysis.

operations management The administration and oversight of business processes to ensure efficient and effective operations.

opportunity recognition The ability to identify and evaluate potential business opportunities in the marketplace. One of eight aspects of the entrepreneurial mindset.

outbound logistics The processes involved in storing, transporting, and delivering finished products to customers. Evaluated as part of the primary activities in a value chain analysis.

outsourcing The practice of contracting external organizations, individuals, or tools to perform business functions rather than handling them internally.

overhead (overhead costs) Ongoing expenses of running a business such as rent, utilities, and administrative salaries.

P&L (P&L statement) See income statement.

packaging The process of enclosing products in containers or wrappers for protection, preservation, and marketing purposes.

pain points Problems, frustrations, or obstacles customers experience when trying to accomplish jobs or tasks. Visualized in the value proposition canvas.

pains See pain points.

para-social One-sided relationships where individuals feel connected to media personalities or brands without reciprocal interaction, common in influencer marketing.

parallel tasks Work activities that can be performed simultaneously rather than sequentially, helping to reduce overall project time. Analyzed with process mapping.

partners External organizations or individuals that collaborate with a business to achieve mutual benefits. Part of the Partners, Collaborators, Stakeholders block in the micro-enterprise for creatives canvas.

partnership A business structure for a company owned by two or more people who share profits, losses, and management responsibilities, with partners typically having unlimited personal liability for business obligations.

passive income Revenue generated with minimal ongoing effort or active involvement from the entrepreneur.

patent Legal intellectual property protection that grants inventors exclusive rights to their inventions for a specified period.

Patreon A membership platform that allows creators to receive recurring funding from their fans.

penetration pricing A pricing objective involving setting a low initial price to attract a large number of customers and gain market share.

people One of the 5 Ps of the marketing mix, referring to all individuals involved in the delivery of a product or service, including employees and customers.

perceived value The value that customers believe they receive from a product or service, which may differ from its objective value.

performance ratio A metric that compares actual results to expected or benchmark performance levels.

PESTLE analysis A planning framework examining six factors in the external environment (political, economic, social, technological, legal, and environmental) that may impact a business.

pilot-in-the-plane principle An effectuation principle where the entrepreneur maintains control over the venture's direction rather than being a passive participant.

pitch competition An event where entrepreneurs present their business ideas to judges for feedback, recognition, and/or funding.

pivot See entrepreneurial pivot.

place One of the 5 Ps of the marketing mix, referring to the channels and locations where products or services are made available to customers.

point of marginal cheapness In the Van Westendorp analysis, the price point below which customers begin to question product quality due to the unusually low price.

point of marginal expensiveness In the Van Westendorp analysis, the price point above which customers consider a product too expensive and demand drops significantly.

political analysis The systematic exploration of political factors, governmental policies, and armed conflicts/wars that may impact business operations and decisions. Part of a PESTLE analysis.

Porter's five forces analysis See five forces analysis.

Porter's value chain analysis See value chain analysis.

portfolio business model Using multiple revenue streams or business units to diversify risk and maximize opportunities.

positioning The marketing strategy process of establishing a distinct place for a product or brand in the minds of target customers.

positioning maps Visual tools that plot brands or products on two-dimensional grids based on key attributes to understand competitive positioning.

post-purchase behavior The fifth stage in the customer decision-making process, encompassing consumer actions and feelings after buying a product, including satisfaction evaluation, usage patterns, and potential repurchase decisions.

PPE See property, plant, and equipment.

pre-orders Sales of products that are paid for before they are manufactured or officially released. Can be used to assess demand, market test, and/or to raise funds for production.

price One of the 5 Ps of the marketing mix, representing the monetary value assigned to a product or service, as well as pricing strategies and tactics used.

price elasticity The responsiveness of demand to a change in price; measures consumer sensitivity to pricing.

price sensitivity The degree to which customers are affected by changes in price.

Price Sensitivity Meter See Van Westendorp analysis.

price skimming See skimming pricing.

pricing The process of determining the optimal price for products or services based on business strategy, costs, competition, customer value perception.

pricing objectives The goals a company aims to achieve through its pricing strategy, such as profit maximization, market share growth, or competitive positioning.

pricing signal Information that price communicates to consumers about quality, value, or brand positioning beyond just cost.

primary activities Core business processes that directly contribute to creating and delivering value to customers. Evaluated through value chain analysis.

primary market research Original research conducted directly with customers through surveys, interviews, focus groups, or observations.

pro forma financial statements Projected financial statements that show expected future performance based on assumptions and estimates.

problem A specific challenge or need that customers face, which a business can address through its offerings. Visualized on the lean canvas.

problem-solving The process of identifying challenges and developing effective solutions. When paired with critical thinking, it is one of eight aspects of the entrepreneurial mindset.

problem/need recognition The first stage of the customer decision-making process where consumers identify a gap between their current and desired state.

process A series of connected steps or activities designed to achieve a specific outcome or result.

process mapping The visual documentation of workflow steps, decisions, and interactions within a business process.

process optimization The practice of improving business processes to increase efficiency, reduce waste, and enhance quality.

process time The total time required to complete a specific business process from start to finish.

procurement The process of acquiring goods, services, or resources needed for business operations. Evaluated as part of the support activities in a value chain analysis.

product Tangible goods that a business creates and sells to customers. Visualized on the value proposition canvas and part of the 5 Ps of the marketing mix.

product development Developing new products for existing markets. One of four growth strategies explored through the Ansoff matrix.

product line A group of related products offered by a company that serve similar customer needs or markets.

product mix The complete range of products or services offered by a company across different categories.

product-based business A company that generates revenue primarily through the sale of physical goods or tangible products.

product-market fit The degree to which a product satisfies strong market demand and meets customer needs effectively.

product/market expansion grid See Ansoff matrix.

production The process of creating goods or services using labor, materials, and equipment.

productivity A measure of efficiency that compares output generated to input resources used.

profit The financial gain remaining after all business expenses are subtracted from revenue.

profit and loss statement See income statement.

profit margin The percentage of revenue that remains as profit after all expenses are deducted, indicating business efficiency and profitability.

profit maximization A pricing objective characterized by setting prices to achieve the highest possible profit.

promotion One of the 5 Ps of the marketing mix, encompassing all communication activities used to inform and persuade target audiences including advertising, public relations, personal selling, direct marketing, and sales promotions.

proof of concept Evidence demonstrating that a business idea or product is feasible and has potential for success.

property, plant, and equipment (PPE) Long-term tangible assets that a company owns and uses in its operations to generate revenue, including land, buildings, machinery, equipment, and vehicles, which are recorded on the balance sheet at their cost minus accumulated depreciation.

prototype An early model or sample of a product used to test concepts, features, and functionality before full production.

prototyping The process of creating preliminary versions of products to validate ideas and gather feedback. An element of design thinking.

psychographic segmentation Dividing markets based on activities, interests, opinions, values, attitudes, lifestyles, and personality traits.

public relations Strategic communication activities designed to build and maintain positive relationships between an organization and its stakeholders.

publicly traded Companies whose shares are available for purchase by the general public on stock exchanges.

purchase decision The fourth stage in the customer decision-making process where consumers choose a specific product or service to buy.

quality The degree to which products or services meet or exceed customer expectations and business specifications or requirements.

question marks High-growth, low-market-share products/businesses, as shown on a growth-share matrix

R & D See research and development.

range of acceptable prices In the Van Westendorp analysis, the price band within which customers consider a product reasonably priced, bounded by points of marginal cheapness and expensiveness.

red ocean Existing market space with intense competition. Avoided through blue ocean strategy.

relational pricing signals Price information that communicates brand positioning relative to competitors or product categories.

relevant One of the SMART criteria for setting objectives, referring to objectives that are meaningful and aligned with broader purposes.

research and development Activities aimed at creating new products, services, or processes through innovation and experimentation. Displayed on the income statement. Also known as R&D.

retail The sale of goods or services directly to end consumers through physical or online stores.

return on investment A performance measure calculating the efficiency of an investment by comparing gains to costs, expressed as a percentage. Also known as ROI.

revenue The income generated from the sale of goods or services. Shown on the income statement.

revenue streams The various ways a company generates income from each customer segment. Visualized on the business model canvas.

revenue-share A business model where partners or collaborators split the income generated from a venture according to agreed-upon percentages.

rivalry among existing competitors The intensity of competition among firms already in the industry. Explored using the five forces analysis.

ROI See return on investment.

royalties Payments made to owners of intellectual property for the right to use their assets, typically based on sales or usage. See also licensing.

S corporation A business structure in the United States for corporations wherein it elects special tax status to avoid double taxation by passing income, losses, and deductions through to shareholders' personal tax returns.

sales volume The quantity of products or services sold during a specific period, often measured in units or monetary value.

saturated market A market where demand for a product or service has been fully met by existing suppliers.

SBA See Small Business Administration.

scalability The ability of a business to grow and handle increased demand without proportionally increasing costs or complexity.

scaling Growing a business by increasing revenue faster than costs, often through systems and processes.

scope creep The uncontrolled expansion of project requirements beyond the original plan, often leading to delays and increasing costs.

search engine optimization (SEO) Optimizing website content and structure to improve visibility and ranking in search engine results.

secondary market research Analysis of existing data and information from external sources like industry reports, government statistics, or published studies.

sector A distinct area of the economy where businesses share similar products, services, or markets, such as healthcare, transportation, or retail.

seed funding Early-stage investment in a startup.

self-funding The practice of financing business operations using personal savings, retained earnings, or internal cash flow.

self-reliance The ability to depend on one's own capabilities and resources without relying on external support. When paired with initiative, it is one of eight aspects of the entrepreneurial mindset.

selling, general, administrative (SGA) Operating expenses that are not directly related to production, including marketing, management, and administrative costs. Shown on the income statement.

SEO See search engine optimization.

sequential process Work activities that must be completed in a specific order, with each step depending on the completion of previous steps. Analyzed with process mapping.

serial entrepreneurship The practice of starting multiple businesses over time, often selling or moving on from previous ventures.

service Intangible offerings that provide value to customers through actions, expertise, or experiences. Visualized on the value proposition canvas. Evaluated as part of the primary activities in a value chain analysis.

service provider A company or individual that offers intangible services rather than physical products to customers.

service-based business A company that generates revenue primarily through providing services rather than selling tangible products.

set-up time The time required to prepare equipment, systems, or processes before production or work can begin.

SGA See selling, general, administrative.

shareholder An individual or entity that owns shares of stock and has ownership rights in the company.

shares Units of ownership in a corporation that represent a claim on the company's assets and earnings.

short-term debt Financial obligations that must be repaid within one year. Shown on the balance sheet.

side hustle A secondary business or income stream pursued alongside primary employment.

situational analysis A comprehensive assessment of an organization's current internal and external circumstances to inform strategic decision-making and planning. Common tools for situation analysis include SWOT, TOWS, and SOAR.

skimming pricing A pricing objective involving setting a high initial price to target early adopters and then gradually lowering the price to attract more price-sensitive customers.

Small Business Administration (SBA) A United States government agency that provides support, loans, and resources to small businesses.

SMART objectives Five criteria for setting objectives: specific, measurable, achievable, relevant, and timebound.

SOAR A strategic planning framework focusing on Strengths, Opportunities, Aspirations, and Results to drive positive change. A common tool for situational analysis.

social analysis The systematic exploration of social factors, trends, and cultural and religious viewpoints that may impact business operations and decisions. Part of a PESTLE analysis.

social enterprise An organization that primarily exists to tackle social or environmental issues. A business structure in the United Kingdom.

social entrepreneurship Using entrepreneurial approaches to address social or environmental problems.

social sustainability A company's ability to operate in ways that support the long-term well-being of employees, communities, and society while maintaining profitable operations through ethical business conduct.

sole proprietorship The simplest business structure available in the United States, where one individual owns and operates the business, with no legal separation between the owner and the business entity, making the owner personally liable for all debts and obligations. States may not require registration for sole proprietorships.

sole trader A business structure in the United Kingdom where an individual runs their own business as a self-employed person with full personal liability for business debts and obligations.

solopreneur An entrepreneur who runs their business single-handedly without employees.

solution The way a business addresses customer problems through its products, services, or approach. Visualized in the lean canvas.

sourcing The process of finding and acquiring goods, services, or materials from suppliers or vendors.

specific One of the SMART criteria for setting objectives, referring to objectives that are clear, well-defined, and unambiguous.

Specific, Measurable, Achievable, Relevant, and Timebound See SMART objectives.

stakeholder Any individual or group with an interest in or who is affected by a business's activities. Visualized as part of the Partners, Collaborators, Stakeholders in the micro-enterprise for creatives canvas.

stars High-growth, high-market-share products and businesses as shown on a growth-share matrix.

startup A newly established business, typically in the early stages of development and seeking to scale rapidly.

starved task A work item that lacks necessary resources, information, or dependencies to proceed effectively.

statement of cash flows A financial statement that tracks the flow of cash from operating, investing, and financing activities.

strategic planning The process of defining strategy and making decisions about allocating resources to pursue this strategy.

strategy A comprehensive plan of action designed to achieve long-term organizational goals and competitive advantage.

Strengths, Opportunities, Aspirations, and Results See SOAR.

Strengths, Weaknesses, Opportunities, and Threats See SWOT.

style boards Visual collections showing design elements, colors, textures, and aesthetics that guide brand or product development.

substitute A product or service that can replace another, potentially reducing demand for the original offering.

succession The process of transitioning leadership and ownership of a business from one person or generation to another.

sunk cost Money that has already been spent and cannot be recovered, regardless of future decisions.

sunk cost fallacy The tendency to continue investing in a project or decision based on previously invested resources rather than future value.

supplier power The ability of suppliers to influence prices and terms of supply. Explored using the five forces analysis.

suppliers Organizations that provide raw materials, components, or finished goods to other businesses.

supply The quantity of goods or services that producers are willing and able to offer at various price levels.

supply chain The network of organizations, people, activities, and resources involved in moving products from suppliers to customers.

support activities Business processes that enable and enhance primary activities, such as human resources and technology development. Evaluated as part of the value chain analysis.

survival pricing A pricing objective wherein prices are set at levels just sufficient to cover costs and stay in business during challenging periods.

sustainability See environmental sustainability.

sustainable competitive advantage A competitive advantage that is difficult for competitors to replicate and can be maintained over a long period.

sweat equity Ownership earned through personal effort and work rather than financial investment.

SWOT A strategic planning framework examining internal Strengths and Weaknesses alongside external Opportunities and Threats. A common tool for situational analysis.

target market The specific group or segment of consumers a business aims to reach with its products or services.

tariff A tax imposed on imported goods, typically used to protect domestic industries or generate government revenue.

task order The sequence in which work activities should be completed to achieve optimal efficiency and results.

taxes Mandatory payments to government entities based on income, property, sales, or other taxable events. Shown on the income statement.

technological analysis The systematic exploration of technology trends and innovations that may impact business operations and decisions. Part of a PESTLE analysis.

technology development The process of creating, improving, and implementing technological solutions to support business objectives. Evaluated as part of the support activities in a value chain analysis.

third place Spaces that are neither home (first place) nor work (second place), where people gather socially. Often important for community-focused businesses.

third-party certifications Independent verification that products, services, or processes meet specific standards or requirements. Examples include Nest's Ethical Handicraft program, fair trade certifications, and B Lab's B Corp Certification.

third-party logistics (3PL) Companies that provide outsourced logistics services including warehousing, transportation, and distribution for other businesses.

threat of new entrants The risk that new competitors will enter the market. Examined through the five forces analysis.

threat of substitutes The risk that customers will switch to alternative products or services. Examined through the five forces analysis.

Threats, Opportunities, Weaknesses, and Strengths See TOWS.

throughput time The total time required for a product or service to move through the entire production or delivery process. Analyzed with process mapping.

time cushion Extra time built into project schedules and planning to account for unexpected delays or complications.

timebound One of the SMART criteria for setting objectives, referring to objectives with specific deadlines or time constraints.

timeboxing A project and time management technique that allocates fixed time periods for completing specific tasks or activities.

TOWS A strategic planning framework that matches external Threats and Opportunities with internal Weaknesses and Strengths to generate strategic options. A common tool for situational analysis.

trade secret Confidential business intellectual property that provides competitive advantage and is protected through secrecy rather than formal registration.

trade show Industry events where businesses display products and services to potential customers, partners, and industry professionals.

trademark Intellectual property using a distinctive sign, symbol, or name that identifies and distinguishes products or services of a particular source.

transactional pricing signals Price information focused on immediate purchase decisions and value perception in specific buying situations.

trend A general direction of change in market conditions, consumer behavior, or industry patterns over time or a current style.

unfair advantage A sustainable competitive edge that cannot be easily copied or bought by competitors. Visualized with the lean canvas.

unique value proposition (UVP) A clear statement explaining how a product or service uniquely benefits customers compared to competitors. Visualized on the business model canvas as value proposition.

unit A single item or standard measure used as a basis for pricing, costing, or sales calculations.

unit economics The profitability of a single unit of a product or service.

UVP See unique value proposition.

valuation The process of determining the economic value of a business or asset.

value chain The series of activities that businesses perform to deliver valuable products or services to customers.

value chain analysis The systematic examination of business activities to identify opportunities for competitive advantage and cost reduction.

value innovation The simultaneous pursuit of differentiation and low cost, creating a leap in value for both the firm and its customers.

value map The section of the Value Proposition Canvas describing how products/services create value through gain creators and pain relievers.

value proposition See unique value proposition. Visualized on the business model canvas.

value proposition canvas A visualization framework focusing on customer profile (jobs, pains, gains) and value map (products/services, pain relievers, gain creators) to ensure product-market fit.

Van Westendorp analysis A market research technique used to determine the range of acceptable prices for a product or service.

variable costs Costs that vary directly with the level of production or sales, such as materials.

VC See venture capital.

venture A new business enterprise, especially one involving risk or uncertainty.

venture capital (VC) Funding provided by firms to startups and small businesses with high growth potential in exchange for equity ownership.

warehousing The storage and management of goods in facilities designed for inventory control and distribution.

waste reduction The practice of minimizing unnecessary use of resources, materials, or time in business processes.

what + how A framework examining both the value proposition (what you offer) and the delivery method (how you provide it). An element of the micro-enterprise for creatives canvas.

wholesalers Businesses that buy large quantities of goods from manufacturers and sell smaller quantities to retailers.

WIP inventory See work-in-progress inventory.

Work-In-Progress (WIP) inventory Partially completed goods that are still in the production process but not yet finished.

workflow The sequence of processes, tasks, or activities through which work moves from initiation to completion.

Appendix B
Helpful Organizations

Throughout the book and in our case studies, we've occasionally shared organizations, events, and websites that the authors recommend, or that the makers we profiled have found useful. This section includes a list of these and other organizations, events, and websites that may offer beneficial resources to you as part of your entrepreneurial journey.

We haven't included local organizations on this list, but there are often great options. Use your favorite search engine to look for local, regional, or national organizations such as the ones on the list below to find out more about education programs and professional development, support services, networking activities, and funding opportunities.

- Arts councils and arts organizations,
- Arts or crafts unions and professional organizations,
- Business improvement districts, business revitalization zones, or community benefit districts,
- Business networking groups,
- Chambers of commerce,
- College or university entrepreneurship centers,
- Community banks, community development financial institutions (CFDIs), credit unions, and mutual banks,
- Economic development organizations and community development organizations,
- Entrepreneur support organizations or incubators,
- Government programs for small business owners,
- Makerspaces,
- Non-governmental or non-profit organizations for artists, artisans, or entrepreneurs, and
- Volunteer accountants and/or volunteer lawyers for the arts.

Artist and Maker Support Organizations

Air Collaborative (aircollaborative.org) is an organization that supports community building in the United States through inclusive collaboration, creative tools, and local leadership.

Assets for Artists (A4A) (www.assetsforartists.org) is a non-profit organization in the United States that offers a six-month capacity building program for artists with limited resources, online and in-person workshops for artists in New England, and online opportunity listings. Additional programs are available for artists in Massachusetts.

British Council (arts.britishcouncil.org) is the United Kingdom's international organization for cultural relations and educational opportunities. Their work in the arts includes fellowship and grant opportunities for artists and creative professionals, online and in-person events, reports and guides, and other programs.

Craft Industry Alliance (craftindustryalliance.org) is a trade association for craft industry professionals. A podcast and blog highlights industry news, while members can access monthly virtual content coworking sessions, roundtable meetings, a member directory, training, online courses, mastermind groups, discounts on business services, and additional curated resources. Individual or corporate membership options are available.

Crafts Council (www.craftscouncil.org.uk) provides support to craft businesses in the United Kingdom. Members can submit their work to the curated online platform for UK makers. The events directory allows you to promote low-cost events. The website offers additional free resources.

Creative Capital for Artists (creative-capital.org) is a non-profit organization in the United States that provides unrestricted project grants, community building services, and professional development including free, online courses in English and Spanish. They also maintain an online list of grants, residencies, open calls, and other opportunities for artists in all disciplines.

Creative Mornings (creativemornings.com) is a global creative community with local and virtual events hosted by chapters in many countries and a global directory of creative companies, professionals, and jobs.

Creative Startups (www.creativestartups.org)/Global Center for Cultural Entrepreneurship is a non-profit organization based in the United States that offers programs for creative entrepreneurs including accelerators with global mentors, innovation challenges and sprints, and training for business librarians through collaboration with partners in the Middle East and throughout the United States. Additional programs are available in select locations.

Creative Workplaces (creativeworkplaces.gov.au) is an Australian government organization that provides resources for artists and arts organizations on workplace issues including payment, safety, accessibility, and cultural relations.

Makerspace Directory (makerspace.com) is a global directory of makerspaces hosted by Make Magazine. You can search or select by country or by type of makerspace.

Nest (www.buildanest.org) is a global non-profit organization that connects artisans, retailers, and philanthropies. Nest makers profiled in this book include Allpa Perú, Bebemoss, Exalting in Beauty, and Larson Wood Designs. *Nest Guild* is a free, online global community of over 3,000 makers and artisan business leaders. *Makers United* includes inclusive local and regional programs for makers in the United States. *Artisan Accelerator* is an intensive incubator program for Nest Guild members that provides support for reaching the international marketplace. The *Ethical Handicraft* seal is a consumer-facing, third-party supply chain certification that indicates the product has been ethically handmade in accordance with Nest standards. Nest also provides free disaster-recovery educational resources, distributes grant funding and awards, and hosts in-person events and workshops.

Springboard for the Arts (springboardforthearts.org) is a non-profit organization in the United States that supports artists and artist-led community development work. They maintain online lists of jobs, grants, opportunities, and accessibility resources for arts organizations and opportunities for individual artists; provide online technical assistance and training; offer career coaching; and provide sliding scale fee-based fiscal sponsorship to allow artists and organizations doing charitable work to receive tax-deductible grants and donations. Additional programs and funding are available for Minnesota-based artists and arts organizations.

US Regional Arts Organizations (US RAO) (usregionalarts.org) is a collective of six regional non-profit organizations providing place-based arts services in the United States. US RAO has a searchable database of grants, opportunities, and resources for artists and arts organizations, as well as links to each of the six regional organizations.

Work in Culture (workinculture.ca) is a Canadian non-profit organization that offers a job board and webinars and events. Additional programs and funding are available for artists and organizations in Ontario.

Entrepreneur and Small Business Support Organizations

Freelancers Union (freelancersunion.org) is a non-profit organization for self-employed people in the United States. They offer educational resources including for doing taxes; online and in-person events; and access to dental, disability, health, liability, life, and vision insurance. Membership is free. Folks in New York City can access additional free resources including coworking and photography spaces and 30-minute consultations with experts.

SCORE (www.score.org) is a non-profit organization that offers free, one-on-one mentoring with experienced advisors, workshops and events, and educational resources to aspiring and established owners of businesses based in the United States.

Small Business Administration (SBA) (www.sba.gov) is a United States government agency that provides funding through loans and disaster assistance, federal contracting assistance, and local resources and technical support through partnerships.

Startup Canada (www.startupcan.ca) is a non-profit organization serving and advocating for Canadian entrepreneurs. In addition to virtual and in-person educational and networking events, they also offer programs to assist Canadian businesses in expanding internationally and to connect with government agencies. They offer pitch competitions and a program to support women-identifying entrepreneurs.

Tory Burch Foundation (www.toryburchfoundation.org) is a global non-profit organization that supports women entrepreneurs through free educational webinars, a content library, a funding finder tool with links to searchable funding databases, and a Fellows program that helps women entrepreneurs in the United States to scale.

Funding Resources

Arts Council England (www.artscouncil.org.uk), **Canada Council for the Arts** (canadacouncil.ca), **Creative Australia** (creative.gov.au), **Creative New Zealand** (creativenz.govt.nz), and the United States **National Endowment for the Arts** (www.arts.gov) are the public art funders of their respective countries. In addition to providing grant funding, they provide education, opportunities to exhibit and perform, networking, and other resources to the artists and artists organizations in their countries.

BDC (Business Development Bank of Canada) (www.bdc.ca/en) is a Canadian, government-owned financial institution focused on entrepreneurs. They offer business loans and consulting services. BDC Capital is the subsidiary that provides venture capital and related services.

Fearless Fund (www.fearless.fund) is a venture capital fund by women of color and for women of color. Programs include Get Venture Ready, a 12-week educational program to prepare participants to gain access to capital, grants, and loans.

Indiegogo (www.indiegogo.com), **Kickstarter** (www.kickstarter.com), and **Patreon** (www.patreon.com) are crowdfunding platforms described in more detail in the Glossary.

Virgin StartUp (www.virginstartup.org) is a not-for-profit organization serving founders in the United Kingdom. They offer fixed-rate business loans, an online community with free and premium memberships, online and in-person networking and events, and mentoring and advice.

Marketplaces and Trade Shows

AIGA (www.aiga.org) is a professional membership organization for designers in the United States and host of the AIGA Design Conference trade show.

DesignerCon (www.designercon.com), also known as DCon, is an annual art and design convention featuring collectible toys, designer goods, and urban, underground, and pop art.

Etsy (www.etsy.com) is an e-commerce platform for unique items including handmade products and arts and crafts supplies. Items for sale on Etsy must be made, designed, handpicked, or sourced by the seller. Etsy Forums, Teams, and Seller Events provide networking opportunities and peer-to-peer advice for sellers.

Faire (www.faire.com) is an online wholesale marketplace. Sellers can reach retailers in Canada, Europe, and the United States, and buyers have thousands of options for no- or low-minimum ordering.

h + h cologne (www.hh-cologne.com) and **h + h americas** (hh-americas.com) are annual trade shows for handicrafts and hobbies.

Impressions Expo (impressionsexpo.com) operates multiple trade shows each year for the decorated apparel and imprinted products industry.

JCK (www.jckonline.com) hosts multiple trade shows each year for the jewelry industry.

Maison&Object (www.maison-objet.com/en) hosts trade shows for interior design, interior decoration, and furniture.

Maker's Row (makersrow.com) is an online marketplace connecting brands with manufacturers in the United States, including small- and medium-sized manufacturers with low minimum orders.

Messe Frankfurt (messefrankfurt.com) is an international organization that hosts many trade shows of interest to makers, including in fashion and apparel, textiles, and chocolate.

NAMTA (www.namta.org) is the International Art Materials Association, a professional membership organization, and host of the Creativation trade show for the creative materials industry.

Needlework Retailer (needleworkretailer.com) hosts the annual Nashville Needlework Market, a trade show for the counted cross stitch, needlepoint, and needlework industry.

NY Now (nynow.com) hosts multi-day wholesale markets in New York City, including activities, educational panels, and networking events for buyers and sellers.

Shoppe Object (shoppeobject.com) has an online marketplace and offers multiple trade shows for the gifts, home goods, furniture, and design industry.

Appendix C

Tax Considerations for Your Business

All business owners, no matter how large or small, have a responsibility to pay and report their taxes and to conduct due diligence on their tax liabilities. As a business owner, your tax liabilities will be determined by where you are doing business, as tax code and policy vary significantly according to the countries, states or provinces, and even cities you are operating in.

The following is a list of some of the major types of taxes you will encounter. This information should serve as a jumping-off point for understanding tax regulations and practices within the specific jurisdiction that you are operating in, and should not be taken as a comprehensive guide or professional tax advice. Always consult with a qualified tax professional for guidance tailored to your specific situation.

- **Corporate Tax:** Taxes levied on the profits of a corporation.
- **Individual Tax:** Income tax paid by individuals, which may include profits from a sole proprietorship or partnership.
- **Self-Employment Tax:** Taxes paid by self-employed individuals in the United States to cover Social Security and Medicare taxes, typically equivalent to the employer and employee portions of these taxes.
- **Sales Tax (VAT/GST):** Taxes collected by businesses on the sale of goods and services, which are then remitted to the government. This may be referred to as Value Added Tax (VAT) or Goods and Services Tax (GST) in various countries.
- **Activity-Specific Local Tax:** Taxes imposed by local governments (cities, counties) on specific business activities or industries.
- **Duties and Tariffs:** Taxes imposed on imported or exported goods, which can impact businesses involved in international trade.

Tax Resources

Sunlight Tax Podcast (https://www.sunlighttax.com/) Artist and Certified Public Accountant Hannah Cole produces this podcast offering detailed and specific tax advice for creative professionals based in the United States.

Volunteer Lawyers and Accountants for the Arts (vlaa.org) This organization matches artists and qualified arts organizations in the United States with volunteer accountants who can provide pro bono tax advice.

Artists' Union England (www.artistsunionengland.org.uk) is a trade union for visual, applied, and socially engaged professional artists in England. Members can access public and products liability insurance, free tax and legal advice, and additional training, resources, and supports.

Index

Note: **Bold** page numbers refer to tables and *italic* page numbers refer to figures.

For Product Safety Concerns and Information please contact our EU representative GPSR@taylorandfrancis.com Taylor & Francis Verlag GmbH, Kaufingerstraße 24, 80331 München, Germany